Thoreau's Living Ethics

PHILIP CAFARO

Thoreau's Living Ethics

Walden and the Pursuit of Virtue

The University of Georgia Press

Athens and London

Title page illustration © 2000 by Abigail Rorer.
Previously published in Henry David Thoreau's
Wild Fruits, ed. Bradley P. Dean (New York:
W. W. Norton and Company, 2000).
Set in Minion by BookComp, Inc.
Printed and bound by Maple-Vail
This book is printed on recycled acid-free paper.

Printed in the United States of America
08   07   06   05   04   C   5   4   3   2   1

Library of Congress Cataloging-in-Publication Data

Cafaro, Philip, 1962–
Thoreau's living ethics : Walden and the pursuit of
virtue / Philip Cafaro.
          p. cm.
Includes bibliographical references and index.
ISBN 0-8203-2610-0 (hardcover : alk. paper)
1. Thoreau, Henry David, 1817–1862—Ethics.   2. Virtues.
3. Thoreau, Henry David, 1817–1862. Walden.   4. Virtues
in literature. I. Title.
B931.T44C34 2004
818'.309—dc22
2003027270

British Library Cataloging-in-Publication Data available

To Kris

As I love nature, as I love singing birds, and gleaming stubble, and flowing rivers, and morning and evening, and summer and winter, I love thee

Contents

Preface

Thoreau's Living Ethics provides the first full, rigorous account of Henry Thoreau's ethical philosophy. It places Thoreau within a long tradition of ethical thinking in the West, from the ancients to the romantics. It relates him to important ethical questions agitating his own society and assesses his potential value to contemporary readers concerned to answer his main ethical questions: How should I live my life? What is my proper place in nature? How can I be a good friend, neighbor, and citizen?

The first chapter explores the genesis of Thoreau's ethical philosophy by considering his early writings and his relationship with Ralph Waldo Emerson. Succeeding chapters focus on *Walden*, Thoreau's mature ethical statement, bringing in his other writings where appropriate. Here I make my case that Thoreau was a real philosopher, both in the modern sense of someone who thought deeply about fundamental ethical issues and whose writings on these issues bear close scrutiny, and in the ancient sense of someone who succeeded in living a good life and thus can help us in our own attempts to do so.

Beyond presenting Thoreau's ethical philosophy accurately, this book has four main goals. First, I want to give professional philosophers another perspective on virtue ethics, one less based on ancient philosophy and more grounded in modern life and experience. Current work in virtue ethics—that branch of ethics focused on human flourishing—begins and all too often ends with Aristotle, but critics have been quick to note the implausibility of his metaphysical biology, his overly static view of human society, and other aspects of his ethical theory that a modern virtue ethics must correct. Thoreau's ethics embraces an evolutionary experimentalism and an appreciation of human diversity that better "fit the facts" about human nature. His conception of virtue incorporates romantic and egalitarian elements that supplement earlier ideals. Thoreau also treats economic, technological, and political issues that are crucial for us but were unimportant or not addressed by the ancients. For these reasons, I contend that Thoreau provides a framework for developing virtue ethics superior to that utilized by most contemporary philosophers.

Second, I want to suggest to environmentalists and environmental philosophers a valuable new way to think about our proper place in the world, one which rejects both narrowly economic and narrowly moralistic answers, and instead opens up consideration of our enlightened self-interest and communal possibilities. The discipline of environmental philosophy, as it has developed over the past thirty years, has focused on arguing for the intrinsic value of nonhuman nature in an effort to foster humility and restraint in our use of the natural world. This is all to the good, yet here as elsewhere positive ideals motivate at least as well as negative proscriptions. Development of an ethics of environmental flourishing seems to me a necessary complement to the "thou shalt nots" usually emphasized in environmental ethics. It will help us understand that what sort of world we create (or destroy) will determine what sorts of people we and our descendants will be.

Third, I want to further Americans' understanding of one of their greatest thinkers, whom they have appreciated as a literary figure and proto-environmentalist, but not yet as a philosopher. More than thirty years ago, Stanley Cavell pioneered taking Thoreau seriously as a philosopher, with rich results. What Cavell did for Thoreau as epistemologist, what recent writers such as Bradley Dean and Laura Dassow Walls have done for his philosophy of science, I would like to do in the equally bountiful area of his ethics. This will lead to a more complete and accurate picture of Thoreau and of American philosophy, which, contrary to popular belief, does not begin with the pragmatists.

Finally, for all my readers, I want to open up important ethical questions with which we should be grappling. The most pressing of these are the questions of the nature of the good life and its proper pursuit, and the development of an environmental ethics for a crowded, fragile, beautiful planet. I have come to believe that these two questions are inseparable. Unless we become convinced that the good life is something else than what we currently pursue, there is little hope that we will preserve a healthy, biologically diverse world for our descendants or that we will appreciate nature and reap the rewards that Thoreau and the other great naturalists assure us are there for the gathering.

Acknowledgments

It is a pleasure to thank the many people who have helped me write and publish this book. The notes and bibliography acknowledge my many debts to the scholarly literature in philosophy and Thoreau studies. Although it is not listed there, I have made extensive use of Marlene Ogden and Clifton Keller's *Walden: A Concordance* (New York: Garland Publishing, 1985).

An early attempt to grapple with Thoreau's ethical philosophy was my Ph.D. dissertation: *Thoreau's Vision of a Good Life in Nature: Towards an Environmental Virtue Ethics* (1997). I thank Boston University and its philosophy department for intellectual training and financial assistance. Thanks to my dissertation committee: Allen Speight, Richard Primack, Lawrence Cahoone, and Erazim Kohak. Special thanks to my first reader, Michael Martin, whose commitment and generosity I have tried to imitate in my own teaching.

Helpful comments on the initial book proposal came from Bryan Norton, James Sterba, Holmes Rolston III, Joel Myerson, David Rothenberg, Matthew Ostrow, Joseph Amato, Joseph Bronars, Joanne Bronars, and David Schmidtz. Commenting on individual chapters or particular issues were Paul Cafaro, John Garber, Gary Collison, Sandra Petrulionis, Jane Bennett, William Chaloupka, Bruce Ronda, SueEllen Campbell, and Philip Koch. My parents, Claire Cafaro and Ralph Cafaro Jr., also provided valuable comments and have furthered this work in many ways.

Thanks to Colorado State University and to my colleagues in the philosophy department for their friendship and encouragement. Special thanks to Pat McKee and Michael Losonsky for advice on publishing and to Holmes Rolston III—always a model of philosophical clarity, creativity, and engagement. Completion of this book was facilitated by two summer study grants from the philosophy department endowment.

Everyone at the University of Georgia Press has been great: patient, helpful, prompt, professional. I especially want to thank Erin McElroy, Sarah McKee, and Nancy Grayson. Press reader David Rothenberg's comments were helpful and always to the point. Jane Curran's copyediting greatly improved the final version. And while I am looking south toward Georgia, thanks to the late Eugene Odum, who first suggested to me that environmentalists had to supplement our "thou shalt nots" with positive ideals.

Two people who read the whole manuscript through (at least once!) deserve special thanks. Brad Dean, Thoreau scholar extraordinaire, has saved me from a few howlers and improved my prose in dozens of instances. He also made more substantial improvements; for example, it was his suggestion to close this book with Thoreau's death. He has encouraged the project from beginning to end.

My wife Kris Cafaro's fine eye for grammar, style, and logical confusion has once again helped me in many ways. She has saved readers of this book from more bloviation than it would be wise to admit to. She also gave me the title and did the bulk of the work of caring for our son Henry Jay while I was completing the manuscript. This book is dedicated to her, with all my love.

Earlier versions of some of the material in this book appeared in the following articles. "Thoreau's Environmental Ethics in *Walden*" in *The Concord Saunterer* 10 (2002): 17–63. "Thoreau, Leopold and Carson: Toward an Environmental Virtue Ethics" in *Environmental Ethics* 23 (2001): 3–17. "Thoreau's Virtue Ethics in *Walden*" in *The Concord Saunterer* 8 (2000): 23–47. "Thoreau and the Place of Economy" in *Center: Architecture and Design in America* 11 (1999): 39–47. "Thoreauvian Patriotism as an Environmental Virtue" in *Philosophy in the Contemporary World* 2 (1995): 1–9. I am grateful to Richard Schneider, Eugene Hargove, Michael Benedikt, and James Sauer, the editors of these journals, for permission to reprint this material.

Thoreau's Living Ethics

The Challenge

"Mr. President and Gentlemen," the tall, thin, large-nosed man at the podium begins, "I greet you on the re-commencement of our literary year. Our anniversary is one of hope, and, perhaps, not enough of labor."[1] It is August 1837. Ralph Waldo Emerson is addressing the Phi Beta Kappa Society in Brattle Street Church, Cambridge, Massachusetts, as part of Harvard College's commencement ceremonies. Along with the new inductees a good portion of Boston's intelligentsia is present, including Oliver Wendell Holmes, Wendell Phillips, and James Russell Lowell. America's most popular and influential nineteenth-century intellectual has begun what remains America's most famous commencement speech. It contains no praise for the successful young scholars or ingratiating jokes. Its short greeting is followed by a complaint and a challenge.

"We do not meet for games of strength or skill, like the ancient Greeks," Emerson continues:

> for the parliaments of love and poesy, like the Troubadours; nor for the advancement of science, like our co[n]temporaries in the British and European capitals. Thus far, our holiday has been simply a friendly sign of the survival of the love of letters amongst a people too busy to give to letters any more. As such, it is precious as the sign of an indestructible instinct. Perhaps the time is already come, when it ought to be, and will be, something else; when the sluggard intellect of this continent will look from under its iron lids, and fill the postponed expectation of the world with something better than the exertions of mechanical skill.[2]

It is an "indestructible instinct," essentially human, to think, and to have thinking flower into poetry and science, religion and philosophy. Emerson's call for specifically American forms of these higher activities is clear and stirring. Whitman in poetry, Melville in literature, C. S. Peirce and William James in philosophy, will all take up this challenge in the coming years, making valuable contributions to world culture through the expression of characteristic American themes, signaling a new American intellectual power and maturity.

But Emerson wants thought to inform our lives, not merely our literary productions, and he speaks not just to geniuses but to the genius in us all. Here he challenges each of his listeners and readers to a direct, personal awakening of our "sluggard intellects." We are to *live* lives of thought; thought must inform our ordinary activities and help us see their significance. Our lives may teach the most important lessons, for Emerson sees an unbroken chain extending from the simplest facts and experiences to knowledge of self, nature, and God. "What would we really know the meaning of?" he asks, and answers: "The meal in the firkin; the milk in the pan; the ballad in the street; the news of the boat; the glance of the eye.... Man is surprised to find that things near are not less beautiful and wondrous than things remote. . . . The perception of the worth of the vulgar is fruitful in discoveries."[3] Such discoveries are, or should be, open to all.

Emerson asserts that maintaining a spirit of discovery throughout life is the key to living well and reaching our highest goals. It enriches our experience, as when the careful observations of the naturalist transform the green mass of a riverbank into hundreds of species of plants, or when the artist's attention to subtle variations of color, light, and shade increases her appreciation of difference and detail. A spirit of discovery and creative thinking is also crucial to freedom: that intellectual independence that completes our political independence. We must think our own thoughts. Not, of course, that we will fail to take advantage of past discoveries or study the world's literary, scientific, and religious traditions. But we will interrogate the ideas of the past and put them to the test of our own experience. Our ideas need not be original with us, yet they should be our own: fully thought through, given content by experience, judged true or false by a confident and commanding intellect. In the end, our important ideas must be acted upon and thoroughly possessed through commitment.

In this way, expansive, creative thinking will further integrity, defined by Emerson as a coherence and focus in our lives, combined with a comprehensive appreciation and interest in human life generally. No part of us should be wasted, no part of us neglected, Emerson believes. We may order our lives so as to pursue our ideals. And we may, through experience, come to better understand the full extent of human life: "Man is not a farmer, or a professor, or an engineer, but he is all. Man is priest and scholar, and statesman, and producer, and soldier."[4] In the current state of society, we parcel these functions out to different individuals. But all express or minister to the needs of human beings, and all teach their own lessons. In their totality, they suggest a complete conception of human being that appreciates our possibilities. Currently, most men sell a good part of their day in order to support themselves and their families. This is not necessarily wrong or unjust, yet it may easily trap us. For the purpose of life is not to prolong life, but to live well. We must avoid sacrificing the whole to a part: the whole range of life's opportunities to narrower realms named Career or Wealth or Prestige.

Emerson identifies the proper coordination of thinking and action as the key to achieving an enriched experience, independence, and integrity. But for all his high valuation of thinking and despite the scholarly occasion, Emerson admonishes his audience that our ability to reflect can undermine these key goals by fostering overspecialization and a subsequent forgetting of our proper ends. "In [an appropriate] distribution of functions," he writes, "the scholar is the designated intellect. In the right state, he is, *Man Thinking*. In the degenerate state, when the victim of society, he tends to become a mere thinker, or, still worse, the parrot of other men's thinking."[5] Cut off from experience, the scholars' thought may become far-fetched and pointless, failing to illuminate his experience. The common man, meanwhile, may fail to reflect on his own actions. Acting "merely mechanically," he pursues economic ends that others have deemed valuable; he worships according to forms and creeds bequeathed by long-dead geniuses and administered by an arm of the "thinking class."

All this is a great loss. For the awakened soul, Emerson believes, can know truth. Even more, it can engage in the divine function of creation: in art, in thought, and, most importantly, in life. "Is not, indeed, every man a student, and do not all things exist for the student's behoof?" Emerson asks. And following Kant, he answers anthropocentrically, yet stirringly: "The one thing in the world, of value, is the active soul. This every man is entitled to; this every man contains within him, although, in almost all men, obstructed, and as yet unborn. The soul active sees absolute truth; and utters truth, or creates. In this action, it is genius; not the privilege of here and there a favorite, but the sound estate of every man."[6]

Since Descartes, a main project of modern philosophy has been to develop and defend rigorous criteria of knowledge. The upshot usually has been either skepticism or a rigid segregation of scientific knowledge from nonsense, trivia, and various kinds of nonscience. One result has been to justify the sort of intellectual division of labor Emerson distrusted: a few knowers and many "doers." Emerson reverses all this here, emphasizing the commonplace miracle of knowledge. He insists that each of us *can* know truth; also, as we have seen, on the value of understanding what is most "common, familiar and low," the stuff of everyday life.[7]

Activity and enriched experience should be the goals of the scholar. "The theory of books is noble," Emerson writes. "The scholar of the first age received into him the world around; brooded thereon; gave it the new arrangement of his own mind; and uttered it again. It came into him, life; it went out from him, truth. . . . It now endures, it now flies, it now inspires." This is how scholarship should work, with the scholar the hero of thought. Yet in practice, "a love of the hero corrupts into worship of his statue. . . . The sluggish and perverted mind of the multitude, slow to open to the incursions of Reason, having once so opened, having once received this book, stands upon it, and makes an outcry, if it is disparaged."[8] Clearly Emerson has in mind popular support for the Christian Bible and popular outrage at perceived slights or deviations from its truth. But there is wisdom in other sacred books, he insists, and above all in the experiences from which, in his view, all books originate. The Christian message itself, even were it the sole and complete truth, could not be learned passively, but only through a struggle to understand the text and to apply its message in life. What holds true for religion holds equally true for politics, literature, or economics.

The dangers to the unlearned are clear. They may never think for themselves and thus lead a merely animal existence. Such lives are incompatible with democracy and Christianity in their full senses.

The dangers to the learned class are somewhat different, although also connected to laziness and passivity. They may become mere parrots or bookworms, neglecting life for books. Anticipating postmodern practices that divorce texts from lived contexts and set them up as their own realities, Emerson criticizes "the book-learned class, who value books as such; not as related to nature and the human constitution, but as making a sort of Third Estate with the world and the soul."[9] This cuts the scholar off from the world, himself and his fellow men, in one fell swoop. Emerson's insight is that even the greatest books can play the role of cereal box reading in our lives, lulling rather than stimulating thought. At bottom, this time-passing stems from laziness and a distrust or fear of life.

Such "bibliomania" may end in existential despair, or misology. Once again, Emerson strikingly anticipates later trends: "Our age is bewailed as the age of Introversion. . . . We, it seems, are critical; we are embarrassed with second thoughts; we cannot enjoy any thing for hankering to know whereof the pleasure consists; we are lined with eyes."[10] Thought becomes a curse, ruining rather than enhancing life. Our moments of appreciation, apprehension, and creation are lost or lose their savor. One answer to this problem, to frankly set aside thought and pursue mindless pleasure, is presumably not open to "the scholar." Is the only option then to take up one's thinking task with a heavy head and live for those moments when the burden mysteriously lifts? Emerson will have none of it:

> Is it so bad then? Sight is the last thing to be pitied. Would we be blind? Do we fear lest we should outsee nature and God, and drink truth dry? I look upon the discontent of the literary class, as a mere announcement of the fact, that they find themselves not in the state of mind of their fathers, and regret the coming state as untried; as a boy dreads the water before he has learned that he can swim.[11]

Certainly we may think too much, overanalyze our lives, and the like. But the answer is to complement introversion with *extroversion:* with a concern for nature: all that is "not-us," human and nonhuman. We are to face our despairs, since "drudgery, calamity, exasperation, want, are instructers in eloquence and wisdom" (such words often get Emerson labeled a Pollyanna; it is well to remember that he had buried his beloved first wife six years before delivering them).[12] We are to value the commonplace and everyday, rather than look to letters as an escape from them. Finally, we are to live.

For above all, the literary class may forget or forgo the need for action. But, Emerson reminds us, real knowledge depends upon it: "The preamble of thought, the transition through which it passes from the unconscious to the conscious, is action. Only so much do I know, as I have lived. . . . So much only of life as I know by experience, so much of the wilderness have I vanquished and planted, or so far have I extended my being, my dominion."[13] No knowledge without action. Only this teaches us, allows for personal growth, gives us something to say. A merely literary life is no life at all. "The true scholar grudges every opportunity of action past by, as a loss of power." And again: "Character is higher than intellect. Thinking is the function. Living is the functionary. . . . A great soul will be strong to live, as well as strong to think."[14]

In current terms, "The American Scholar" treats "virtue ethics": that half of ethics that concerns itself less with our duties toward others and more with personal excellence and societal flourishing. Here Emerson hearkens back to an older ethical tradition. While modern ethical philosophy argues for altruism, ancient ethical philosophy started from an enlightened self-interest. While the modern ethicist's main question is, "What are my duties to others and their responsibilities to me?" the ancients' main question was, "What is the good life and how can we go about living it?" Modern ethicists typically ask, "What is a just society?" and answer by specifying rights that all should enjoy and a fair distribution of material goods. The ancients asked, "What is a flourishing human society?" and answered by specifying norms, educational training, and political institutions that they hoped would create the best kinds of people.[15]

Recently, philosophers have begun to ask the ancients' questions again, questions that have lost none of their importance during hundreds of years of philosophical neglect. This revival of "virtue ethics" bids fair to broaden contemporary ethical philosophy, as we keep what we would almost all recognize as valuable in the modern conception—support for universal human rights and regard for the least favored members of society—and add a concern for the pursuit of excellence and human flourishing.

We can see that Emerson is a virtue ethicist by the very terms he uses. He speaks of "heroism" and "nobility," words that connote superior effort and achievement. He speaks of "being a man" and "a great soul" and of respecting one's genius. All these terms are foreign to modern ethics, which focuses largely on spelling out particular rights and on justifying egalitarianism, rather than on self-cultivation or superior achievement, which, when successful, tend to accentuate human inequality.

Emerson does speak of duties, but they are not the common moral duties. Rather they are duties of self-cultivation, on the one hand, and duties to enrich the nation's culture, religion, politics, and public life generally, on the other. These latter are the scholar's social duties, the former his personal duties. The wages of attention to these duties, Emerson believes, will often be "poverty and solitude." Rather than worldly success, then, the scholar "is to find consolation in exercising the highest functions of human nature. . . . He is the world's eye. He is the world's heart. He is to resist the vulgar prosperity that retrogrades ever to barbarism, by preserving and communicating heroic sentiments, noble biographies, melodious verse, and the conclusions of history."[16] If it sounds strange, to us, to speak of these as duties, perhaps that shows our impoverished view of ethics. Modern ethicists have generally failed to distinguish higher from lower human functions, noble and heroic lives from tame and ignoble ones.

It is easy, in our time, to speak of the value of the individual but harder to make demands on him: easier to flatter your audience than to challenge it. Emerson counsels his young listeners that living a life that is truly one's own involves burdens of solitude, uncertainty, and the hard work of thought.[17] Five years earlier, he had given up the well-paid pulpit of one of Boston's principal churches in order to pursue an independent course of thinking and worship. Now, he tells the graduates that such choices might be in their futures, too, and that pursuing the greater good might demand giving up certainty and comfort. The cardinal virtue that makes possible such efforts, Emerson says, is "self-trust," closely allied to the virtues of "bravery" and "freedom."[18]

Here is Emerson's bedrock democratic demandingness, which Henry Thoreau will come to share. All men and women have great possibilities open to them. Yet no change in the political arrangements will actualize these possibilities. We must do that ourselves, one person at a time. Emerson, following Kant, extols egalitarian morality and justice, yet unlike Kant he also demands self-cultivation and achievements outside the strictly moral realm: "Every thing that tends to insulate the individual,—to surround him with barriers of natural respect, so that each man shall feel the world is his, and man shall treat with man as a sovereign state with a sovereign state;—tends to true union as well as greatness."[19] The final clause is key. Justice or a "true union" is important, but so is "greatness" of effort and accomplishment. A social order or moral theory that fails to recognize and demand such greatness, no matter how respectful of individual rights, is a failure.

Emerson looked at his society and found that it failed to guarantee the rights of its citizens, most flagrantly its enslaved black citizens. But it also fell short in "greatness." In both cases, the main cause was an overemphasis on commerce and economic prosperity. "Public and private avarice make the air we breathe thick and fat," Emerson told his young charges. "The mind of this country, taught to aim at low objects, eats upon itself." But we can reach higher and achieve more, he concludes. "We will walk on our own feet; we will work with our own hands; we will speak our own minds. . . . A nation of men will for the first time exist, because each believes himself inspired by the Divine Soul which also inspires all men."[20]

In short, Emerson tries to inoculate his listeners against bookishness and passivity, while at the same time encouraging and challenging them with the importance of thinking and literary labors. The maturation of thought may complete the democratic promise of America, and the learned class, Emerson's immediate audience, should lead the way. Only thus can they live their lives well, only thus can they (in their role as scholars) improve the lives of their countrymen. As ministers, they should de-emphasize doctrine and encourage their parishioners to think for themselves (to take up "an original relation to the universe" and its Creator, as Emerson phrased it in *Nature*).[21] As teachers, they should discourage drill and rote memorization and encourage creative thinking in their wards. Even in their high literary productions, American thinkers should illuminate and celebrate common American life or suggest improvements.

For both the literary class and for ordinary people, there are new possibilities and challenges, and the stakes are great. We may remain subhuman: repeating dead forms, thinking others' thoughts, acting merely mechanically (no great accomplishment, no matter how much dirt we move). Or we may achieve a kind of divinity, by thinking our own thoughts and living our own lives. We thereby achieve a genuine independence, fulfilling the promise of our earlier religious and political emancipations.

Achieving these goals is not a "right" that has been granted us by God, Nature, or some constitutional convention. Success will take effort. Yet success lies within our power. Emerson's very phrasing suggests and encourages this thought: "the time is already come, when [our lives] ought to be, and will be, something else." The "ought" has come in its due time; the times are right to turn this "ought" into an "is" (reversing philosophy's typical, interminable head scratching about the move from "is" to "ought," itself sometimes a weight on activity); we *will* make something better of ourselves. Here a congratulatory note does enter Emerson's speech. Not congratulations on past achievements, but rather on our abounding opportunities: on having been born at precisely the right time to achieve our own and America's potential. "This time, like all times," Emerson says to his young scholars, "is a very good one, if we but know what to do with it."[22]

Emerson's ethics had important intellectual precursors. His stress on individual faith was squarely in the Protestant tradition. The American political tradition, too, emphasized the value of the individual and held out great, democratic hopes for the common man. Emerson was well versed in Greek and Roman literature and philosophy with their focus on virtue and nobility. He was a lifelong disciple of Goethe, from whom he took the romantic conception of *Bildung* or self-cultivation, with its emphases on aesthetic appreciation, artistic creation, personal expression, and diversity of experience. All these traditions informed Emerson's ethics. Understanding them helps us understand him.

Focusing on intellectual forerunners, however, might give the impression that this was mainly a matter of Emerson developing theories and responding to intellectual influences. This would be a fundamental mistake. For it is not literature but life that sets us the challenge that Emerson articulates in "The American Scholar." That's why Emerson's listeners paid attention, and readers have been inspired ever since by what Oliver Wendell Holmes called "our Intellectual Declaration of Independence."[23]

First Responses

Graduating from Harvard in 1837 was a young student named Henry David Thoreau. We may imagine him listening in rapt attention to Emerson's speech, fired by its challenge to heroic literary effort. How the future author of *Walden* must have thrilled to these words: "Nature is the opposite of the soul, answering to it part for part. . . . The ancient precept, 'Know thyself,' and the modern precept, 'Study nature,' become at last one maxim."[24] He leaves the hall in a trance, his school days behind him, his vocation suddenly clear . . .

Unfortunately, Thoreau probably wasn't there to hear Emerson's talk. He had attended the main graduation ceremonies the previous day and even given a short speech of his own on "The Commercial Spirit of Modern Times." But Thoreau's biographers think he probably took his degree and his prize money and headed home that same day.

No matter. "The American Scholar" would be printed and distributed widely as a pamphlet, and Thoreau had read an earlier version of "the challenge" in Emerson's great, extended essay *Nature*, published a year earlier. Thoreau had taken *Nature* out of the Harvard library twice, once in the spring, then again a few months later. Besides, Thoreau and Emerson were neighbors and about to become close friends. Thoreau had lived in Concord most of his life; Emerson had moved there three years earlier. When Thoreau returned home after college, he and Emerson became properly acquainted. They began to take long walks together in the fall of 1837. Emerson's notebooks are full of talk about his "young friend Henry," who began his own journal, probably at Emerson's suggestion. Emerson guided Thoreau's reading and acted as editor and agent for his first literary projects. Within a few years, Thoreau was living at the

Emersons as a member of the family. A few years after that, in 1845, he would begin his experiment at Walden Pond on a lot owned by Emerson. When Thoreau writes that he was born in the ideal place in the nick of time, his words refer equally to the proximity of Walden and Waldo.

Thoreau's early writings show him groping for ways to praise and explore the pursuit of virtue. An early essay, "The Service," written when he was twenty-three, is an idealistic call for readers to strive for great things, very much in the vein of Emerson's challenge in "The American Scholar." Hortatory and pretentious, it contains such oracular pronouncements as the following:

> The weak person is flat, for like all flat substances, he does not stand in the direction of his strength, that is, on his edge, but affords a convenient surface to put upon. He slides all the way through life. . . . The brave man is a perfect sphere, which cannot fall on its flat side, and is equally strong every way.

> What first suggested that necessity was grim, and made fate to be so fatal? . . . Must it be so,—then it be good.

> There is as much music in the world as virtue. In a world of peace and love music would be the universal language, and men greet each other in the fields in such accents, as a Beethoven now utters at rare intervals from a distance.[25]

Such statements express the venerable philosophical belief in a perfect harmony between nature and the right sort of human striving: the cosmic optimism at the heart of much ancient ethical theory. They also show the personal optimism and energy necessary to *live* such an ethics. But the assertions are so general, metaphorical, and extravagant as to provide no concrete guidance or sense of how they would be justified or qualified. The essay as a whole is an unconvincing compound of clever wordplay, whistling in the dark by an inexperienced young man, and the typical philosopher's belief that abstractions best reveal truth and compel assent. When Margaret Fuller, editor of the short-lived transcendentalist journal the *Dial,* rejected the piece, she did no injury to Thoreau's literary reputation.

A later essay, "Sir Walter Raleigh," is more successful, being more focused. It is in the genre of Emerson's and Carlyle's "hero pieces," in which an exemplary life teaches moral lessons. The essay is largely dependent on secondary sources, but Thoreau makes good use of them. The swashbuckling Raleigh was a man of action and intellect—as heroic with the sword as with the pen, Thoreau says—providing another occasion to consider the proper relationship between thought and action, literature and life. Raleigh, a "proper knight" and "born cavalier" with "somewhat antique and Roman virtues," allows Thoreau to explore older, broader conceptions of heroism and virtue of which he approves.[26] He quotes Raleigh's *History of the World*, at length and approvingly, on the virtues of an ancient hero: "His justice and sincerity, his temperance, wisdom, and high magnanimity, were no way inferior to his military virtues . . . he was grave and yet very affable and courteous; resolute in public business, but in his own particular, easy and of much mildness. . . . To these graces were added great ability of body, and much eloquence, and very deep knowledge in all parts of philosophy and learning."[27] Here is an ancient conception of virtue that combines moral integrity with intellectual and physical abilities in a comprehensive ideal of human excellence. Arguing for such a conception of virtue will be a main goal in *Walden*—as its recovery has been a key achievement of the current virtue ethics revival.

Thoreau on Raleigh also anticipates philosophers' recent interest in moral character, in opposition to the nearly exclusive focus on discrete actions that characterized philosophical ethics throughout most of the twentieth century. After describing one of Raleigh's adventures, Thoreau remarks: "His behavior on this occasion was part and parcel of his constant character . . . nor indeed is it of so much importance to inquire of a man what actions he performed at one and what at another period, as what manner of man he was at all periods."[28] Then Thoreau goes further, suggesting that our characters point toward ideals that are the real business of ethics. "When we reconsider what we have said in the foregoing pages," he writes toward the end of the essay:

> we hesitate to apply any of their eulogy to the actual and historical Raleigh, or any of their condemnation to that ideal Raleigh which he suggests, for we must know the man of history as we know our contemporaries, not so much by his deeds, which often belie his real character, as by the expectation he begets in us—and there is a bloom and halo about the character of Raleigh which defies a close and literal scrutiny, and robs us of our critical acumen.[29]

The passage undercuts itself playfully at the end: why should we credit any of Thoreau's judgments about Raleigh, when he as much as admits that hero worship has clouded it? But doesn't the passage also give an accurate account of how heroes work in ethics, and wouldn't ethics be a poor thing without them? The quotation acknowledges an ineliminable idealism in ethics; still, we can no more dispense with the realistic assessment of character than we can always remain within it. In fact, Thoreau does criticize particular acts of Raleigh's and mark certain deficiencies in his character. Thoreau's treatment of heroism is far subtler here than in "The Service," engaging difficulties and paradoxes with which he will struggle fruitfully in subsequent ethical writings.

We may learn much from such heroes as Raleigh. Still, the example is "far-fetched"—from the sixteenth rather than the nineteenth century, from England rather than America. Thoreau's key innovation will be to make himself the hero of *Walden* and to identify the real challenges facing him and his contemporaries: not battling Spaniards and sailing ships to the New World, but battling conformity and settling America in such a way as to "keep the new world new." This is to face "the challenge" directly and demand the most from oneself. As many of Thoreau's readers have pointed out, it is presumptuous to treat yourself as a hero. *Walden* forces serious readers to specify exactly what is being presumed (is it that we can live better lives than we do? that some people are better than others?). In presuming and personalizing ethics in this way, Thoreau will clarify the challenge that life presents to himself and his society. His particularity will ensure that along with his growing, impressive ability to express himself, he will have something useful to say.

Similarly, Thoreau's exploration of natural history needed time to mature. In *Nature,* Emerson had ably and stirringly examined the natural world as a resource for human development. Now as a literary assignment, he gave Thoreau several recently published books on the natural history of Massachusetts, and Thoreau reviewed them under that title for the *Dial*. Thoreau showed a transcendentalist's disdain for the many dry and dusty facts they contained and mostly substituted his own poetry and generalizations for a discussion of the matter of the books ("science is always brave; for to know is to know good," "vegetation is but a kind of crystallization," and the like).[30] Still, his curiosity was aroused by some of these facts. "Entomology extends the limits of being in a new direction," he wrote. "It suggests besides, that the universe is not rough-hewn, but perfect in its details. Nature will bear the closest inspection."[31] In coming years, Thoreau proved the truth of this last assertion, devoting ever more time to inspecting the flora and fauna of Concord and becoming a fine field naturalist. A detailed knowledge of nature informs all his later writings. Once again, only through an appreciation and exploration of particularity—in this case, nature's myriad species and various landscapes—could Thoreau fully reap the harvest of knowledge, expression, and personal development that Emerson had confidently promised in *Nature*.

In "Natural History of Massachusetts," Thoreau chides his authors for their dryness and failure to address the general reader—proof, to him, that they have failed to understand nature. How could adding knowledge to beauty lead to such dullness? he wondered. "The true man of science," he concluded the piece, "will know nature better by his finer organization; he will smell, taste, see, hear, feel, better than other men. His will be a deeper and finer experience. . . . With all the helps of machinery and the arts, the most scientific will still be the healthiest and friendliest man, and possess a more perfect Indian wisdom."[32] Beyond the obvious romantic influence, an ancient philosophical faith is expressed here: in the unity of knowledge; in the necessary congruence of knowledge, virtue, and wisdom; in the need to prove one's philosophy by living it. Such beliefs have largely been abandoned by modern philosophy and rejected by modern science. In *Walden*, Thoreau will make his case for them, and for nature as the main source of human strength and the main resource for human development.

Here, of course, he will follow the master's lead, but in a way that will take his mature philosophy quite a way from Emerson's anthropocentrism. In *Nature* Emerson had located nature's purpose and value solely in human development. "All the facts in natural history," he had confidently and unequivocally stated, "taken by themselves, have no value. . . . The instincts of the ant are very unimportant, considered as the ant's; but the moment a ray of relation is seen to extend from it to man [they] become sublime."[33] Thoreau restates this belief in the centrality of human consciousness at various points in his career. But already in "Natural History of Massachusetts," his attention is drawn to nature's freedom or *wildness*, and this category will eventually become central to his philosophy. In time, he will seek to understand nature's stories themselves, scientifically (while still mining them for literary or imaginative purposes); furthermore, he will propose that some of those stories be allowed to continue without human interference or control. An appreciation of wildness will also lead Thoreau to insist that nature has value in its own right and to question the Kantian belief that lawfulness is the key to ethics. In treating these issues, Thoreau will develop his own philosophy and explore what remain some of the deepest, most vexing questions in ethics.

At this early stage in his writing career, Thoreau is groping. He has found his themes (with a little help from his friend), but he has not yet lived enough to say much about them or appreciate the difficulties and complexities of actualizing them. "The Service," for example, suggests that what we really need to succeed in life is effort and courage and a worthy aim. True enough, but empty.

For now, Thoreau's writings are more important for working up themes and as training in the craft of writing than for what they accomplish themselves. And even more important than writing, at this stage, is living. Thoreau moves into Emerson's house for two years. He learns the discipline of different kinds of work, from teaching to surveying to pencil making. He improves his acquaintance with nature and with what naturalists have written about it. Friendships deepened or cut off by death; infatuation and a rejected marriage proposal to a young woman; discussions with the literary greats and social reformers who visit Concord; family life at the Thoreaus and the Emersons. All this is grist for Thoreau's mill, which in due time will turn out its masterpiece.

Although I am not blind to Thoreau's literary merits, this is a study of Thoreau as philosopher, which requires some explanation before we proceed. Despite the efforts of Stanley Cavell and a few others, Emerson and Thoreau are not widely read by professional philosophers today. A recent excellent study titled *Emerson's Ethics* was written by an English professor. The best study of Thoreau's ethics to date, in my opinion, was written by a professor of American Studies.[34] The most valuable works on Emerson's and Thoreau's ethics remain literary studies that have wandered fruitfully beyond the usual disciplinary boundaries.

I am indebted to these works, yet I want to claim Emerson and Thoreau for mainstream philosophy. For one thing, they are an important part of the American philosophical tradition. Emerson strongly influenced university philosophy from the mid- to late-nineteenth century, as it made the same transition he had, casting off the certainty and authority of Christian orthodoxy for a more exciting, uncertain, wide-ranging, fragmented reflection. William James is on record regarding Emerson's influence on pragmatism; indeed, if C. S. Peirce first articulated pragmatism's characteristic epistemological doctrines, Emerson first articulated its ethical tenets, particularly the corrigibility and empirical testability of values. Beyond the universities, Emerson's popular lectures brought philosophical speculation—the intelligent discussion of ethics, theology, metaphysics, and other philosophical topics—to tens of thousands of his fellow citizens.

As Emerson's direct intellectual influence has waned, Thoreau's has waxed. Gandhi read *Walden* and "Resistance to Civil Government" as a young lawyer in South Africa, later recalling that Thoreau's ideas influenced him greatly as he developed his political philosophy. Martin Luther King Jr. acknowledged a similar debt. All the key American environmental thinkers, from John Muir to Aldo Leopold to Rachel Carson, show Thoreau's clear influence. Many current attempts to articulate an environmentalism for the twenty-first century, from those of conservation biologist Daniel Botkin to those of simplicity advocate David Shi, look to Thoreau for inspiration.[35] More than any other nineteenth-century American thinker, Thoreau remains a vital presence in important, current intellectual debates.

A scrupulous intellectual history will acknowledge the importance of Emerson and Thoreau. But regardless of their past importance, Emerson and Thoreau contain some of our best reflections on ethics. Like all great philosophers, they address central questions clearly and searchingly and avoid pat answers. Like many great philosophers, their questions were not always immediately recognized as central by other philosophers, but the recent revival of virtue ethics and the growth of environmental ethics show professional philosophers finally catching up to them. On these topics—the pursuit of virtue and our proper relationship to nature—they can be read with greater profit than all but a handful of contemporary philosophers. *Walden,* in particular, remains a remarkable if largely neglected philosophical resource, as I hope to show.

Life

Henry Thoreau went to Walden Pond to take up Emerson's challenge. *Walden,* published seven years after Thoreau's two-year sojourn, records what he learned there and subsequently, as he worked to improve his life.[1] It is both an achievement and a record of achievements. It poses its own challenges but, its author hopes, offers readers help in meeting them.

Let us consider two key passages, beginning at the beginning with the epigraph, the only sentence that is repeated in *Walden:*

> I do not propose to write an ode to dejection, but to brag as lustily as chanticleer in the morning, standing on his roost, if only to wake my neighbors up. (ii, 84)*

This passage foreshadows much that follows. There is the mention of neighbors, and the implied questions of who they are and how best to speak and live with them (surprisingly recurrent themes in this book written by a solitary). There is the notion of awakening, one of Thoreau's key moral tropes. There is all that is suggested by the comparison with Coleridge's "Ode to Dejection," a poem lamenting the mature adult's alienation from nature:

> All this long eve, so balmy and serene,
> Have I been gazing on the western sky,
> And its peculiar tint of yellow green:
> And still I gaze—and with how blank an eye!
> . . . those clouds . . . those stars . . .
> Yon crescent Moon, as fixed as if it grew
> In its own cloudless, starless lake of blue;
> I see them all so excellently fair,
> I see, not feel, how beautiful they are!

Coleridge (or the poem's narrator) presents this as a necessary alienation, the consequence of the growth of reason, as "that which suits

---

* Parenthetical citations throughout the book are from the 1971 Princeton University Press edition of *Walden.*

a part infects the whole / And now is almost grown the habit of my soul."[2]

Thoreau shared this romantic sense of loss. "Once I was part and parcel of nature," he wrote in middle age; "now I am observant of her."[3] Throughout his writings, he notes the danger of knowledge killing off love, science killing poetry, thought killing feeling. Yet *Walden* presents an alternative to romantic despair over the inevitable loss of our initial innocent connection to nature; indeed, it makes a mature, knowledgeable relationship to nature central to living a good life. In sustaining romantic hopes while warding off romantic misology, Thoreau will tackle central philosophical questions about the place of reason in a good human life, including its value and limitations as a guide to right living.

The epigraph suggests that Thoreau has made a choice here. Like Coleridge, he could have written an ode to dejection: faced west at sunset, rather than rising to greet the sun in the east. A journal entry, written while he was composing *Walden*, confesses: "Now if there are any who think that I am vain glorious—that I set myself up above others— and crow over their low estate—let me tell them that I could tell a pitiful story respecting myself as well as them—if my spirits held out to do it, I could encourage them with a sufficient list of failures—& could flow as humbly as the very gutters themselves."[4] Here, in the relative privacy of his journal, Thoreau lets himself moon a bit. He certainly knew these moods and the disappointments that led to them. In fact, he explored them, as essential human experiences having much to teach him.

But Thoreau knows that such dejected, twilight thoughts provide no impetus and no guidance for right living. "That man who does not believe that each day contains an earlier, more sacred, and auroral hour than he has yet profaned, has despaired of life, and is pursuing a descending and darkening way" (89). Note the word "despair" here, from the Latin *de* (without) + *sperare* (hope). Such hopelessness leads to lethargy and laziness. Despair is an important term in *Walden,* often marking our "stuckness" in the quotidian and our failure to demand more from our lives and ourselves. "The mass of men lead lives of quiet desperation. What is called resignation [acceptance, brute endurance] is confirmed desperation" [the final surrender, a fatalism that is truly fatal] (8).

Rather than despair, we must build on a recognition of the essential goodness of life (*esse qua esse bonum est,* wrote Augustine, specifying *his* ethical starting point). "We should impart our courage, and not our despair," Thoreau writes, "our health and ease, and not our disease, and take care that this does not spread by contagion" (77). The epigraph's crowing cock puts a simple "yes" to life at the center of ethics. We can get from this simple "yes" to more complex affirmations, but never from a "no" to a "yes." And this first premise, or necessary practical postulate, cannot be proven. Affirmation or negation always remains the main choice facing each of us.

Consider a second key passage, one of the most often-cited in *Walden*:

> I went to the woods because I wished to live deliberately, to front only the essential facts of life, and see if I could not learn what it had to teach, and not, when I came to die, discover that I had not lived. I did not wish to live what was not life, living is so dear; nor did I wish to practice resignation, unless it was quite necessary. I wanted to live deep and suck out all the marrow of life . . . to know it by experience, and be able to give a true account of it in my next excursion. (90–91)

The passage develops into a stirring peroration to life and life's grand possibilities (experiencing deeply, knowing truth, sharing this knowledge with others). But Thoreau makes it clear that these possibilities can be explored only by those who live *deliberately*. The term encompasses both the ability to consider alternatives and the ability to act—to instantiate one alternative rather than another. The presence of *liber* and *liberate* suggests an essential connection between such deliberation and human freedom.

If choosing to speak a basic "yes" to life is one key antidote to despair, another is deliberation: thinking through particular options and actively choosing the best ones, rather than falling into the easiest ones. Deliberation is an act of optimism, signaling the belief that we have choices; that we can distinguish better from worse choices; that we can act on that knowledge and improve our lives. "I know of no more encouraging fact," Thoreau writes, "than the unquestionable ability of man to elevate his life by a conscious endeavor" (90). Throughout *Walden,* he renews his call for "deliberate" action in constructing a house (45), choosing a career (73), reading a book (101), building a fireplace (241).

Deliberation is the key to living well, affirming human freedom, and meeting life's challenges. Life is glorious, Thoreau insists, and so the stakes are high. For we may come to the end of our lives and find that we have not lived. We may waste our lives on inessential trivialities. We may fail to learn what life has to teach. Like the penitential brahmins described in *Walden*'s third paragraph, we may lead lives that deny or deform our human nature (4). In all these ways we may, and often do, deny life.

Awakening

Walden anchors its ethical discussions in powerful, richly extended metaphors: morality as economy, morality as cultivation, morality as flourishing. Just as we must pay particular attention to first principles and initial arguments in works of academic philosophy, so here we must attend to these key orienting metaphors. One of the most important equates morality with awakening.

Two calls to wakefulness bracket the text of *Walden:* the epigraph's crowing of the cock and the text's final sentences: "There is more day to dawn. The sun is but a morning star" (333). In between, Thoreau returns to the theme often, asking us, for example, to awaken to the fact that we have choices in life (8), or describing his literary labors and itinerant naturalizing in terms of alert wakefulness (17). The metaphor's most extended use occurs midway through *Walden*'s second chapter, "Where I Lived, and What I Lived For."

"Every morning was a cheerful invitation to make my life of equal simplicity, and I may say innocence, with Nature herself," Thoreau begins, once again emphasizing our free choice of whether or not to engage life's opportunities. "I have been as sincere a worshipper of Aurora as the Greeks. I got up early and bathed in the pond; that was a religious exercise, and one of the best things which I did" (88). The sacrament's power comes from its bodily immediacy—what could be more immediate than a plunge, first thing in the morning, into a clear, cold pond?— and its ability to thrust us into the state of excitement and awareness it celebrates. If you doubt that wakefulness is a matter of degree, or despair of your own ability to wake up more fully, such a plunge will instantly dispel these worries! The metaphor's power comes from how literally Thoreau takes it, here at the start of the discussion, and from the diverse ways it transcends that literal meaning, in what follows. The passage continues: "The morning, which is the most memorable season of the day, is the awakening hour. Then there is least somnolence in us; and for an hour, at least, some part of us awakes which slumbers all the rest of the day and night" (89). Now Thoreau begins to speak metaphorically, yet the statement also seems literally true to experience. Waking from a full night's sleep, early, before the neighbors begin bustling about, we may feel a freshness within and without, a hopefulness and sense of possibility that even the best days, as they fill up with details, somehow obscure. Morning is a natural beginning; making the effort to wake with the world, at dawn, emphasizes this.

Then again, how we will experience our mornings remains to some extent open, no matter when we arise. We may all have to get up eventually, to some degree, but the spirit in which we do so can make all the difference. "Little is to be expected of that day, if it can be called a day, to which we are not awakened by our Genius, but by the mechanical nudgings of some servitor, are not awakened by our own newly acquired force and aspirations from within . . . to a higher life than we fell asleep from" (89). Hope is the key to true awakening: hope, anchored in feelings of excitement and in the belief that we can live better lives than we ever have before. "We must learn to reawaken and keep ourselves awake, not by mechanical aids, but by an infinite expectation of the dawn" (90).

Thoreau's admonition speaks directly to anyone who has ever unwillingly dragged himself or herself out of bed to the shrilling of an alarm clock. But I think that to fully appreciate "awakening" as a metaphor for personal renewal, you need to have watched a sunrise recently and felt the radiance on your face, the sense of promise warming your bones. We must anchor our metaphors in personal experience. The more we do so, the truer they will prove themselves, if indeed they are true.

Just as the metaphor of "awakening" allows us to descend more fully into our experience, it points to its transcendence: to an ability to look beyond experience, hopefully. The passage continues: "To him whose elastic and vigorous thought keeps pace with the sun, the day is a perpetual morning. It matters not what the clocks say or the attitudes and labors of men. Morning is when I am awake and there is a dawn in me. Moral reform is the effort to throw off sleep" (89–90). To call moral reform, the improvement of character, an effort to throw off sleep emphasizes yet again that this opportunity is widely available; in a sense, it is as easy as waking up. It isn't for lack of some esoteric knowledge that we fail to live better lives, but for lack of effort.

But Thoreau's "moral reform" is quite different from the common conception, in his day or ours. It is personal, not social; it does not ask for justice toward others, but that we be just *toward ourselves* and develop our highest faculties. "The millions are awake enough for physical labor," Thoreau continues, "but only one in a million is awake enough for effective intellectual exertion, only one in a hundred millions to a poetic or divine life" (90). If that is so, we have all of us—including the author of *Walden*—mostly been sleepwalking through life. "I have never yet met a man who was quite awake," Thoreau asserts. "How could I have looked him in the face?" (90).

The power of the metaphor, I think, comes from its juxtaposition of the ease and the difficulty of waking up. If we could continue after our dip in the pond, piling sacrament upon sacrament, and be fully alive, truly grateful, completely aware, for just one day—what a day that would be! And, the metaphor suggests, we might simply wake up and *see* the right path to all this, as easily as we wake up and see the world waking up outside our window. For these are the great miracles, of course: the living, changing, lovely world; our ability to see and understand and appreciate it. The goal seems so near! To really think, really create, really live, means to be *present*, the way we are when we plunge into a pond and WAKE UP. Yet we continue to slumber.

Again, the power of the metaphor comes from its juxtaposition of incremental and heroic striving, and Thoreau's blurring of the line between them. It is as if, like some con man or "travelling patterer" (218), he and his metaphor have signed us up to purchase something that we are not sure we want, despite its obvious goodness, despite lacking any clear reason to remain suspicious. "Who would not be early to rise, and rise earlier and earlier every successive day of his life, until he became unspeakably healthy, wealthy, and wise?" (127). Yet we prefer endurance to excellence.

Self-Culture

The challenge is to live well. Another key metaphor, which suggests how to think about this and begins to help specify its content, is "flourishing." Thoreau quotes a Sufi mystic, who compares the worthy or noble man with the cypress tree: evergreen, perpetually fresh, "always flourishing" (79). We have taken good care of our *material* "flourishing," Thoreau says at another point; now let us pursue those higher activities that "conduce to our culture" (110). The notion of flourishing (= "flowering") suggests beauty of character and higher achievements than mere endurance or physical growth. It suggests a healthy self and a movement beyond the self, into positive relationships with others and achievements in which others may share. Related to flourishing is fruiting; Thoreau warns that we cannot pluck life's "finer fruits" if we devote ourselves too exclusively to the "coarse labors of life," or to moneymaking and the pursuit of luxury (6, 15).

Interestingly, recent scholars have used "flourishing" to translate the Greek word *eudaimonia*, the final end or general human goal in the ethics of Plato, Aristotle, and other ancient Greek philosophers.[5] Traditionally *eudaimonia* has been translated by our trivial word "happiness," but its overtones of subjectivity (you are happy if you say so) and pleasure maximization seriously mischaracterize the Greek original. Thoreau uses the word "happiness" only once in *Walden* (193), in passing, perhaps for this reason.

A related word for our chief goal is "cultivation," used in the sense of "self-culture." Organic growth is a key metaphor for personal development in *Walden*—"Why has man rooted himself thus firmly in the earth, but that he may rise in the same proportion into the heavens above?" (15)—with the theme of self-culture becoming fully explicit in the chapter "The Bean-Field": "I said to myself, I will not plant beans and corn with so much industry another summer, but such seeds, if the seed is not lost, as sincerity, truth, simplicity, faith, innocence, and the like, and see if they will not grow in this soil, even with less toil" (163–64). Thoreau presses for "human culture" (40), "intellectual culture" (103) and a village that looks after "our own culture" and spends as much on mental as bodily "aliments" (108). He asks for a "noble" culture that educates into an appreciation of beauty and learning—"instead of noblemen, let us have noble villages of men" (110)—and insists that this opportunity is and should be open to all, the Irish immigrant no less than the Boston brahmin (205).

The metaphor of cultivation suggests the hard work necessary to improve ourselves, particularly when it is returned to its agricultural roots, as Thoreau does in *Walden*, hoeing real beans as he cultivates himself. At the same time, cultivation and related organic metaphors suggest that such improvement is as widely available as life itself. The student, we are told, "should not *play* life or *study* it merely . . . but earnestly *live* it from beginning to end" (51). The injunction "live!" repeated again and again in *Walden* points to engagement and commitment, but also to ubiquitous possibility: anyone who is alive can improve his or her condition. It asserts the essential goodness of our situation in the world, where nature preserves us (not without some effort on our part, of course), and our greatest opportunities grow out of the simplest aspects of our lives: the child's rapt attention to flowers or insects and his or her "whys?" are kin to science; the same expressive impulses behind careless finger paintings or nursery rhymes lead to the highest achievements in art and poetry. Life is an "experiment" (9), an "adventure" (15) that is open to all, if we will take it that way. We, like Thoreau, may "improve our opportunities" (246).

The romantic concept of *Bildung*—often translated as "self-culture" or "self-development"—is thus central to Thoreau's ethics, as it was to Emerson and many of the transcendentalists.[6] Romantic *Bildung* involves fully cultivating all our human capabilities, particularly our intellectual, aesthetic, and spiritual capabilities. To the ancient ethicists' emphasis on knowledge and virtue, the romantics added a new stress on individuality, authenticity, and creativity. To the modern concern with a specifically moral goodness—fulfilling our duties, treating others well—the romantics added an appreciation of all those hyphenated "self" words: self-expression, self-improvement, self-actualization.

One particularly important aspect of self-culture for Thoreau is the need to enrich and diversify our experience. "It is something to be able to paint a particular picture, or to carve a statue, and so to make a few objects beautiful," Thoreau writes, "but it is far more glorious to carve and paint the very atmosphere and medium through which we look, which morally we can do" (90). The last, qualifying phrase is meant seriously. Appreciating and enriching our experience is a key *moral* imperative for Thoreau. It makes us more fully human. Knowledge and self-development depend upon it (91, 323–24). More simply, enriching our experience helps us lead more interesting and enjoyable lives. The fact that our actions remain important keeps this ethical position from degenerating into mere aestheticism. The passage continues: "To affect the quality of the day, that is the highest of arts. Every man is tasked to make his life, even in its details, worthy of the contemplation of his most elevated and critical hour" (90).

In service to this goal, Thoreau repeatedly advocates trying new activities and pursuing diverse adventures (3, 208, 324). Just as often, he shows us how to get more out of our ordinary experiences: by carefully attending to them, thoroughly reflecting on them, patiently improving them (246, 329). *Walden* is filled with descriptions of common activities: reading, fishing, hoeing beans, laying a course of bricks, watching a sunset. Yet as Thoreau experiments with these simple activities, they become charged with possibility: means, now, to connection and knowledge; paths inward through the self and outward into nature; even sacraments, tying us closer to our native Earth in love and gratitude. Finding the great, unsuspected possibilities hidden in ordinary life is a big part of what *Walden* offers to help us achieve.

Thoreau repeatedly emphasizes the aim of developing our natural capabilities or, in his more usual term, our proper "faculties." He speaks of his "best faculties" being concentrated in his head (98), warns that we must not allow our "nobler faculties" to slumber (104, 222), discusses how we may keep our "higher or poetic faculties in the best condition" (215), recounts "recovering" his physical and mental faculties after coming in from a cold and blustery winter's day (254). The metaphor of the penitential brahmins emphasizes the danger of forfeiting our natural capabilities through repeated engagement in pointless or life-denying activities (4). We, like the brahmins, may choose wrongly, failing to use our faculties or using them in perverse ways, so that they atrophy or become permanently deformed.

This emphasis on normal or inherent human faculties provides a naturalistic grounding for Thoreau's ethics. It also links his discussion to the current "capabilities approach" to ethics and human development.[7] For Thoreau, certain faculties define our humanity and make us who we are; we should therefore make the most of them. Or—a weaker claim that would still be valuable for Thoreau's hortatory purposes—we (most of us) have these faculties; therefore we can make more of them, as easily as not.

Thoreau lays particular stress on exploring and developing the full range of human capabilities, making this part of his ethical ideal. As often as he faults workers for failing to cultivate their intellects, he criticizes intellectuals for letting their bodies atrophy. As often as he condemns his neighbors for too exclusive a focus on economic matters, he denounces the idle rich for failing to attend to economics and learn the lessons that economic life can teach. Rather than pursuing a narrow way, we should broaden our interests and ourselves. "Man's capacities have never been measured," Thoreau states, "nor are we to judge of what he can do by any precedents, so little has been tried" (10). It is only by pushing ourselves in these various directions that we can begin to know and enjoy our capabilities.

Thoreau's discussions of particular human faculties adds content to the general notions of "flourishing" and "self-cultivation," further clarifying his ethical ideal. And emphasizing these goals de-emphasizes others. Nowhere, for example, does Thoreau suggest that we should try to maximize pleasure in our attempt to live the good life—the utilitarian desideratum. In fact, he argues that pursuing this objective is ignoble and contemptible, a turning away from more worthy goals. Similarly, he disparages the pursuits of wealth and power, perennially popular candidates for the good life (in real life, if not within philosophy). When Thoreau talks about "enriching our lives," he clearly does not mean this in terms of money or increased material possessions.

Flourishing, self-culture, enriching our experience, developing our faculties. These related terms point us in certain directions: toward activity rather than passive enjoyment, for example. Yet they also remain open to individual, idiosyncratic interpretation. The focus may be on self-cultivation, but we need not assume (and Thoreau does not assume) that our selves are essentially the same. If you are a rosebush and I am a cabbage patch, our proper cultivation will be different. So will our fruits. In either case, we can improve our lives and take pride in the results. In contrast to modern ethics' focus on rules and commands, *Walden* provides open-ended guidance for self-development. In contrast to modern ethics' concern to specify the proper limitations on personal assertiveness, *Walden* encourages such assertiveness. In the end, Thoreau insists that your particular path is up to you.

Our Chief End

This emphasis on personal choice is underscored by a third key term Thoreau uses to describe his ethical aspirations: pursuing his "chief end." Consider again a passage we have already discussed:

> I went to the woods because I wished to live deliberately, to front only the essential facts of life . . . to live deep . . . to know [life] by experience, and be able to give a true account of it in my next excursion. For most men, it appears to me, are in a strange uncertainty about it, whether it is of the devil or of God, and have *somewhat hastily* concluded that it is the chief end of man here to "glorify God and enjoy him forever." (90–91)

The phrase Thoreau emphasizes is nicely ambiguous. The full quotation actually goes some way toward specifying Thoreau's conception of the good life, which includes a rich experience, the pursuit of knowledge, artistic creation, and reverence. That conception is in many ways out of the ordinary, but Thoreau's conclusion sets these goals up as constituents of a "chief end" to which his readers must respond.

Thoreau's contemporary readers, predominantly Protestants, would have immediately recognized the source of the quotation that concludes the passage as the catechism given in the *New England Primer,* widely used in the religious instruction of the young. "Q: What is the chief end of man? A: To glorify God and enjoy him forever."[8] To refer to this catechism is to refer to a "chief end" that has been explicitly acknowledged by many of his readers, in language that they understand and accept to some degree. Thoreau cleverly piggybacks his own elevated conception of the good life onto another conception to which his neighbors at least pay lip service, letting his readers' religious convictions do some of the motivational work for him. In fact, he will challenge these convictions. But it is in such words as the catechism speaks that his readers acknowledge higher goals and some chief goal in life, and Thoreau begins here.

What might it mean that his readers have "*somewhat hastily* concluded" on a chief end? Perhaps that they have chosen wrongly and that there is a better one. But "to glorify and enjoy God" might well express Thoreau's own vision of living well, based on his own particular definitions of the terms in question. So the "hasty conclusion" might mean that the terms are correct, yet their common interpretation false. Then again, such suggestive words are essentially empty without a certain amount of interpretation, which each individual must provide for himself or herself. There could be many valid readings, but some degree of mental effort is necessary for any genuine one. Still another possible interpretation focuses on our actions: most of us conclude our efforts to live up to our chief end "somewhat hastily," failing to pursue the good life through mere laziness. Along these lines, the quotation might even refer to a widespread hypocrisy: we acknowledge a grand purpose to our lives, we gravely insist that our children memorize these words. Yet we often fail to even attempt to live up to them.

Thoreau certainly means to challenge his readers' interpretations of their "chief end." But irrespective of any particular interpretation, he wishes to warn them against a premature belief that they understand what such rich and consequent words mean and what their acceptance would entail. Perhaps Thoreau's most important contention is that *resting* in any particular interpretation of these words, or in any particular forms for living up to them, is mistaken. This point holds regardless of our definition of our chief end. "Happiness," "flourishing," or even "maximizing pleasure," all challenge us. Their pursuit demands a continual effort of translation and interpretation and will. To rest in doctrine—*this* is God, the Bible, or my particular sect, says so—is to abdicate my personal responsibility to know God. To rest in a particular understanding of what God demands from us—these particular forms of worship, these particular relationships to our neighbors—is to close off the possibility of a transformative religious experience or genuinely new testament that might call into question our current forms of life.

Taking the words of the catechism seriously—believing that we are making a statement that refers to God, the author of the universe, who demands that we *glorify* him—means accepting a task that is almost by definition beyond our abilities. We can know God's nature only very imperfectly and can only glorify him in words and deeds that fall laughably short of his own glory. Nevertheless we must make the effort, or forthrightly renounce this as our chief end. To fail to take our chief end seriously is to fail to take ourselves seriously.

The congregation repeats that its chief end is to *enjoy* God, yet Thoreau sees little joy in his neighbors' religion: "Our hymn-books resound with a melodious cursing of God and enduring him forever. . . . There is nowhere recorded a simple and irrepressible satisfaction with the gift of life, any memorable praise of God" (78). The worshippers on the hard benches certainly don't look like they are enjoying God, life, or anything else. They no doubt hope to get closer to God in the great by and by and enjoy him then "forever." But if this world is God's creation, displaying an order and beauty that all may see, then perhaps we are somewhat hasty in dismissing it. Perhaps a proper reverence demands an appreciation for *this* creation—the only one, after all, with which we have yet formed an acquaintance.

The catechism defines our chief end in religious terms, but religion easily enough becomes another discrete activity in our lives, performed in church on Sunday mornings. In contrast, *Walden* specifies reverence within various concrete areas of life: fishing, reading, cooking meals, heating a house. Thoreau describes his experiment in farming as a means toward reverent association with the Earth, conceived as God's creation (and even more radically, conceived of as itself divine). He seeks to make farming a sacrament expressing joy in the world and our necessary work within it. Such examples undermine the convenient belief that we may worship God at select times and places and go our secular way in between times. Our chief end should not be so lightly dismissed. Thoreau's attempts at everyday sacramentality show both a will to reverence and a determination to focus his efforts toward his chief end. There is a strong connection between this reinterpretation of everyday activities and the reinterpretation of important ethical terms. Both further our goal of living the best lives possible.

Thoreau offers these reinterpretations as a way of challenging his neighbors to take seriously their chief end, *however they may conceive of it*. Elsewhere in *Walden*, he speaks of the good life in more secular terms. Whether speaking in sacred or secular language, he insists that our highest goals and ideals must be part of our daily lives. If they do not infuse our lives, they do not really specify our chief end. We should then honestly discard them and discuss our real goals in life, low as these may be.

Any putative chief end must be the conceivable point of all our actions. The simplicity of *Walden*'s chapter headings illustrates Thoreau's determination to find beauty, joy, and value in the mundane. "Economy," "Reading," "House-Warming," "Visitors." These activities and aspects of our lives may in the end be elaborated in quite complicated ways. They may turn out to mean something more, or something different, than what we had originally envisioned. But they should be put to the worthiest possible use: a chief end that we may wholeheartedly endorse.

For finally, neither reason, nor tradition, nor society, can define our chief end. Each of us must choose, saying, through our actions, "this is good" or, at least, "this shall be." Whatever our chief end, we should take it seriously and make it our own and "earnestly live [life] from beginning to end" (51).

Awakening, self-cultivation, pursuing our chief end. These metaphors and key terms emphasize somewhat different aspects of our ethical situation. What they share is a demanding open-endedness. They challenge us to strive, while resisting any complete specification of what we should be striving toward.

Whether or not a general account of human flourishing is possible—and *Walden* several times suggests that it is not (16, 71, 326)—each of us can know which paths are better for us personally and act on that knowledge. The possibility of improvement through our own efforts should cheer us. The possibility that our lives can become more fully *our* lives—our actions consciously and therefore freely chosen, our experiences consciously and therefore deeply experienced—should likewise cheer us, beyond the further hope that the choices will be better and the experiences more pleasurable. Thoreau alternately harangues his readers for our inertia and failure to demand more from life and entices us onward with fair possibilities, noble ideals, and accounts of his own successes: Thoreau snug and secure in his well-built cabin, facing winter's blasts (256); Thoreau floating on the calm summer waters of Walden Pond, flute or fishing pole in hand, a symbol of personal equilibrium and harmony with his surroundings (174–75). As long as we are alive we should strive to live well. Anything less is a premature "resignation" from life's pleasures and possibilities, which devalues life and demoralizes us.

Because *Walden* is a work in virtue ethics, it is hard for some readers—and most contemporary philosophers—to see it as a work of ethics at all. For we tend to define ethics as the discipline that specifies proper interpersonal relations, or even more narrowly, our strict obligations toward one another.[9] So it is not surprising that recent philosophers have neglected *Walden* and focused, when they've attended to Thoreau at all, on "Resistance to Civil Government," with its emphasis on justice and basic political obligations. Thoreau returns the favor, repeatedly invoking the ancient moralists in *Walden*—not only Greek and Roman but also Indian and Chinese—while largely ignoring modern moral philosophers.

Thoreau clearly found the ancients' broader conception of ethics compelling. "Our whole life is startlingly moral," he writes. "There is never an instant's truce between virtue and vice" (218). Our decisions about what careers to pursue, whom to befriend, or how to spend our time and money, all imply value judgments. Like our judgments about how we should treat other people, they involve distinguishing different courses of action and calling some better than others—if only implicitly, through our choosing one course of action over another. But better in relation to what? The answer would seem to be: better in relation to furthering our own (and perhaps others') happiness, success, flourishing, excellence, or personal achievement, however we define these. So in a sense, we are all committed to some ethical judgments here. The ancients' philosophical hope was that we could, through deliberation, improve those judgments.

To call something an ethical question, though, says that it involves value judgments *and* asserts its importance. It is precisely the sense that these personal decisions are important—that they help make us who we are and that this matters—which Thoreau works so hard to instill in his readers.[10] Self-development is the challenge and opportunity presented, by life, to all, "the teamster on the highway" driving for "Squire Make-a-stir" and the Irish immigrant John Field, no less than Ralph Waldo Emerson or Henry David Thoreau. The humblest reader of *Walden* cannot escape the injunction: "However mean your life is, meet it and live it" (328). Here Thoreau parts company most decisively with the ancients, who generally didn't worry about the virtues of hoi polloi. Plato and Aristotle spoke mainly to their society's intellectual and economic elite, directing their ethical exhortations to youths whose social position already predisposed them to see their own flourishing as important. A key goal for Thoreau is to inculcate that sense of self-importance more widely.

The Good Life

Taking *Walden* as a whole produces a clear picture of Thoreau's view of the good life—or, at least, of the good life for him. This includes health, freedom, pleasure, friendship, a rich experience, knowledge (of self, nature, and God), reverence, self-culture, and personal achievement.[11] This list is somewhat arbitrary, since many other terms are used to cover these "goods": health is often referred to as "hardiness," for example, while "freedom" is used interchangeably with "independence." Many terms overlap, and all are open to interpretation. To list them is not to say anything about their relative importance or proper balance in a complete life. Still, the list gives an accurate summary of Thoreau's ideal. I think it also fairly summarizes what many of us want out of life, although we will each understand and balance these goods somewhat differently.

Thoreau specifies his pursuit of these goods, or goals, in detail, often in terms of his relationship to nature. For example, freedom, for Thoreau, includes not just the absence of physical coercion, but also having the time to explore his surroundings, the ability to walk the local landscape without being arrested for trespassing, and the intellectual openness and energy to think his own thoughts. He considers pitfalls and explores possibilities for maximizing such freedom. Rather than polishing an exact, abstract definition of freedom and attempting to justify its value in terms of a general theory of human nature or ethics, Thoreau assumes freedom as an ideal shared by his readers. He then tries to enrich and complicate our understanding of it by considering freedom's physical, intellectual, and social aspects or by introducing startling comparisons between our lives and the lives of slaves, Indians, and other exotic characters. By increasing our sense of what is possible and sharing his own achievements, Thoreau hopes to motivate his readers to more fully explore and achieve their own freedom. This mimics the hortatory and voluntary character of much ancient virtue ethics, as opposed to modern ethics' typical emphasis on rules and obligations. We cannot, after all, be forced to be free or to value freedom. It also anticipates the commonsense approach of many current writers in virtue ethics, who take the widespread acceptance of certain goals as prima facie evidence for their objective value and importance, while exploring their meaning and cultivation in detail.[12]

Similarly, Thoreau assumes a widely shared belief in the importance of worthwhile, enjoyable social relations for living the good life but radically reinterprets this in *Walden*. Dwelling apart from people awakened him to possibilities for "sympathy," "society," and "friendship" with nonhuman beings, he reports in his chapter "Solitude." Solitude also helped Thoreau order his life, clarify his thoughts, and, he intimates, draw nearer to God—goals presumably shared by some of his readers. Farther from common experience here, he describes, in detail, some of his methods for focusing and for attending to nature, implicitly inviting his readers to try them. Such solitude is not for everyone, Thoreau suggests, but many of his readers might benefit from it, coming back from their own "seasons in the wilderness" as better people, with new insights to share with their neighbors.

Like the orienting metaphors already discussed, the goods or goals of virtue ethics are open-ended: while rudimentary achievements are valuable, there is always room for further striving. For example, *Walden* shows the pleasure and value to be gained from a basic knowledge of nature, as Thoreau carefully watches and faithfully describes the squirrels in his woodpile, the wasps in his walls, or the mice underneath his floorboards. It also displays the expressive and poetic possibilities opened up by such knowledge. After *Walden,* Thoreau pursued more rigorous, scientific knowledge of ecological topics such as seed dispersal mechanisms and patterns of forest succession. But these artistic and scientific achievements did not come at the expense of a basic appreciation and interest in a wide variety of natural phenomena. Of course, our attempts to know and love nature, like our attempts to know and love people, can never be more than partially successful. The trick is to enjoy and fully live our successes, while remaining open to nature's puzzles and mysteries. In all our endeavors, current achievements should be savored, setting the stage for further ones.

How should we balance the "goods" making up the good life? That is largely up to us as individuals. We may hope that pursuing one will support the others, and they often do. Working to enrich our experience should make our lives more pleasurable. Cultivating deep friendships can lead to self-knowledge. But there are also trade-offs. For example, Thoreau sometimes wondered if his intense communion with nature unfitted him for normal social relations. Similarly, the pursuit of scientific knowledge or literary achievement may be lonely and demanding: all in all, not promising the most pleasurable life. Nevertheless, sacrificing some pleasure may lead to greater intellectual or artistic accomplishments and perhaps to pleasures of a different, higher sort.

Or consider the relative value of health, defined as basic physical well-being. Ancient virtue ethicists typically took one of two tacks in relation to health. The first is exemplified by Aristotle, whose *Nicomachean Ethics* commonsensically suggests that health is a necessary component of a happy, flourishing life. Disease makes life unpleasant and keeps us from doing many things. Get unhealthy enough and you die, permanently fore-closing all opportunities to flourish. The second tack is taken by Stoics like Marcus Aurelius, who insists that "anything which happens equally to a bad and a good man cannot be either bad or good." Ill health cannot force us to forsake our principles or live ignobly, and this is all-important. "Where it is possible to live, it is also possible to live the good life."[13]

Thoreau takes both these contradictory positions in *Walden*. He lists "leisure and independence and health" as the fruits of his stay at the pond (60). He talks about how factory workers ruin their lungs and how merchants in town become soft and flabby. He extols the benefits of being out in all weathers and acquiring a strong, rude health that infuses our whole spirit. "Man was not made so large limbed and robust," he exclaims, "but that he must seek to narrow his world, and wall in a space such as fitted him" (27). Get out! Get active! Be healthy!

At other times, though, Thoreau speaks of his willingness to sacrifice health to higher goals. "No man ever followed his genius till it misled him," he writes in his discussion of vegetarianism in the chapter "Higher Laws." "Though the result were bodily weakness, yet perhaps no one can say that the consequences were to be regretted, for these were a life in conformity to higher principles" (216). If a choice arises, Thoreau will put principle over health, just as he will put freedom and self-culture over pleasure. These are higher goods, he believes. Still, there is no principle that tells us exactly when we should put principle over health, or exactly how to balance the various goods in a good human life.

It is important to recognize that the existence of trade-offs does not mean that we are not trading off genuine goods. Even at his most stoical, Thoreau does not forget that we must sometimes make real sacrifices to live according to principle. Nor need such trade-offs undermine our complex ideals of the good life. Our ideals can still guide us, since uncertainty as to particular trade-offs does not indicate complete uncertainty in all cases. I may hesitate over whether to award the palm for the best life to the world-class athlete or the dedicated, but somewhat flabby, scientist. Nevertheless, they both win out over the beer-guzzling couch potato. Not all choices and not all lives are equally good ones.

Should an account of the good life focus more on success out in the world or on personal character? Contemporary virtue ethicists usually focus on character, but without any explicit justification for this. Contrarily, in their pre-reflective moral judgments, many people place a high value on professional success, social influence, creative achievement, or other "external" aspects of life. Reason does not seem to demand that we privilege either of these aspects in judging human excellence; as one contemporary philosopher puts it, after a rare discussion of this issue, "a person may have [legitimate] objectives other than personal well-being."[14] Furthermore, our pursuit of "internal" goals such as character development or acquiring knowledge necessarily seems to involve attempts at external achievement. Given all this, a comprehensive overview of the good life arguably should encompass both aspects.

Thoreau does this, tying his literary and intellectual efforts at the pond to his personal development. As he points out in *Walden*, this "trade . . . with the celestial empire" was indeed "a labor to task [and develop] the faculties of a man" (21). By trying to express in words the sights and sounds of the surrounding woods, fields, and ponds Thoreau enriched his experience of them. By doing ecological fieldwork and writing natural history essays, he learned more than if he had merely read the latest results in the scientific journals. But in committing ourselves to these attempts, we, like Thoreau, commit ourselves to judging our lives to some extent based on their success or failure. So the good life, for a writer, must include writing good books, or poems, or plays; the good life, for a scientist, must include making significant contributions to his or her chosen discipline; the good life, for a parent, must include raising happy, healthy children. On the other hand, personal ability and character help determine success in such projects. In the end, a convincing account of the good life must consider both character and personal achievement: our selves and our creations.

Similarly, we might wonder whether we should praise most highly those who live balanced lives or those who excel in one or two areas. Thoreau argues that specialization cheats us out of many of life's most interesting experiences and the knowledge that comes from them: the division of labor is "a principle which should never be followed but with circumspection" (50). In *Walden* he is his own sawyer, carpenter, and mason; his own farmer, fisherman, and cook; his own prophet, priest, and—until *Walden* started to sell—congregation. *Walden*'s success is a good argument for generalism. Still, some degree of specialization does help us improve our abilities and focus on what we do well. Not everyone is as talented as Henry Thoreau!

In the final analysis, reason does not force us to favor either of these poles: character or success, comprehensive excellence or specialized brilliance. This complicates ethical judgment. How do we rate the sleazy yet gifted genius? The mediocrity with a heart of gold? The successful scientist who sacrifices personal relationships and her family's happiness to live in her lab? The pianist who gives up the effort to develop his world-class talents and contentedly teaches music in a suburban high school? Perhaps we should not press too hard for a general account of the good life that provides simple answers to the questions these examples raise. In any event, it is up to each of us to strike what we often still call "a proper balance" in our own lives.

Higher Goals

Often then and reasonably enough, Thoreau simply presupposes our shared conceptions of happiness or fulfillment and the general goods that constitute them, describes what he believes are improved means to achieve these goods, and leaves their proper balance up to the individual. Such goods as pleasure, freedom, and friendship are widely valued. Enjoying or achieving them is arguably the point of many of our efforts, half-hearted or half-baked as these sometimes are. We thus are already committed to them. If any further justification for their pursuit or importance is needed, Thoreau can appeal to the reader's intuition or personal experience.[15]

But Thoreau also wants to recall us to what he considers the higher ends of self-culture, the pursuit of knowledge and creative achievement. These goals are widely slighted or rejected, Thoreau believes; hence their inclusion in his conception of the good life is more contentious. Beyond modeling their pursuit himself, he has two basic ways to advocate for these higher goals.

First, Thoreau appeals to higher ends that his readers' already hold, if only formally. As we have seen, he makes much of the catechism's "chief end" of knowing and serving God, to which many of his readers are already committed as a basic religious conviction. Then he asks them to take it seriously. "Are you really living reverently?" Thoreau asks. "What then are your sacraments, and how do they inform your life?" Or again: "I know you go to church every Sunday. Still, it isn't quite clear whether you worship God or Mammon. Which is it?" Such questions have no purchase on non-Christians, but honest Christians must answer them or forthrightly renounce their beliefs. Thoreau takes a similar tack in his later political piece "A Plea for Captain John Brown," quoting the abolitionist at length and then commenting simply: "You don't know your testament when you see it."[16]

Thoreau's second main way to commend higher ends is to appeal to the greatness of human nature. "Men labor under a mistake," he writes at the beginning of *Walden,* foolishly pursuing wealth or possessions through greed, gross sensuality, or simply lack of imagination. In this way "the better part of the man is soon ploughed into the soil for compost" (5). Again: "The gross feeder is a man in the larva state" (215). Defining our happiness in terms of sensual pleasure is childish, a failure to grow up and appreciate the proper pleasures of adulthood and to recognize those "higher laws" by which adults freely abide. Or again: "Every man is the lord of a realm beside which the earthly empire of the Czar is but a petty state, a hummock left by the ice" (321). The human soul or spirit is immeasurably superior to mere matter. Exploring and developing *this* is our greatest task.

Such appeals to a better or higher human nature are squarely within the Western philosophical tradition. Consider a classic example from Aristotle's *Nicomachean Ethics.* Aristotle rejects pleasure as the primary criterion for judging the goodness of our lives because he believes this slights human nature, saying "the many, the most vulgar, would seem to conceive the good and happiness as pleasure, and hence they also like the life of gratification. Here they appear completely slavish, since the life they decide on is a life for grazing animals."[17] A human being has capacities and is capable of achievements that far exceed those of the other animals. To ignore these possibilities and focus solely on physical pleasure is to sell ourselves short. The question is not which sort of life furnishes the most pleasure, but which is the best life. While pleasure is a genuine good-in-itself and thus a necessary part of the best human lives, a life devoted solely to maximizing the gross physical pleasures is poor and ignoble.

Aristotle says quite a bit more against views that put pleasure at the center of the good life, but the quotation above pithily indicates the issues raised: the appeal to higher capacities; the appeal to either a *real* or a *better* human nature (higher than the nature of "grazing animals," who do not look up at the stars and wonder, but who look down at the ground and masticate); the insinuation that to live a life devoted to pleasure is in some sense to abdicate our freedom and become passive ("slavish"); the counter-thought that Aristotle's position is elitist, perhaps a counsel of perfection but in any case unsuited to the mass of men who lack ambitions higher than pleasure seeking ("the many, the most vulgar" are said to prefer pleasure over honor or the pursuit of knowledge). Thoreau sounds all these themes and provokes the same aggrieved charges of elitism and perfectionism.

Such appeals to human nature are legion. Perhaps the strongest objection to them is that if we define human nature as what human beings, in fact, *are*, there is no clear standard that we can apply to distinguish between higher and lower, or better and worse, aspects of human nature. We seem to need some standard that transcends human nature in order to judge it. Even if we find such a standard—no easy task in itself—we will no longer have an appeal to human nature, but an appeal beyond it.

There is also the related problem that some people do not seem cut out for higher pursuits. They may have little desire to pursue knowledge or self-culture, or meet with little success when they do pursue them. *Walden* gives us just such a character in Alek Therien, the carefree French-Canadian woodchopper (144–50). Thoreau presents Therien's simple, non-intellectual goodness very sympathetically. Therien is humble, industrious, kind, and considerate of others: "he thoroughly believed in honesty and the like virtues" (150). His life shows many interesting parallels to Thoreau's. Like Thoreau, Therien lives alone in the woods and gets his living outdoors. Like Thoreau, he is a skilled workman and loves wild nature. Therien was the healthiest man Thoreau knew, never tired, even at the end of a long day of physical labor. "He interested me because he was so quiet and solitary and so happy withal," Thoreau wrote, "a well of good humor and contentment which overflowed at his eyes" (146).

Yet Therien is thoroughly simpleminded. He shows no self-knowledge or desire for self-knowledge: "Hearing Plato's definition of a man, —a biped without feathers,—and that one exhibited a cock plucked and called it Plato's man, he thought it an important difference that the *knees* bent the wrong way" (149). Thoreau suggests that Therien lives his life as if this or something similar really were the most important difference between an animal and a man, rather than our ability to reason and thus to strive morally and intellectually. Thoreau tries to get Therien to entertain proposals for social or personal reform: "to take the spiritual view of things" (150). He fails, and describes Therien as infantile, slumbering, not fully human.

But Thoreau still admires Therien, quoting an approving townsman who saw him as "a prince in disguise" (148). Of all the characters who appear in *Walden*, only Thoreau and Walden Pond itself are treated in greater detail. This implies some crucial and unfathomed ethical import in Therien's life and example. "It would have suggested many things to a philosopher to have dealings with him," Thoreau wrote (148). "In him the animal man chiefly was developed," he believed, while "the intellectual and what is called spiritual man in him were slumbering as in an infant" (146–47). Thoreau's virtue ethics is called into question by Therien, who seems to be happy and well suited to his life despite his childishness, his lack of intellectual curiosity, and his passiveness and failure to strive. He is being true to *his* nature, Thoreau suggests—a nature unable to call its own nature into question—and so he is largely beyond criticism. It hardly makes sense to exhort or blame someone for not striving, if they cannot strive. Nevertheless, Therien represents less than the best a human being can aspire to. Then again, perhaps Therien's simple joyfulness and acceptance are worth having in the world, as contributing to its diversity. Despite his high valuation of moral and philosophical striving, Thoreau had said earlier: "there never was and is not likely soon to be a nation of philosophers, nor am I certain it is desirable that there should be" (56).

If Thoreau's intellectual efforts call Therien's simple acceptance of life into account, Therien's easily achieved goodness, in turn, calls Thoreau's strivings into account. Who, then, represents human nature? Who is the better man? Perhaps Alek Therien and Henry Thoreau simply lead different lives, with each exhibiting his proper virtues. If so, a pragmatic resolution would be to ask the reader to try to understand her own nature, cultivate her own suitable virtues, and not bother comparing her successes or achievements with radically different people. If you are a modern Alek Therien, you will not be reading *Walden* and so cannot be insulted by it; if you read and understand the book, you have the capacity and therefore the duty to pursue higher ends. Yet as reasonable and nonjudgmental as this sounds, taking this road creates its own practical and philosophical problems. Practically, we may demand less from ourselves than we should. Philosophically, we may undermine legitimate comparisons. Perhaps the fact that someone cannot aspire simply shows his inferiority, even if it does not prove his culpability in that inferiority. Wasn't Henry Thoreau a better man than Alek Therien? And how should *we* live: those of us, the vast majority, whose intellectual aspirations, talents, and energy lie somewhere between the extremes portrayed by Thoreau and Therien? Reason itself, apparently, cannot tell us.[18]

Still, our responses to the "elevationist" arguments of Thoreau and Aristotle are important. In lieu of proof of the superiority of our higher goals, we remain free to pursue them. Whether a person values pleasure or higher ends helps define his vision of the good human life, which helps set the framework within which he makes his important life decisions. Philosophers cannot prove the superiority of virtue to pleasure. This makes it all the more important that they live virtuous lives themselves, if they mean to challenge us to strive for higher goals and encourage us in the belief that we can achieve them. As Socrates' career suggests—and the author of *Walden* insists—a philosopher owes us a life and not just arguments.

Pleasure and Intellect

Earlier I included pleasure as part of Thoreau's ethical ideal. Given his strenuous conception of the good life, it might seem strange to count pleasure among its components. I admit that Thoreau does not directly advocate the pursuit of pleasure in *Walden* and at times takes a very ascetic line, even denigrating pleasure. This usually occurs when he is advocating pursuit of some higher goal. For example, he dismisses "petty fears and petty pleasures" when compared to the "exhilaration and sublimity" of attaining knowledge (96). In a letter to his friend Daniel Ricketson, he writes: "What matters it how happy or unhappy we have been, if we have minded our business and advanced our affairs?"[19]

Nevertheless, pleasure is an important good for Thoreau. His keen, detailed reporting in *Walden* of the sights, sounds, smell, and feel of things betrays the strong sensual enjoyment he finds in nature. Thoreau often describes feelings of merriment, joy, delight, ease, contentment, and subjective happiness in straightforward, positive words. At other times, these are easily enough inferred from his descriptions themselves:

> Sometimes I rambled to pine groves, standing like temples, or like fleets at sea, full-rigged, with wavy boughs, and rippling with light, so soft and green and shady that the Druids would have forsaken their oaks to worship them. (201)

> The first sparrow of spring! The year beginning with younger hope than ever! The faint silvery warblings heard over the partially bare and moist fields from the blue-bird, the song-sparrow, and the red-wing, as if the last flakes of winter tinkled as they fell! (310)

He remarks "the pleasant hillside" on which he built his house and the "pleasant spring days" during which he built it (41). The leaves of the sumac, the flowers of blackberries, St. Johnswort, and cinquefoil, the new vegetation peeping forth out of winter's weeds are all "pleasant" (114, 155, 309).

Furthermore, *Walden*'s very first pages ask readers to interrogate their own feelings concerning their routinized lives and to consider whether their lives are enjoyable. Attention to our feelings provides important evidence, apparently, for whether we are living well. Life should be pleasant. If it is not, something needs to change. Thoreau, like Aristotle and most subsequent virtue ethicists, believes that our natural human activities, properly engaged in, should bring us pleasure.

Throughout *Walden*, Thoreau contrasts the pleasure of activity with the dullness of passive consumption or merely possessing things. Designing and building his shack, he asks, "Shall we forever resign the pleasure of construction to the carpenter" along with the experience and knowledge that such building affords (46)? Sometimes Thoreau emphasizes the pleasure afforded by simple activities such as fishing, hoeing, or walking, when we fully engage in them; at other times, he reminds us of the pleasures to be gained through higher activities such as reading and thinking (99); at still other times, he points toward the "indescribable pleasures" of contemplation and mystical vision (134). All this suggests that using all our mental and physical faculties will lead to pleasurable lives; more pleasurable, in fact, than lives devoted directly to the pursuit of pleasure.

Thoreau does argue the superiority of principle over pleasure, most sustainedly in the discussion of hunting and vegetarianism in the chapter "Higher Laws." There Thoreau finds appetite, desire, and physical pleasure pushing him in one direction, principle—in this case, "cause no unnecessary suffering"—pushing him in the other. Sacrificing pleasure to principle here is noble and instantiates a specifically human excellence, he believes. So, more generally, does his effort at Walden Pond to live a more focused, "principled" life devoted to the pursuit of knowledge and artistic creation. Practicing asceticism, cultivating contempt for the pleasures and comforts of the flesh, fits us for such sacrifices and reminds us that they may be necessary in order to pursue higher goals. This is all to the good.

The fact is, though, that Thoreau finds pleasure in asceticism. He enjoys seeing how low he can fare; it is an interesting experiment. When *we* make it, we find that simple food tastes good if we have worked up an appetite; also, that when the fare gets repetitive, occasional changes from the routine are memorable and enjoyable. In these ways, the ascetic may find more enjoyment around his cooking fire than the gourmand being waited on at his sumptuous table. A certain indifference to physical comfort makes possible new experiences and hence new pleasures: the pleasure of wandering through a pitch-dark wood late at night and arriving home safe and snug, for example (169); or the pleasure of sitting under a few boards in a hard rain, baking a loaf of bread and tucking into it, feeling the warmth and goodness spreading through your body (45).

Pleasure thus seems to be part of the good life for Thoreau, even if not the whole or the most important part. Despite his experiments in asceticism by the pond, Thoreau's overall position is more one of Aristotelian balance than Stoic self-denial (although like Aristotle in the *Nicomachean Ethics,* he never works this issue out to his complete satisfaction and keeps coming back to it). Pursuing pleasure should be part of something larger—living a good life—and subordinate to this. Still, pleasure's part in constituting the good life, and in telling us when we are on the right track, is substantial.

While Thoreau shows a certain ambivalence toward pleasure, he expresses no such doubts about the importance and value of intellectual activity in his account of the good life. Some of *Walden's* grandest passages praise contemplation or the pursuit of knowledge:

> In accumulating property for ourselves or our posterity, in founding a family or a state, or acquiring fame even, we are mortal; but in dealing with truth we are immortal, and need fear no change nor accident. The oldest Egyptian or Hindoo philosopher raised a corner of the veil from the statue of the divinity; and still that trembling robe remains raised, and I gaze upon as fresh a glory as he did, since it was I in him that was then so bold, and it is he in me that now reviews the vision. (99)

We can know ourselves and the world around us. Nothing is worthier than this. The effort is "divine" and "immortal." So are we, when we make it. So are those realities that the pursuit of knowledge reveals: above all, that immortal Nature of which Thoreau sings in *Walden's* penultimate chapter, "Spring."

It is no accident that Thoreau employs a sexual metaphor for the pursuit and acquisition of knowledge, since this goal has a centrality for him that sex and physical pleasure have for many other men. Like Socrates in Plato's *Symposium,* Thoreau channels his sexual energy and considerable passion into the pursuit of knowledge and the cultivation of virtue (like Alcibiades in the *Symposium,* Thoreau's friends sometimes mistook faithfulness to higher aims for emotional frigidity). It is also no accident that Thoreau's metaphor leaves the sexual act unconsummated, since the goal of such knowledge, for him, is appreciation and celebration of the world around him, not its "improvement," control, or domination (such domination through knowledge has often been expressed in terms of sexual conquest).

Traditionally, philosophy has emphasized the importance of self-knowledge, and Thoreau places himself squarely within this tradition:

"If you would travel farther than all travellers, be naturalized in all climes, and cause the Sphinx to dash her head against a stone, even obey the precept of the old philosopher, and Explore thyself" (322). Self-knowledge is the endlessly fascinating challenge that life presents to us all. It is also a key to right living. But in Thoreau's view, self-knowledge is equally a matter of introspection and "extro-spection." We must search our own hearts and minds, but also carefully attend to our effects on the world around us, in order to know ourselves. The "self" that Thoreau seeks to know is varied: now his personal ego; now that rational soul or "divine spark" that he shares with all humanity, past, present, and future; now his ideal self, which he would fain realize in this world or the next. Self-knowledge involves situating himself in relation to his human and nonhuman neighbors; juxtaposing his personal history with the history of the successive races who have inhabited the shores of Walden Pond; comparing his own thoughts with the speculations of philosophers from many different times and cultures. In the end, self-knowledge is inseparable from "knowledge of the history of the human race" (103) and a fully developed physics, metaphysics, and cosmology: it demands "a universal knowledge" (21). Impossible goals, of course, but that is all right. We *should* pursue impossible goals. We will live better lives if we do so.

Thoreau seeks to understand the grand spiritual truths expressed in the world's scriptures and the objective, universal truths of science. But he also respects the practical knowledge of local fishermen, trappers, and village artisans. The universe or its maker *may* be one, supporting universal truths, yet human beings have diverse experiences and live diverse lives within it. This leads to diverse knowledges. Thoreau tries to make these his own, to some extent, by listening to people's stories and testing their truths in his own life. Following Emerson, he insists that other people's insights must be put to the test of his own experience. Just as much as he can experience and confirm in his own life, so much can he truly know. Knowledge and experience should inform one another; knowledge confirmed by experience, experience enriched by knowledge.

Thoreau thus places a very high value on the pursuit of knowledge and on thinking well. In addition, he interprets *all* the basic components of the good life in an intellectualized way. Consider again freedom—surely one of Thoreau's most important and oft-praised goods. "I sometimes wonder that we can be so frivolous, I may almost say," writes this anti-slavery advocate, "as to attend to the gross but somewhat foreign form of servitude called Negro Slavery, there are so many keen and subtle masters that enslave both north and south. It is hard to have a southern overseer; it is worse to have a northern one; but worst of all when you are the slave-driver of yourself" (7). Here is the familiar theme of the need to attend to our own reform, the point made even sharper by comparison with the gross injustice of slavery that, while emphatically every American's business, is "somewhat foreign" to his readers' persons. The question each of us must ask is: "Am *I* free?" We value freedom, but we may be wage slaves, beholden to "Squire Make-a-stir." We value freedom, but we may allow our gross desires to dictate our actions and may live unprincipled lives. Such slavery is worse than chattel slavery, in the sense that it is wholly self-imposed. We cannot blame it on anyone but ourselves. Escape from such slavery depends on *thinking* our way out of it, for "what a man thinks of himself, that it is which determines, or rather indicates, his fate. Self-emancipation even in the West Indian provinces of the fancy and imagination,—what Wilberforce is there to bring that about?" (7–8).[20]

You are important enough to have a fate, Thoreau reminds his reader, who may have forgotten. It is a fate of which you may take charge, if you can command a clear view of yourself. This attempt may fail through wishful thinking, since thinking highly of ourselves hardly ensures that personal excellence will follow. It may entangle us in riddles: no matter how deeply I come to know myself, am I not confronted with a mysterious and somewhat unpredictable personality? Yet Thoreau's claim here goes to the heart of the hope of any virtue ethics. We may know ourselves and what is best for ourselves and may act on that knowledge. Then our lives will no longer be a fate imposed from without, but our own free creation. Our emancipated self will be a better self, and part of what will make it better will be our newfound self-knowledge and self-control, with their attendant freedom.

Beyond this practical aspect, Thoreau sees true freedom in the play of the intellect itself, whether in personal expression and artistic creativity, in the detailed and precise observation and reasoning of science, or in the planning and building of a house or a new pencil-making process. Again, there is our freedom to soar beyond the trivial and mundane, in meeting a friend or a great intellect of the past in the higher realms of thought. Thoreau does not underestimate the value of physical freedom: the freedom given by a strong pair of legs and the good sense to walk out of doors each day: the freedom that is so outrageously abridged by "Negro Slavery." But physical freedom is not enough for a *human* being. A free man or woman should not settle for mere physical freedom.

Other important components of the good life are treated in a similar manner. Friendship, for Thoreau as for Plato, serves to further self-knowledge. Enriching our experience, as presented in *Walden*, involves thinking through old activities as well as trying new ones. Pleasure is found in both physical and mental pursuits. True reverence cannot be unthinking: we must "sacrifice *in our minds* not only our first but our last fruits also" (166, emphasis added).

The good life is thus a life of the mind. But an expanding mind, curious and connected, not a highfalutin mind searching for esoteric knowledge unrelated to the realities surrounding and sustaining it. Thoreau expresses this in yet another paean to the life of thought:

> The intellect is a cleaver; it discerns and rifts its way into the secret of things. I do not wish to be any more busy with my hands than is necessary. My head is hands and feet. I feel all my best faculties concentrated in it. My instinct tells me that my head is an organ for burrowing, as some creatures use their snout and fore-paws, and with it I would mine and burrow my way through these hills. I think that the richest vein is somewhere hereabouts; so by the divining rod and thin rising vapors I judge; and here I will begin to mine. (98)

This interesting, strange celebration of intellect shows how Thoreau steadfastly refuses to disconnect the rational from the physical even as he praises and commits himself to a life of thinking. The metaphors of cleaving and burrowing are aggressive and "dirty"; the metaphor of "mining" suggests a heedless pursuit of wealth and the crassest material possession. Yet subsequent chapters question the wisdom or possibility of such possession and show instead a sort of "mining" or "making one's own" that celebrates and protects the natural world. They describe a "digging into nature" leading to a "richness" of experience that need not impoverish it. The key is to take intellectual, imaginative, and creative possession of the land with our "best faculties" setting our goals, rather than merely serving our grosser physical desires.

So *Walden* praises the life of the mind—while insisting upon the necessary and legitimate claims of the body. Thoreau's life at Walden Pond is physical, sensual, active: the opposite of the cramped and crowded, office- and house-bound lives of so many of us. "I never feel that I am inspired unless my body is also," he had written in an early journal entry: "It too spurns a tame and commonplace life. They are fatally mistaken who think while they strive with their minds, that they may suffer their bodies to stagnate in luxury or sloth. The body is the first proselyte the soul makes. Our life is but the Soul made known by its fruits—the body.

The whole duty of man may be expressed in one line—Make to yourself a perfect body."[21] Once again, we see the comprehensiveness of Thoreau's ethical vision, encompassing body and soul, internal development and external achievement, pleasure and thought. Our conception of the good life should be as broad as life itself.

In service to this comprehensive vision, Thoreau strives to live a higher, "divine" life without dismissing ordinary pursuits, occupations, and responsibilities. He moves to the pond and digs into the earth to grow beans, not to some ivory tower to study and write while others "do the dirty work" necessary to sustain him. Ideally, reason and effort should inform all our ordinary activities. Learning all we can of life, both its ordinary and extraordinary aspects, we will make it our own. In the end, Thoreau believes, we will see that it is all extraordinary.

Virtue

The past twenty-five years have seen the rise of "virtue ethics" as an alternative to Kantian and utilitarian ethical theories. Academic philosophers have returned to this more comprehensive approach to ethics, often through the study of ancient Greek philosophy.[1] This process of philosophical restoration has involved recovering the ancients' conception of virtue as personal excellence, recovering an ethical space for the pursuit of excellence, and recovering a broad account of virtue that acknowledges the full spectrum of human interests and activities. As I show below, Thoreau anticipated these recovery projects in *Walden* and went considerably further than most contemporary philosophers in articulating a plausible and challenging account of virtue.

While recovering more robust conceptions of human excellence and flourishing has been the main goal of some philosophers, others have explored virtue ethics because of the perceived failures of mainstream approaches to justify our moral duties; or, contrarily, because these approaches seem to justify too much, making excessive moral demands upon us. In the second half of this chapter, I explore Thoreau's suggestions for harmonizing personal aspiration and social duty in a comprehensive ethical philosophy. But first I examine his account of personal virtue.

Recovering the Ancient Concept of Virtue

As we have seen, Henry Thoreau went to Walden Pond to become a better person, defining this broadly to include increased knowledge, an enriched experience, character development, creative achievement, and greater personal integrity. Significantly, in describing his own goals or prescribing goals for his readers, he often speaks of cultivating "virtue" or "the virtues" (80, 164, 172, 218, 315). But what exactly does he mean by this? In particular, does he refer to a narrow modern conception of virtue or to the broader conception of Plato, Aristotle, and other ancient writers?[2]

In the modern sense, a virtuous person is a morally good person: someone who treats others well and does her duty. The emphasis may be on kindness, compassion, and a loving spirit, as in the Christian gospels, or on reason and a strict adherence to principle, as in Immanuel Kant's ethical philosophy. Either way, the desired outcome is usually altruistic action. For as Kant says, we have a strong tendency to favor "the dear self," and virtue helps us overcome this.[3] The virtues, in this view, are character traits that help us act morally, such as temperance, humility, generosity, and benevolence. Virtue here is synonymous with moral excellence.

In the ancient view, virtue equals excellence in a more comprehensive sense. The virtues are all those qualities the possession of which makes a person a good person and more likely to succeed in characteristic human endeavors. So in addition to moral excellence, ancient virtue (Greek *aretē*, Roman *virtus*) includes physical, intellectual, aesthetic, and spiritual excellence. The Greeks spoke of strength, speed, and dexterity as the virtues of Olympic athletes; intelligence and quick-wittedness as the virtues of rhetoricians; creativity and a sense of harmony and balance as the virtues of sculptors and painters. Ancient philosophers tried to justify these common ethical judgments by linking them to plausible conceptions of human nature and human flourishing. Aristotle, for example, argued that human beings had characteristic functions; he defined the virtues as those qualities that helped people successfully perform those functions and thus lead flourishing lives.[4] But whether in popular speech or in the accounts of the philosophers, ancient virtue involved the perfection of the individual self, rather than its taming or abnegation.

The concept of virtue has had a long and complex history in Western philosophy. It has been moralized by the Roman Stoics and spiritualized by medieval Christians (who added the three "theological virtues" of faith, hope, and charity to the ancient four cardinal virtues of courage, temperance, justice, and wisdom). It has been secularized by the great Enlightenment moralists and aestheticized by the romantics. The history of this concept cannot be fully recounted here. Suffice it to say that there is a great gulf between the typical modern and the typical ancient views: between virtue as moral goodness and virtue as comprehensive human excellence (including moral goodness). A scholar of Latin and Greek, Thoreau was aware of how those languages themselves preserved the memory of a broader conception of virtue, and he wrote in an early journal entry: "The state of *complete* manhood is virtue. . . . This truth has long been in the languages. All the relations of the subject are hinted at in the derivation and analogies of the Latin words *vir* [man] and *virtus* [virtue]; and the Greek αγαθος [good] and αριστος [best]. . . . The analogies of words are never whimsical and meaningless, but stand for real likenesses."[5]

As the passage suggests, Thoreau approved of a broad conception of virtue. He employed it throughout his writings and tried to embody it in his life. In *Walden*, he deliberately quotes older sources and archaic uses of the word "virtue" that emphasize this distinction and suggest his sympathy with earlier views. For example, in the chapter "The Bean-Field," Thoreau quotes seventeenth-century horticulturist John Evelyn's assertion that "the earth . . . especially if fresh, has a certain magnetism in it, by which it attracts the salt, power, or virtue (call it either) which gives it life, and is the logic of all the labor and stir we keep about it, to sustain us" (162). Clearly a field cannot act morally! For Evelyn, as for Thoreau, "virtue" implies power: that force through which a field or a man may flourish and bring forth the proper fruits. Thoreau quotes a similar archaic use of "virtue" by Cato the Elder (243).

Virtue is thus essentially active for Thoreau; as he had written earlier, "even virtue is no longer such if it be stagnant."[6] In the modern view, the virtues are valuable largely because they limit our self-assertion and keep us from doing what we should not do. The modest person will not brag about his achievements, the honest person will not lie for personal advantage, the just person will not take more than her fair share. The ancient view instead stresses that actively cultivating the virtues is key to our self-development and happiness. They allow us to do what we should do and become better people. Thoreau echoes this life-affirming view when he writes: "The constant inquiry which Nature puts is Are you virtuous? Then you can behold me. Beauty—fragrance—music— sweetness—& joy of all kinds are for the virtuous."[7]

Thoreau, like the ancients, links his notion of virtue to personal flourishing. In *Walden*, he tries to show how the virtues of simplicity, integrity, and resolution serve to focus and clarify our lives; how generosity and sympathy may improve our relations with our neighbors; how curiosity, imagination, and reverence help us appreciate the world around us. These connections between virtue and flourishing serve to specify genuine virtues and spell out their proper development and use.

For the ancients, the virtues were less ends in themselves ("virtue is its own reward," *we* say) than the necessary means to achieve character-istic human goals. Hence Thoreau's repeated injunction to strive for worthwhile ends. Hence his suggestions that virtue, by itself, is not virtue or is not complete virtue:

Still we live meanly, like ants; though the fable tells us that we were long ago changed into men . . . our best virtue has for its occasion a superfluous and evitable wretchedness. Our life is frittered away by detail. (91)

How long shall we sit in our porticoes practising idle and musty virtues, which any work would make impertinent? (331)

Virtue is not merely an internal matter of character or conscience for Thoreau, as it is for most modern ethicists, but an external matter of actual achievement out in the world. While Kant, for example, can write that virtue depends solely on human beings *willing* to do good, regardless of whether they succeed, the author of *Walden,* like the ancients, holds that genuine virtue must prove itself in life.

This ancient conception of virtue can be seen most clearly in the "complemental verses" by the Cavalier poet Thomas Carew that end *Walden*'s first chapter. As so often, Thoreau's words are slyly suggestive. The verses are hardly complimentary to those who refuse to recognize higher goals in life, but the ethic of aspiration they express may well complement our more conventional ethic of social obligation:

Thou dost presume too much, poor needy wretch,
To claim a station in the firmament,
Because thy humble cottage, or thy tub,
Nurses some lazy or pedantic virtue. (80)

Carew contrasts "lazy or pedantic virtues" that are presumably easy to achieve and that allow us to live in "dull society" with others, with "fair blooming virtues," whose neglect "Degradeth nature, and benumbeth sense, / And, Gorgon-like, turns active men to stone" (80). As examples, Carew rejects "necessitated temperance" and "forc'd falsely exalted passive fortitude" as virtues, because these qualities are life-denying; also, perhaps, because we may take them on through fear, insensibility, or laziness. Carew's adjectival qualifications suggest he might recognize a genuine temperance or fortitude, in the service of action and life. Certainly Thoreau would. Elsewhere, he reminds us that temperance can keep us from pursuing unnecessary and frivolous goals, while true fortitude is not mere passive acceptance of our lot, "forced" on us by circumstances, but is rather itself a force enabling us to act in adversity.

The conventional social virtues become degraded through an acceptance of "mediocrity," while rarer, more difficult-to-achieve virtues are ignored altogether. "But we advance," Carew says:

Such virtues only as admit excess,
Brave, bounteous acts, regal magnificence,
All-seeing prudence, magnanimity
That knows no bound, and that heroic virtue
For which antiquity hath left no name,
But patterns only, such as Hercules,
Achilles, Theseus. (80)

Already in his early essay "The Service," Thoreau had rejected any pseudo-Aristotelian account of virtue as a mean of effort or achievement: "their mean is no better than meanness, nor their medium than mediocrity."[8] Here he quotes Carew to challenge the complacency that seeks to specify some point beyond which we need not strive: either because we are already sufficiently virtuous; or because we have no strict duty to do so; or because higher, difficult to achieve goals are unimportant. Magnificence (the bestowal of great gifts on others) and magnanimity (literally "great-souledness," the superior development of one's whole personality) are almost by definition impossible for most people to achieve. But that does not make them any less virtues for Carew or Thoreau. We may assume that the inhabitant of the one-room house by Walden Pond would interpret magnificence and magnanimity quite differently than the Cavalier poet, but this emphasizes all the more what these aristocrats of human aspiration do share: a demanding and open-ended conception of virtue.

The idea of rare, "heroic virtue" transcending words might seem errant romanticism. Nothing is more embarrassing to many modern Thoreauvians than their hero's emphasis on heroism. Yet Thoreau believes that an appreciation of exceptional human achievement completes ethics. No matter what valued quality we are looking at—intelligence, generosity, bravery—the least amount is valuable, while each of us should strive to increase our share of it. Indeed, since "effort is the prerogative of virtue," those with the greatest abilities will have the greatest demands made upon them.[9]

Hercules, Achilles, and Theseus are semi-divine, achieving greatness through heaven-sent abilities or being rewarded for their achievements with immortality. Similarly, *we* might believe that Albert Einstein or Mother Teresa, paragons of intelligence and compassion, transcend human limits and live on beyond death in their achievements. In his *Nicomachean Ethics,* Aristotle felt compelled to round out his account of human excellence by recognizing "bestiality" and "divine virtue," the conditions that fell below and rose above mere human vice and virtue.[10] He left it an open question how often humans beings achieve these states. Just so, Thoreau makes a place for such extremes of vice and virtue. And with Carew, he rejects the apotheosis of mediocrity: "Thou dost presume too much, poor needy wretch, / To claim a station in the firmament" (80). This is not to demean people of modest abilities, but rather to rebuke sloth and remind us to appreciate rare forms of excellence.

This conception of virtue makes sense. Yet it is apt to rub modern readers the wrong way, because it is essentially inegalitarian, stating forthrightly that some people are better than others. Even worse, it suggests that we may be better or worse not solely through our own efforts, but according to the vagaries of heredity, upbringing, or other fortuitous circumstances. For after all, few of us have the intelligence or creativity of a Thoreau, no matter how hard we strive. Hence we may be tempted to limit our conception of virtue to what is within all (almost all?) people's power. We may be tempted to say that people who treat others with respect, or at least avoid treating others with disrespect, or at least sincerely try to do this and repent of their failures, are sufficiently virtuous—*this* is what is really important. If we are religious, we may hope that these morally virtuous people will be rewarded with immortality, that "station in the firmament" that Carew and Thoreau have heretically denied them.

In this way, we would return to our narrow modern conception of virtue—mistakenly, I believe. For such a retreat undermines our ability to appreciate humanity's greatest successes. Instead, we should retain a broad and challenging conception of human excellence and acknowledge life's essential unfairness. Some people are better than others, and not necessarily through their own efforts. This realization may challenge us in two ways: first, to mitigate life's unfairness for others and second, to cultivate our own personal excellence.[11] How to balance these challenges is a nice problem. Thoreau gives several answers to it in *Walden*, including the laconic statement: "we may waive just so much care of ourselves as we honestly bestow elsewhere" (11). In any case, the injunction to strive holds true for all of us, regardless of our particular endowments. "Shall a man go and hang himself because he belongs to the race of pygmies, and not be the biggest pygmy that he can? Let every one mind his own business, and endeavor to be what he was made" (326).

Recovering the Pursuit of Virtue

Thoreau recognizes that besides recovering the concept of virtue, we must recover an ethical space for virtue's pursuit. *Walden's* introductory chapter sets up a framework for this pursuit: put economic life in its properly subordinate place; elevate, or at least consciously adopt, your main goals in life; select the best means to achieve them; strive! Yet we cannot strive, and Thoreau cannot report the results of his own strivings, without affirming our right to do so. "Economy" concludes by addressing this issue (72–80).

The *Walden* self-improvement project was apparently somewhat at odds with the ethical sensibilities of Thoreau's townsmen. "But all this is very selfish," Thoreau has some of his neighbors say. He then "confesses": "I have hitherto indulged very little in philanthropic enterprises. I have made some sacrifices to a sense of duty, and among others have sacrificed this pleasure also" (72). Challenging conventional morality (and much modern moral philosophy), Thoreau asserts that we have not merely a right, but a duty, to pursue self-development. Philanthropic activities may be a shirking of this duty; routine acts of kindness to others may be easier to undertake than difficult projects of self-improvement. To suggest that we might have to sacrifice the *pleasure* of philanthropy in order to fulfill a *duty* of self-development challenges the modern equation of selflessness and dutifulness. To suggest that we at least sometimes perform benevolent, philanthropic actions out of pleasurable indulgence neatly combines the Kantian reminders that duty commands (we are not, in fact, free to choose whether to indulge in it) and that duty rightly overrides the claims of pleasure, with an admonition not to accept conventional accounts of our duties. Thus, unlike some contemporary virtue ethicists who question the usefulness of the concept of moral obligation, Thoreau affirms such obligation but contests its content.

Thoreau goes on to suggest that individuals may contribute more to the common good through self-development and personal achievement than through charitable efforts:

What *good* I do, in the common sense of that word, must be aside from my main path, and for the most part wholly unintended. Men say, practically, Begin where you are and such as you are, without aiming mainly to become of more worth, and with kindness aforethought go about doing good. If I were to preach at all in this strain, I should say rather, Set about being good. (73)

In taking the time to investigate nature, reflect on his experiences, and compose *Walden,* Thoreau arguably contributed more to humanity than he could have in many lifetimes of visiting the sick and giving money to the poor of his native town. But we miss Thoreau's point if we focus on his own exceptional achievement. Even a person of average abilities who takes the time to fully experience life and carefully observe nature improves himself or herself. Since society is made up of individuals, such personal improvement improves society. And this person may, like Thoreau, go on to teach his neighbors some of what he has learned, benefiting the larger community a second time. He might do all this without ever feeling it was his duty to do so and without it ever *being* his duty to do so. The common good rests partly on the development of personal excellence and its free propagation and not solely on benevolence and adherence to duty.

Thoreau says he would preach self-development rather than charity, but this is not to preach against charity. Philanthropic acts are often useful, and sometimes even obligatory. But they do not fully define the good life. We may legitimately demand more from each other, not asking for a double dose of charity or perfect "justice as fairness," but rather for a different sort of tonic altogether:

> A man is not a good *man* to me because he will feed me if I should be starving, or warm me if I should be freezing, or pull me out of a ditch if I should ever fall into one. I can find you a Newfoundland dog that will do as much. Philanthropy is not love for one's fellow-man in the broadest sense.... Comparatively speaking, what are a hundred [philanthropists] to *us,* if their philanthropy do not help *us* in our best estate, when we are most worthy to be helped? (74)

Here, once again, is the insistence on a legitimate self-interest.[12] Also the reminder that beyond those standard duties that we owe each other, there exists the pursuit of excellence: the progress from our hitherto "best estate" to one yet higher. To appreciate it, we must supplement our commonsense, Christian understanding of human goodness with the ancients' sense of goodness as personal excellence. The pursuit of excellence, like the pursuit of justice, exalts human nature. This pursuit, too, can be an object of our cooperation. The fact that such cooperation can be enjoyable, and that we may experience it as fulfilling rather than self-abnegating, should not blind us to its importance.

Philanthropy "in the broadest sense" includes friendship as well as justice: Emerson and Thoreau talking philosophy, as well as Emerson lecturing against slavery or Thoreau putting an escaped slave on a train for the Canadian border. A true "love" of "humanity" makes demands on us at our strongest, just as it sustains us at our weakest. But society, in Thoreau's time and ours, fails to recognize this. As Thoreau complains:

> Philanthropy is almost the only virtue which is sufficiently appreciated by mankind. Nay, it is greatly overrated. . . . I once heard a reverend lecturer on England, a man of learning and intelligence, after enumerating her scientific, literary, and political worthies, Shakspeare, Bacon, Cromwell, Milton, Newton, and others, speak next of her Christian heroes, whom, as if his profession required it of him, he elevated to a place far above all the rest, as the greatest of the great. They were Penn, Howard, and Mrs. Fry [philanthropists and penal reformers]. Everyone must feel the falsehood and cant [Kant?] of this. The last were not England's best men and women; only, perhaps, her best philanthropists. (76)

Both Christianity and modern secular ethics insist that we need not be particularly intelligent or accomplished to be morally good, and that moral goodness is definitive of human goodness (or infinitely more important than other kinds of human goodness, which comes to the same thing). Common moral thought seconds this, adding that we need not be particularly imaginative, artistic, or physically fit, or have achieved much in our lives or careers, to count as good people.[13] All such abilities and successes are distinct from *moral* goodness and distinctly secondary to it. Taken far enough, this viewpoint blinds us to much of human virtue and achievement and undermines the incentive to pursue excellence.

Many readers, in this democratic age, are likely to question the need or the possibility of specifying a country's "best men and women." It is difficult to imagine finding consensus on the "greatest of the great" in a large, complex society, given the many pursuits in which individuals may excel. More fundamentally, most moderns share a commitment to equal basic rights and responsibilities for all human beings. Modern moral theories typically ground this moral equality in some form of substantive or factual equality: we are all ensouled, we are all rational, we are all parties to an implicit contract, we are all sensitive beings who can suffer harm. These theories imply that those areas where humans are unequal are *in*essential.

But Thoreau is right to contest this, for any ethics of aspiration will be essentially inegalitarian. It will need heroes—exemplars of great virtue—to spur us on and show what is possible (this is not the same as asserting that all people have a duty to be heroes). As the above quotation shows, modern ethics puts forward its own candidates for superiority and heroism—paragons of selflessness and service to others—which a fuller understanding of human virtue will supplement or even contest. Most important, virtue ethics sets up a framework for judging our actions, characters, and achievements that implicitly applies to all of us and even ranks us to some degree. If we take intelligence, courage, justice, compassion, generosity, and integrity as the virtues constitutive of human excellence, then we cannot help but judge ourselves inferior to someone who has *all* of them to a greater extent than we ourselves do or superior to someone whom we outshine in the same way. However we define the good life, we cannot well deny that some people live much better lives than we do, and some much worse. While there are limits to how clearly and in what detail we may specify *the* definitions of human virtue or flourishing, we all make these judgments to some degree, agreeing on many obvious judgments and disagreeing on more difficult ones.[14]

None of this argues that we do not have important, other-directed moral duties. By most accounts Thoreau was a good neighbor, a conscientious family member, and a valued, if sometimes difficult, friend. He was as harsh as any of his contemporaries in his condemnation of such basic injustices as slavery and imperialism; Thoreau was, after all, the author of "Resistance to Civil Government" and a leading defender of John Brown. In arguing for justice for the wronged slave or Indian, he appeals to our common humanity and condemns the prejudice and greed that lead us to deny it.

Still, when Thoreau turns to consider his life and his neighbors' lives as free human beings, he insists on emphasizing those higher capabilities that the term "humanity" implies. He demands that each of us live up to these capabilities—and not merely render bearable the existence of others. "Do not stay to be an overseer of the poor," he writes, "but endeavor to become one of the worthies of the world" (79). This quotation implies, reasonably, that we must sometimes choose between helping others achieve a basic well-being and the pursuit of personal excellence. It may appear, less reasonably, to assert the absolute superiority of the latter course. Yet in the end, I believe Thoreau is striving for a balance between these two aspects of our ethical lives. Above all, he desires that this balance occur at a high level: one that demands much from "wealthy" and "poor" alike.

Thoreau's high expectations and the moralistic hectoring that accompany them seem elitist to many of his readers. They seem the very opposite to me. "Instead of noblemen [as in Europe] let us have noble villages of men," Thoreau writes (110). This democratic demandingness makes a healthy combination of modern egalitarianism and the ancient pursuit of excellence. Articulating such a true "philanthropy" is a major task facing contemporary ethical philosophy, I believe, and one that each of us faces in our own lives.

Recovering Full Human Virtue

Thoreau reappropriated an ancient conception of ethics because it helped make sense of his project of self-improvement. Similarly, he reappropriated the ancients' broad conception of the virtues and even outdid them in comprehensiveness. Rather than praising only moral excellence, Thoreau commends the following qualities as virtues in *Walden:*

adventurousness	dignity	hopefulness
affection	earnestness	hospitality
alertness	economy	humanity
appreciation of	enterprise	humility
beauty	expressiveness	humor
aspiration	exuberance	imagination
austerity	faith	independence
beauty	fidelity	industry
bravery	flexibility	innocence
charity	focus	integrity
chastity	frankness	intelligence
cheerfulness	friendliness	justice
civility	generosity	liberality
cleanliness	geniality	living in the present
clear-headedness	grace	loftiness
close watching	gratitude	love
compassion	hardiness	magnanimity
confidence	harmony	magnificence
contentment	health	manliness
conviviality	heroic striving	nobility
creativity	heroism	originality
cultivation	holiness	patience
curiosity	honesty	persistence

philanthropy	self-respect	strength
physical endurance	sense of history	studiousness
pride	sensibility to beauty	sympathy
prudence	sensitivity	temperance
punctuality	serenity	tenderness
purity	simplicity	tirelessness
rectitude	sincerity	trust
refinement	skill in particular	truthfulness
resolution	crafts	vigor
reverence	spontaneity	wakefulness
sagacity	stillness	wildness
self-knowledge	stoicism	wisdom (passim).
self-reliance		

It is too simple to say that Thoreau calls these qualities virtues, since sometimes he refers to a trait as a virtue in one place and a vice in another. Humility is a virtue when shown in gratitude for nature's gifts (166), but a vice when it undermines self-respect and personal striving (50). Industry is a virtue when applied consciously to noble ends (20), but a vice when mindlessly pursued (70). Furthermore, listing these qualities tells us little about their relative importance, how they might be combined in a balanced character, or how such contradictory virtues as humility and magnificence can be reconciled. Still, the list gives a good sense of Thoreau's ideal of human excellence.

To the Christian virtues, Thoreau adds the virtues of the ancients and the romantics. Moral virtues are certainly well represented. These include both character traits that further social harmony—such as sympathy, benevolence, and generosity—and what one philosopher has called the "executive" virtues—qualities such as prudence, resolution, and integrity, which allow us to act responsibly and effectively.[15] But Thoreau also follows the ancients, praising intellectual virtues such as curiosity, imagination, clearheadedness, and wisdom.[16] He praises physical virtues, such as beauty, strength, and hardiness (Thoreau closes a letter to a friend with the words: "Methinks I am getting a little more strength into those knees of mine; and, for my part, I believe that God *does* delight in the strength of a man's legs).[17] He draws on the romantic tradition, including virtues associated with aesthetic appreciation and creativity, such as expressiveness and sensibility to beauty. Thoreau recognizes the value of widespread or easily attainable virtues, such as cheerfulness and cleanliness, but also rare, difficult-to-achieve virtues, such as magnanimity and wisdom.

But it is easy to praise various character traits—how do we know which really are virtues? By linking virtue to human flourishing. In *Walden*, praise for a virtue is usually accompanied by descriptions of the various successes it makes possible. So, for example, hardiness and simplicity make possible greater freedom (70–71), while those who lack these virtues are condemned to drudgery (205–6). Alertness, vigor, and persistence lead to many fascinating experiences and discoveries in natural history. Chastity and austerity help us follow our consciences and act morally (220–21). Compassion and sympathy help us appreciate society's outcasts (see especially the chapters "Brute Neighbors" and "Former Inhabitants"). And so on, through all the character traits praised in *Walden*.

In this way, Thoreau grounds his account of virtue in his account of human flourishing. However, Thoreau is less sure than Aristotle that he can specify a universal human nature, or build a single, all-embracing ideal of human excellence upon it. He is skeptical, too, of the "unity of the virtues" thesis upheld by most philosophers: the view that human virtue is a singular whole and that to fully possess one of the virtues one must possess all of them. Instead, Thoreau suggests that there may be real, irreconcilable ethical trade-offs. The virtues of the hard-working farmer and the "idle" poet may both be genuine and may both help define possibilities for human happiness and flourishing. Yet perhaps one and the same person cannot possess them.[18] The smooth, civilized virtues of the gentleman differ from the woodsman's rough, wild virtues; again, perhaps we cannot combine all that is best in both their characters.[19] The virtues of heroic societies are no less authentic than the Christian virtues that succeed them. Their loss is a genuine loss, and it is more difficult than most moralists imagine to distinguish moral progress from moral change.[20]

Taking another look at the virtues Thoreau praises in *Walden*, we can place them into rough categories, based on the spheres of life they primarily deal with:

PERSONAL VIRTUES: *Help us act effectively and own our actions.*
Aspiration, austerity, bravery, confidence, contentment, deliberation, earnestness, economy, enterprise, hopefulness, independence, industry, innocence, integrity, living in the present, manliness, persistence, pride, prudence, punctuality, resolution, self-reliance, serenity, simplicity, spontaneity, stoicism, temperance, wakefulness.

SOCIAL VIRTUES: *Foster good relations with others and avoidance of immorality.* Affection, charity, chastity, cheerfulness, civility, compassion, conviviality, dignity, fidelity, frankness, friendliness, geniality, generosity, harmony, hospitality, humanity, humility, humor, justice, liberality, love, philanthropy, purity, rectitude, self-respect, sincerity, sympathy, tenderness, trust.

INTELLECTUAL VIRTUES: *Contribute to knowledge of the world around us and successful action within it.* Adventurousness, alertness, clear-headedness, curiosity, cultivation, focus, honesty, imagination, intelligence, patience, sagacity, self-knowledge, sense of history, studiousness, tirelessness, thoughtfulness, truthfulness, wisdom.

AESTHETIC VIRTUES: *Further the creation and appreciation of beauty in art and nature.* Appreciation of beauty, close watching, creativity, expressiveness, faith, gratitude, originality, refinement, reverence, sensibility to beauty, sensitivity, skill in particular crafts, wildness.

PHYSICAL VIRTUES: *Facilitate physical activity, health, and well-being.* Beauty, cleanliness, flexibility, grace, hardiness, health, physical endurance, stillness, strength, vigor.

SUPERLATIVE VIRTUES: *Promote or mark extraordinary human excellence.* Exuberance, heroic striving, heroism, holiness, loftiness, magnanimity, magnificence, nobility.[21]

Of course, this categorization is somewhat artificial. Many of these character traits could be put in more than one category: "patience" is equally a personal, a social, and an intellectual virtue; "hardiness" has both mental and physical aspects and could be considered a personal as well as a physical virtue. Still, setting out the list in this way shows why Thoreau believes these traits are virtues, since each category refers to some aspect of life essential to human flourishing. If we compare Thoreau's list with the lists of the virtues accepted by philosophers today, we get an even better sense of his comprehensiveness, since most contemporary philosophers do not acknowledge any virtues that do not fit into the first two categories of personal and social virtues.

Thoreau's broad conception of the virtues validates his own talents and preferences, of course. But it also seems to assert a more plausible conception of human excellence than is put forward, explicitly or implicitly, within most current moral theories. Since dutiful and benevolent actions do not exhaust our important activities, human excellence arguably involves more than moral excellence. Since we do, in fact, want to live happy and flourishing lives, our ethical theories should reflect this. Contemporary ethics gives us credit when we are excellent moral beings, but Thoreau's ethics gives us credit when we are excellent human beings. Since we are human beings, this broader conception of virtue should prevail.

In some ways, this list of virtues might overemphasize the commonality between Thoreau's ideal and contemporary ethics, particularly regarding the relative importance of intellectual and moral virtue. As one philosopher notes, current usage allows the terms "good" and "stupid" to be predicated of one and the same person.[22] Most ethicists accept this, but Thoreau does not. While he commends the moral virtues, he devotes approximately equal space to praising the intellectual virtues. Even more revealing, his table of vices includes stupidity, laziness, and insensibility. He is as likely to praise industry, patience, and honesty as *intellectual* virtues leading to increased knowledge as he is to praise them as *moral* virtues leading to proper conduct toward others (20, 269, 327). He is more likely to put "executive" virtues such as enterprise and resolution in service to his own projects, rather than in service to conventional philanthropy. All this places Thoreau closer to the broader, worldly view of human excellence given by Aristotle and farther from the narrower, moralistic view advocated by Kant.

Furthermore, Thoreau manifests ambivalence, at best, toward the key Christian virtues of charity, compassion, and humility. Charity is often misguided, he believes, failing to elevate the giver or benefit the receiver (75–76). It cannot substitute for a searching attempt to understand the causes of human degradation and may simply perpetuate this degradation. In itself, compassion may be fruitless or debilitating: "all disease and failure helps make me sad and does me evil, however much sympathy it may have with me or I with it" (78). We must take care that our sympathy for the weak does not weaken us and perhaps leave us resentful of the strong and dismissive of all worldly success. Charity and compassion are not ends in themselves for Thoreau, as they are for the Christian moralist. They are only good to the extent that they further human life.

Similarly, Thoreau is as likely to count humility a vice as a virtue, depending on whether it motivates greater appreciation, striving, and achievement (328, 331). We should remain humble in the face of our shortcomings and grateful to God or nature for their many gifts. But we should also take pride in our accomplishments, Thoreau believes, telling us twice that he intends "to brag as lustily as chanticleer in the morning." Nowhere does Thoreau strike a more jarring note, for many readers, than in his pride. Indeed, *Walden* may force us to specify more clearly the difference between pride and arrogance.

For Christians pride is a vice, since human beings are infinitely inferior to God and essentially equal to one another. We often go wrong in our social dealings precisely through a desire to assert our superiority over others. Contrarily, the ancients tended to view pride as a necessary part of a good life. Since self-knowledge and striving to live well helped define the good life, if one lived well, one knew it and commended oneself for it. Humility was at best a just judgment of one's own mediocrity, at worst a failure to understand true human excellence and whether one had achieved it or not.[23]

Thoreau clearly endorses the ancient view, perhaps because he sees a connection between valuing pride and taking human accomplishments seriously. "If I seem to boast more than is becoming," he writes, "my excuse is that I brag for humanity rather than for myself" (49). There are certain objective standards that we must take seriously if we are to strive for excellence. If we do take them seriously, we may celebrate our successes as well as lament our failures. Thoreau continues: "Notwithstanding much cant and hypocrisy,—chaff which I find it difficult to separate from my wheat, but for which I am as sorry as any man,—I will breathe freely and stretch myself in this respect, it is such a relief to both the moral and physical system; and I am resolved that I will not through humility become the devil's attorney. I will endeavor to speak a good word for the truth" (49). The truth is that we may live better lives than we do. The "respect" in which Thoreau "stretches" his "self" is a respect for human nature and human possibility, which will enlarge those individuals who take them seriously. (While admitting here to speaking some cant and sometimes falling into hypocrisy, does Thoreau also confess to telling some "stretchers" in *Walden* about his personal accomplishments?) *This* is our life, yet "most men [most Christians] are in a strange uncertainty about it, whether it is of the devil or of God" (91). Thoreau suffers from no such uncertainty. Life is glorious, both human life with its many possibilities and that wild life surrounding us in all its beauty and complexity. "One world at a time," he advises—this world.[24]

While Thoreau discounted or reinterpreted these important Christian virtues, he emphasized less traditional virtues, such as simplicity, integrity, and independence. These are cardinal virtues for Thoreau, because he believes their possession is especially crucial to human flourishing.[25]

Thoreau's simplicity clearly is not simplicity of thought or experience, which he seeks to complicate and enrich. It refers rather to limiting our use of external goods and focusing on the tasks at hand. Such simplicity allows us to understand the effects of our actions and better order our lives: "Our life is frittered away by detail. . . . Simplicity, simplicity, simplicity! I say, let your affairs be as two or three, and not a hundred or a thousand; instead of a million count half a dozen, and keep your accounts on your thumb nail" (91). The hope is that by acting consciously and focusing more narrowly on our true ends, we may achieve "simplicity of life and elevation of purpose," the former making the latter possible (92). Indeed, Thoreau sometimes seems to assert a necessary correlation between simple means and higher goals, on the one hand, and complex means and vulgarity, on the other.

Simplicity allows focus. More than that, it forces us to confront our means and our ends. Thoreau presents himself in *Walden* as self-assured and wise. But he went to the pond at twenty-seven, with big hopes and uncertain prospects, unsure of himself and his vocation as a writer, largely a failure in the eyes of his neighbors. Like many young people, he felt pulled in different directions, and he simplified his life in order to fairly try out several pursuits that had been calling to him insistently. Simplification allowed him to pursue the disciplined work of writing, free from a variety of distractions. It allowed him to put to the test what he himself recognized as the romantic ideal of living close to nature. Thoreau came back from the pond convinced of the value of simplicity for such demanding pursuits and experiments.

Thoreau sees a strong correlation between simplicity and the other virtues. He often pairs simplicity and independence, for example (15). If we live simply, we need not mortgage our time to any bank or employer and can spend it as we wish (63). Elsewhere Thoreau links simplicity and honesty; speaking simply allows us to focus on the sense and truth of our words (46). Simplicity, to borrow a concept from ecology, is a "keystone" virtue. It plays an important role in stabilizing and focusing our lives, and allows the development of a rich character manifesting diverse virtues.

Integrity is another key virtue often mentioned in *Walden* (6, 23, 326–27). Thoreau's integrity encompasses both the modern moralist's injunction "Treat others respectfully!" and the ancient moralist's "Order your life so as to further your true human ends!" Thoreau's reform essays give numerous examples of immoral actions and institutions, from slavery to grave robbing. Here unprincipled offenders sacrifice the rights and dignity of others. *Walden* focuses instead on our offenses against ourselves: "The laboring man has not leisure for a true integrity day by day. . . . The finest qualities of our nature, like the bloom on fruits, can be preserved only by the most delicate handling. Yet we do not treat ourselves nor one another thus tenderly" (6). In response, Thoreau asks us to consciously choose our life goals and integrate all aspects of our lives toward their achievement. At best we may "meet with a success unexpected in common hours" (323), as the most mundane or trivial activities—hoeing beans, fishing—transform themselves into sacraments or teach us vital lessons. At worst, we will have given our goals and ideals a fair try. For both self-regarding and other-regarding actions, integrity is often undermined by greed, misplaced expediency, or some other failure in our personal economy. Integrity is furthered when we live consciously and act "according to principle."

Independence or freedom is also a key virtue for Thoreau, perhaps the most frequently mentioned virtue in *Walden*. Thoreau moved to the pond, as he twice tells us, on the Fourth of July (45, 84). He describes freedom in both negative and positive terms. Negatively, Thoreau cultivates a freedom *from* economic demands (12, 33), social requirements (167–68), and various sorts of fear (fear of ridicule, fear of failure, fear of death). Positively, Thoreau's freedom is a freedom *to* develop his particular talents (70–71), think his own thoughts (57), create his own artistic work (17–19), and generally live his own life. Negative freedom does not appear to be an end in itself for Thoreau. It finds value and completion in positive freedom: the full flourishing and expression of individual personality.

Thoreau's account suggests interesting questions concerning the nature and value of freedom. How much independence do we want in our lives? How much did Thoreau want in his (he did eventually move back to town)? Some degree of independence seems necessary for genuine thinking and for making our lives our own. Yet Thoreau's experiment might tell us more about the varieties of liberty and community, than about the absolute value of independence. Living alone, Thoreau drew closer to his nonhuman neighbors. Solitude helped him to see the "infinite extent" of his "relations" (171) and to appreciate his dependence on a benevolent nature or God (132, 134). "As long as possible live free and uncommitted" (84), Thoreau enjoins, but *Walden* shows him thoroughly committed to the pond and his wild neighbors, not through ownership, but through knowledge and love. Thoreau's positive freedom—the flourishing and expression of his true nature—seems to demand this commitment.

By emphasizing these favored virtues and reinterpreting the traditional Christian virtues, Thoreau shifts our account of human excellence in three important ways. First, he broadens that account to include the full range of human excellence: physical, intellectual, spiritual, and aesthetic excellence, in addition to moral excellence. Second, he emphasizes the ethically open-ended nature of our lives, since simplicity, integrity, and independence may be put in service to a wide variety of goals. Virtue leads not to conformity, but to diversity. Third, by reminding us of our duties to ourselves, Thoreau adds an ethics of aspiration to our more conventional social ethics. Morality is more than "a certain set of rules, called etiquette and politeness, to make [our] frequent meeting tolerable" (136), nor is it just "hospitalality" (152): the charitable maintenance of as many tons of human flesh as possible.[26] Ethics involves ideals, achievements, and personal satisfaction, as well as restraint, renunciation, and personal limitation. Taken together, these shifts represent a serious challenge to conventional moral thought and modern moral philosophy.

Romantic Virtue

As we saw in the previous chapter, Thoreau's conception of the good life was strongly influenced by the ideals of romanticism, particularly in its focus on *Bildung* or self-culture. In *Walden,* this leads him to emphasize those virtues that aid us in enriching our personal experience. For instance, Thoreau praises—and exhibits—the proper virtues of the field naturalist: patience, stillness, alertness, attentiveness, physical endurance, keen hearing, keen eyesight, careful observation, precise description, careful measurement, and the ability to make fine distinctions (see in particular the chapters "Brute Neighbors" and "Winter Animals"). Such qualities are usually ignored by philosophical moralists, yet Thoreau portrays them as genuine virtues, since they enrich our experience and improve our lives. As we cultivate these virtues, we deepen our knowledge and appreciation of the landscape around us. If we fail to do so, *it* remains dull and *we* remain bored and ignorant. Thoreau insists that when this happens, as it so often does, the failure lies in us, not in the world: "the poem of creation is uninterrupted; but few are the ears that hear it" (85).[27]

Similarly, Thoreau emphasizes the virtues of the creative artist: imagination, empathy, creativity, boldness, discipline, alertness (again), hard work, patience (again), expressiveness, accuracy, invention, apt symbolism, dramatic flair. Like the naturalist's ability to observe and comprehend nature, the artist's ability to imagine and create new realities enhances his own experience and enriches others'. Indeed, acquiring knowledge and creating new works of art are divine acts for Thoreau (99, 326–27). It is no accident that an elaborate parable inspired by the *Bhagavad-Gita* substitutes "an *artist* of Kouroo" for the warrior Arjuna as its hero. The aesthetic and creative virtues are genuine virtues for Thoreau, as important as conventional moral virtues. "The perception of beauty is a moral test," he wrote in his journal.[28]

Another prominent aspect of Thoreau's romanticism is his concern for authenticity and diversity. "If [a person] has lived sincerely, it must have been in a distant land to me," he writes, somewhat cryptically, in the book's second paragraph (4). By *Walden*'s final chapter we know what he means, yet he is still demanding that we leave the beaten track, step to the music we hear "however measured or far away," "meet and live" the lives we are actually leading (323, 326, 328). In between, he tells us that "there are as many ways [to live] as there can be drawn radii from one centre" (11) and that despite his moralizing, he "does not mean to prescribe rules to strong and valiant natures" (16). Above all he is not looking for followers, for "I would not have any one adopt *my* mode of living on any account. . . . I desire that there be as many different persons in the world as possible; but I would have each one be very careful to find out and pursue *his own* way, and not his father's or his mother's or his neighbor's instead" (71).

As disappointed as Thoreau is with many of his neighbors' life choices, he is more disappointed to think that they have not really been chosen. Personal authenticity and social diversity are important virtues, in Thoreau's view. So are those qualities that further them, such as intelligence, independent thinking, persistence (stubbornness!), confidence, commitment, self-reliance, self-knowledge, and integrity.

These emphases lend open-endedness and optimism to *Walden*'s ethics, but also a certain uncertainty. "Man's capacities have never been measured," Thoreau crows, for all of us, "nor are we to judge of what he can do by any precedents, so little has been tried" (10). And again: "What youthful philosophers and experimentalists we are! There is not one of my readers who has yet lived a whole human life" (331). We may discover new possibilities in life. Old ways may be replaced by new ways, to our advantage, *and there may be no end to the process.* As *Walden* concludes: "There is more day to dawn. The sun is but a morning star" (333). A simple yet awesome gift has been given us, to be able to remake ourselves and improve our lives. Just as we may transcend our current lives, Nature, the source of our being, may transcend itself.

This complicates ethical justification, since nature cannot serve as the unchanging foundation for any ethical theory. It renders particular ethical judgments uncertain, since there is no unchanging nature, human or otherwise, to which we may appeal for guidance. Yet Thoreau is right to embrace an experimental, open-ended ethics. The railroad and the telegraph taught him—and a further century and a half of technological and social transformation have taught us—that our modern world is a world of radical change. Darwin and the paleontologists have forever undermined belief in an unchanging human nature, even in our deep prehistory. In addition, a genuine embrace of human diversity demands some concessions from philosophy's universalistic pretensions.

No purely naturalistic or universal ethical philosophy will work for us now, yet no alternative clearly compels rational assent. How to combine an optimistic experimentalism with robust, convincing justifications of our ethical judgments, thereby providing some guidance for aspiring human beings, might be the central theoretical problem in contemporary ethical philosophy. (I return to Thoreau's treatment of this issue in the chapter "Foundations.") This theoretical problem is also a practical problem for each of us. Perhaps it has increased the value of tolerance, flexibility, confidence, imagination, and all those virtues that enable us to press on in the face of ethical uncertainty.

Virtue and Duty

As we have seen, Thoreau's ethics in *Walden* is best seen as an ethics of aspiration, looking back to the ancients and forward to the contemporary virtue ethics revival. This revival has reopened important areas of our lives for intelligent philosophical scrutiny. A danger, though, is that in clearing a space for virtue ethics, we will throw out what is of value in an ethics of duty. Some contemporary virtue ethics proponents have charged that the notions of *moral* obligation and *moral* duty are incoherent or inherently misleading and have denied the existence of specifically moral obligations.[29] "There is an everyday notion of obligation, as one consideration among others, and it is ethically useful," writes Bernard Williams. This notion of obligation includes both "importance" and "immediacy." But moral obligation goes further; it is "inescapable." "Moral obligation applies to people even if they do not want it to," Williams objects. He believes we would be better off jettisoning the concept.[30]

But, in fact, just this notion of moral obligation is an important part of our ethical experience, and the concept is as necessary for virtue ethics as for any other plausible ethical approach. Certainly this is Thoreau's position, as he shows in numerous passages in *Walden:*

> Look at the teamster on the highway, wending to market by day or night; does any divinity stir within him? His highest duty to fodder and water his horses! (7)

> I do not speak to those who are well employed . . . but mainly to the mass of men who are discontented, and idly complaining of the hardness of their lot or of the times, when they might improve them. There are some who complain most energetically and inconsolably of any, because they are, as they say, doing their duty. (16)

Thoreau here questions people's notions of their duties, while invoking the force of the concept of moral duty to emphasize these issues' importance. The teamster *does* have a higher duty than to move goods from one point to another and take care of livestock. Those who use "doing their duty" as an excuse for running in life's unhappy treadmills are deluding themselves as to their true duties. The grudging quality of their obedience may suggest seriousness and selflessness to some moralists; to Thoreau, with his belief in life's essential goodness, it suggests laziness or confusion.

Similarly, in discussing his own life, Thoreau makes good use of the concept of duty, while contesting conventional understandings of its content. We have already noted this clever little passage: "I confess that I have hitherto indulged very little in philanthropic enterprises. I have made some sacrifices to a sense of duty, and among others have sacrificed this pleasure also" (72). The passage works so well because of its mixture of acceptance and contestation. It begins by implying that Thoreau fully accepts conventional conceptions of duty ("I confess") but then suggests that his philanthropic neighbors may be "indulging" themselves: pursuing pleasure rather than the true path of duty. This brings us up short and makes us question whether *we* have attended sufficiently to the content and seriousness of our obligations. Meanwhile, Thoreau wriggles off the moralistic hook.

To take another example, Thoreau asserts that he has not shirked his personal responsibilities by studying and enjoying nature, as some of his neighbors have charged. Rather, he has met those responsibilities, brooking no obstacles. "For many years I was self-appointed inspector of snow storms and rains storms," he writes, "and did my duty faithfully" (18). The notion of *self-appointed* duties—tasks that we impose on ourselves, yet that rise to the importance of moral obligations—shows yet again the importance of personal choice and diversity in Thoreau's ethical thought. Thoreau also wants to illustrate a proper obedience, which is glad, not grudging, and which testifies to the essential goodness of our situation. Doing our duty need not be grim and need not be treated grimly. Thoreau notes that, among his self-appointed tasks, he has "watered the red huckleberry, the sand cherry and the nettle tree, the red pine and the black ash, the white grape and the yellow violet, which might have withered else in dry seasons" (18).

In these and similar passages, Thoreau asserts that we have an important and immediate obligation to cultivate virtue and make the most of life. For what could be more important to us than our own lives, what more immediate than the opportunities they present? We may well debate the exact nature and extent of this obligation. We may expect diverse responses from those who take it seriously. Nevertheless, the call to strive is clear.

Thoreau's examples suggest that no clear distinction can be made between Williams's notions of important and immediate obligation and inescapable *moral* obligation. A moral obligation is simply a sufficiently important or immediate obligation. Thoreau believes the injunction to strive for personal excellence is indeed inescapable. We cannot ignore it without failing in our "chief end" and greatest opportunity.

It remains open to the reader to deny a moral obligation to pursue self-development: to deny its importance, its universality, its coherence, or its very existence. Another virtue ethicist, less demanding or optimistic than Thoreau, might accept his account of the superiority of a life of striving but deny that the average person can or should pursue it. A Kantian or utilitarian, suspicious of virtue ethics' elitism or committed to a parsimonious account of our duties, might deny the existence of any strong (or *moral*) duties to further self-knowledge or develop the intellectual virtues. I take it as evidence for the indispensability of the notion of moral obligation that it can help us distinguish these positions.

Just as Thoreau retains the concept of moral duty, he accepts the common view that we have important moral duties toward one another. In "Resistance to Civil Government," Thoreau argues that Americans have a duty to actively oppose slavery and imperialism. To make this argument, he employs a conception of moral duty as universal, binding on all, and commanding absolutely. Slavery and imperialism are such egregious injustices, Thoreau asserts in "Resistance," that we have an absolute, unavoidable duty to oppose our own government if it supports them. This is not a matter of expediency, but of justice. Arguing against theologian William Paley, a prominent advocate of submission to civil government, he writes:

> Paley appears never to have contemplated those cases to which the rule of expediency does not apply, in which a people, as well as an individual, must do justice cost what it may. If I have unjustly wrested a plank from a drowning man, I must restore it to him though I drown myself. This, according to Paley, would be inconvenient. But he that would save his life, in such a case, shall lose it. This people must cease to hold slaves, and to make war on Mexico, though it cost them their existence as a people.[31]

In a sense, moral duty overrides expediency and all conflicting interests by its very definition. This is true whether or not duty ever calls for the absolute sacrifice of one's life, regardless of how often duty and expediency do, in fact, conflict, and regardless of whether Thoreau is right in this particular instance. Of course, we should not assert such duties lightly. However, "when a sixth of the population of a nation which has undertaken to be the refuge of liberty are slaves, and a whole country is unjustly overrun and conquered by a foreign army, and subjected to military law, I think that it is not too soon for honest men to rebel and revolutionize. What makes this *duty* the more urgent is the fact, that the country so overrun is not our own, but ours is the invading army."[32] Because these injustices are being sustained or perpetrated by our government, in our name, we have a direct responsibility to oppose them.

"Those cases" in which we *must* set aside expediency are precisely those where fundamental human rights are at stake, and, especially, where the abrogation of such rights rises to the level of a denial of human beings' humanity. "I think that we do not even yet realize what slavery is," Thoreau writes in a later essay, "Slavery in Massachusetts": "If I were seriously to propose to Congress to make mankind into sausages, I have no doubt that most of the members would smile at my proposition. . . . But if any of them will tell me that to make a man into a sausage would be much worse—would be any worse, than to make him into a slave,—than it was to enact the Fugitive Slave Law, I will accuse him of foolishness, of intellectual incapacity, of making a distinction without a difference. The one is just as sensible a proposition as the other."[33] Later in this same essay, Thoreau speaks of his "brothers and sisters ... being scourged and hung for loving liberty" and asks his readers to consider the incongruity of supporting a government that kept order and protected property while enslaving their own family members. He charges his government with "robbing a poor innocent black man of his liberty for life, and, as far as they could, of his Creator's likeness in his breast." In "A Plea for Captain John Brown," he quotes Brown's words asserting the equality of all human beings: "It is my sympathy with the oppressed and the wronged, *that are as good as you,* and as precious in the sight of God."[34]

The moral argument against slavery, then, rests on our common humanity and on an admonition to act consistently. Do not treat human beings as things when they are not things. Do not treat one group of human beings radically different from the rest, when they are not radically different from the rest. To deny any of this is to fail to understand the nature of morality and justice, as Kant and other modern moralists have correctly defined them. In secular terms, it is to deny our common humanity and the clear commands of reason ("I will accuse him of foolishness, of intellectual incapacity"). This secular conception of moral duty has a religious origin, to which Thoreau explicitly refers:

And he said to them all,
   If any man will come after me, let him deny himself, and take up his cross daily, and follow me.
   For whosoever will save his life shall lose it: but whosoever will lose his life for my sake, the same shall save it.
   For what is a man advantaged, if he gain the whole world, and lose himself, or be cast away?[35]

For Thoreau, moral obligation is, indeed, inescapable and demanding. As he wrote in "Slavery in Massachusetts": "I wish my countrymen to consider, that whatever the human law may be, neither an individual nor a nation can ever commit the least act of injustice against the obscurest individual, without having to pay the penalty for it."[36] The penalty is simply to *be* immoral and unjust (Christians believe in further penalties, and society adds others for practical reasons). This conception of duty is necessary, pace some contemporary virtue ethicists, in allowing us to assert, along with Thoreau, a set of basic duties toward others that we are bound to follow. We thus preserve the rights of that "obscurest individual."

Many false resolutions are possible, as we balance self-interest and the interests of others. As we have seen, Thoreau believes we may lose ourselves in routine activities and conventional duties and fail to pursue excellence. In *Walden*'s "Conclusion," he mocks our dullness and timidity: "If you are chosen town-clerk, forsooth, you cannot go to Tierra del Fuego this summer: but you may go to the land of infernal fire nevertheless" (320). Also in this concluding chapter, however, Thoreau rejects any blanket denial of our conventional moral duties:

> It is said that Mirabeau [French revolutionary statesman and rogue, praised by Friedrich Nietzsche in *The Genealogy of Morals*] took to highway robbery "to ascertain what degree of resolution was necessary in order to place one's self in formal opposition to the most sacred laws of society." . . . A saner man would have found himself often enough "in formal opposition" to what are deemed "the most sacred laws of society," through obedience to yet more sacred laws, and so have tested his resolution without going out of his way. It is not for a man to put himself in such an attitude to society, but to maintain himself in whatever attitude he find himself through obedience to the laws of his being, which will never be one of opposition to a just government, if he should chance to meet with such. (322–23)[37]

Thoreau here clearly rejects the idea that any individual can evade the moral law, no matter how superior he or others deem himself. The "sacred laws" of morality and justice exist. The context implies that they do not limit the pursuit of virtue, which is not equivalent to mere novelty or diversity of experience. For both the timid town clerk and the deluded superman, Thoreau advises the renewed pursuit of self-knowledge. Such self-knowledge will make its demands on us, and with "resolution" and "obedience" we may meet those demands. We need not sacrifice our own integrity in order to uphold the integrity of others.

The question of how to mesh an ethics of personal aspiration with an ethics of interpersonal duty remains largely unexplored in contemporary philosophy. It also remains a real question in many people's lives. Thoreau gives us several important aids toward the more comprehensive ethical view that could begin to answer it.

First, Thoreau writes about both these aspects of ethical life: interpersonal duty in the anti-slavery and reform articles, personal aspiration in *Walden* (with some overlap). This is already more than most contemporary philosophers. Second, he gives us a detailed, blistering account of our ethical failures, finding the same causes for our injustice toward others and our failure to pursue personal excellence: laziness, thoughtlessness, gluttony, and greed. Third, Thoreau gives us justifications for both sorts of judgments that illustrate their common grounding in a respect for human nature and human potential. The same human capabilities that demand Kantian respect also allow for Aristotelian development, in Thoreau's account.[38] The same appeals to integrity, consistency, and principle that ground our moral duties also support our higher aspirations. In either case, the call to strive is unmistakable.

Resolution

In his journal for 1845, Ralph Waldo Emerson wrote: "I owed— my friend and I owed—a magnificent day to the *Bhagavat-Gita*. It was the first of books; it was as if an empire spoke to us, nothing small or unworthy, but large, serene, consistent, the voice of an old intelligence which in another age and climate had pondered and thus disposed of the same questions which exercise us."[39] Thoreau valued the *Bhagavad-Gita* as highly as any other book, both for the sublimity of its cosmology and for its noble ethical ideals. It is probably not accidental that *Walden*, like the *Gita*, is divided into eighteen chapters, or that both works move from images of despair and uncertainty in their initial pages to statements of triumphant, life-affirming resolution in their final ones.[40] This sacred Hindu scripture points us toward one possible resolution of the conflict between duty and virtue, for it sees adherence to duty as the highest virtue.

The *Gita*, part of the much larger Indian epic *Mahabharata*, tells the story of the noble hero Arjuna's growing understanding and acceptance of his duty. Surveying the battlefield at Kuru, Arjuna is dejected to think of the great slaughter to come, and especially troubled by the thought of killing his relatives and teachers, whom fate has placed on the enemy's side. He questions his "charioteer," the god Krishna, who convinces him that the field of Kuru is also a field of Dharma or "duty," and that it is his duty as a warrior to fight. In the process, Krishna describes the various yogas, or disciplines, that a person may follow to achieve focus and enlightenment. In fighting, Krishna tells Arjuna, he plays his proper role in the Cosmos. By defeating the forces of evil and upholding sacred Dharma—which means "order" as well as "duty"—Arjuna helps preserve the world. From despair and uncertainty, Arjuna progresses to enlightenment and resolution. He goes on to glorious success in the battles that conclude the *Mahabharata*.

As Hinduism's premier ethical scripture, the *Gita* suggests that each of us have our own "fields of duty" to which we are called. No matter how lowly they seem, they are ours, and we, like the greatest of heroes, may fulfill our sacred duty within them. Thoreau echoes this position in *Walden:* "However mean your life is, meet it and live it; do not shun it and call it hard names" (328). The ancient scripture also suggests that different members of society may have very different duties, tied to particular stations in life, admonishing: "better to do one's own duty imperfectly than to do another man's well." Thoreau finds this moral particularism appealing. Toward the end of *Walden*, he provides a parable that evokes the *Gita* with special reference to his own artistic vocation:

> There was an artist in the city of Kouroo who was disposed to strive after perfection. One day it came into his mind to make a staff . . . he said to himself, It shall be perfect in all respects, though I should do nothing else in my life . . . and as he searched for and rejected stick after stick his friends gradually deserted him, for they grew old in their works and died, but he grew not older by a moment. His singleness of purpose and resolution, and his elevated piety, endowed him, without his knowledge, with perennial youth. . . . By the time he had smoothed and polished the staff Kalpa was no longer the pole-star; and ere he had put on the ferrule and the head adorned with precious stones, Brahma had awoke and slumbered many times. . . . When the finishing stroke was put to his work, it suddenly expanded before the eyes of the astonished artist into the fairest of all the creations of Brahma. He had made a new system in making a staff, a world with full and fair proportions. (326–27)

Clearly Thoreau is himself the artist of this parable, while the "world" he has made is *Walden*. Thoreau indicates that, like Arjuna, he too has unusual duties to perform, which might conflict with conventional moral duties to friends and family. The comparison with the *Gita* suggests that the devoted performance of such tasks involves sacrifice, elevation, and transcendence of the self; also, that such dutiful action helps sustain and enrich the world.

Krishna's teachings in the *Bhagavad-Gita* aim to foster Arjuna's resolve. The virtues it praises are valued precisely for conducing to resolution, focus, and dutifulness, as well as spiritual enlightenment:

> Fearlessness, purity, determination in the discipline of knowledge, charity, self-control, sacrifice, study of sacred lore, penance, honesty;
> Nonviolence, truth, absence of anger, disengagement, peace, loyalty, compassion for creatures, lack of greed, gentleness, modesty, reliability;
> Brilliance, patience, resolve, clarity, absence of envy and of pride; these characterize a man born with divine traits. . . .

The divine traits lead to freedom, the demonic lead to bondage; do not despair, Arjuna; you were born with the divine.[41]

Walden praises many of these same virtues. Both works emphasize discipline and renunciation. Both assert that the highest virtues are rare and difficult to obtain. Both insist, in the *Gita's* words, that "no effort in this world is lost or wasted." Like the *Gita, Walden* places a premium on the virtues fostering adherence to duty, while insisting, somewhat paradoxically, that these also lead to genuine freedom.

Comparison with the *Gita* clarifies Thoreau's commitment to an ethics of duty. Still, when it comes to the *content* of duty and the proper method for determining that content, he strongly disagrees with the ancient scripture. "Kreeshna's argument, it must be allowed, is defective," Thoreau writes in an extended discussion of the *Gita* in his first book, *A Week on the Concord and Merrimack Rivers:* "No sufficient reason is given why Arjoon should fight. . . . The duty of which [Krishna] speaks, is it not an arbitrary one? When was it established? The Brahman's virtue consists not in doing right, but arbitrary things. . . . What is 'a man's own particular calling'? What are the duties which are appointed by one's birth? It is in fact a defence of the institution of caste, of what is called the 'natural duty' of the Kshetree, or soldier, 'to attach himself to the discipline,' 'not to flee from the field,' and the like."[42] It is precisely this deference to tradition among his neighbors that Thoreau will later condemn in *Walden,* partly through the metaphor of the "penitential bramins." Thoreau's practical challenge to such traditionalism is simply to move a little outside Concord village and live his own life in full sight of his neighbors. His philosophical response is to deny that conservative appeals to tradition successfully define our duties, or a person's "particular calling." Only the individual can do that, Thoreau insists. "I must conclude that Conscience," he wrote in *A Week,* "was not given us for no purpose, or for a hinderance."[43]

Like the author of the *Gita,* Thoreau sometimes uses warlike metaphors to praise rigorous adherence to duty and the pursuit of difficult goals.[44] He appears to have had more than his share of the martial virtues; Emerson wrote in his funeral address that "there was something military in his nature not to be subdued, always manly and able," and he connected this discipline to Thoreau's tireless moral and intellectual striving.[45] But the man who condemned the blind obedience of marines in the Mexican-American War—an obedience, he wrote, that makes a man "a mere shadow and reminiscence of humanity"—and who railed at Massachusetts policemen returning escaped slaves to their Southern owners, could never stomach an ethical philosophy that made discipline, effectiveness, or obedience ends in themselves.[46] Only when married to conscience do such virtues acquire their highest value. Without it, they easily become vices.

Thoreau believes that the *Gita*'s view is "the wisest conservatism," "a sublime conservatism."[47] Yet it countenances all sorts of abuses, provided they are sufficiently timeworn. It leads to social stagnation and undermines novelty in the world. Above all, it is an abdication of personal and moral freedom. Such conservatism offers only a bogus moral certainty, as Thoreau believed attentiveness to conscience would show.

We may better understand Thoreau's and the *Gita*'s different valuations of personal choice and moral certainty if we return to the parable of "the artist of Kouroo." Thoreau's own pursuit of excellence involved artistic creation and the solitude, focus, and self-absorption necessary to achieve it. He well knew the conflicts between the demands of art and everyday life and between personal and familial duties. The parable presents the artist's fantasy of perfection and importance: the work itself becoming a world; the creation of this ideal world balancing out any moral failures in the real one. Such single-mindedness *is* faithfulness to duty, Thoreau wants to believe. Only thus are the greatest achievements possible. Such faithfulness to duty takes precedence over all conventional duties to friends and family. In the face of great artistic (even cosmic) achievements, any conventional moral failures are unimportant. Perhaps the passage is directed specifically at budding artistic geniuses. Perhaps all of us, like the artist of Kouroo, may choose new commitments and follow them through, whatever it takes—provided we fully dedicate ourselves to them.

But back in the real world, Thoreau was a dutiful friend and family member, putting down his own literary projects to work in the household pencil factory when his father's illness required it, for example, or heading off immediately to Long Island at Emerson's request to search for Margaret Fuller's remains after her shipwreck. As opposed to a Gauguin, who abandoned his family to sail to Tahiti and pursue his art with no distractions, Thoreau carved out substantial time for his own literary labors, while continuing to fulfill his familial duties. Neither his personality nor his ethical philosophy left room for a Gauguin-like resolution to the conflict between duty and the pursuit of personal virtue or artistic achievement—even had he felt inclined toward such a resolution.[48] Both the Kouroo parable and the discussion of "philanthropy" at the end of *Walden*'s first chapter assert a certain freedom to pursue personal excellence and achievement. Yet both also justify this freedom, in part, by reminding readers that society gains by providing it to its members. The exact balance to be struck remains uncertain—necessarily, in Thoreau's view. Moral certainty lies beyond reach, since neither tradition nor divine revelation can answer these questions once and for all. Arjuna has Krishna as his charioteer or divine guide, whose words of advice are buttressed by religious revelation, in the vision of Krishna's totality (section eleven of the scripture). Arjuna, his allies and enemies, and all the worlds are merely fragments of that totality. Any moral guidance coming from the author of the universe has dispositive power. Any uncertainty as to his message may fairly be referred to *our* insufficiencies, rather than God's.

But the artist of Kouroo is alone. His inspiration comes from he knows not where ("one day it came into his mind to make a staff"), and he must take his resolution himself. His friends pursue their works as he pursues his and become "dead" to him. (We remember with sadness Emerson's and Thoreau's early closeness and later estrangement, in part over Emerson's negative judgment of *A Week,* Thoreau's first major "work.") The artist or striver after virtue must choose his own path, guided partly by tradition, but primarily by his own inner light.

Still, Thoreau greatly admired Hindu scripture's call to discipline in service to higher goals. "Depend upon it," he wrote a friend, some years after he left the pond, "that, rude and careless as I am, I would fain practice the *yoga* faithfully. 'The yogin, absorbed in contemplation, contributes in his degree to creation: he breathes a divine perfume, he hears wonderful things. Divine forms traverse him without tearing him, and united to the nature which is proper to him, he goes, he acts, as animating original matter.' To some extent, and at rare intervals, even I am a yogin."[49] In the face of ethical uncertainty, the self-discipline of the yogi becomes even more important. Thoreau insists that each person must give himself or herself the rule for how to live. Resolution is universally a virtue, but some moral decisions can be resolved only by the individual, in action. Virtue and duty remain our key ethical concepts, but those concepts must still be applied by each of us in our own lives.

Economy

"My purpose in going to Walden Pond," Henry Thoreau writes early in *Walden*, "was not to live cheaply nor to live dearly there, but to transact some private business with the fewest possible obstacles; to be hindered from accomplishing which for want of a little common sense, a little enterprise and business talent, appeared not so [much] sad as foolish" (19). As we have seen, the "business" referred to includes living a good life, "private" not because it is best pursued alone, but because no one can do it for us.

Whatever his original intentions, an important part of Thoreau's experiment at the pond turned out to involve answering basic economic questions. What is the best way to earn a living? How much time should I spend at it? How much food and what kind of shelter are necessary to live, or to live well? Thoreau believed that these questions were best posed and answered by individuals attending carefully to their own lives, rather than by reformers attending to institutions. He argued that the real importance of our economic lives lies not in how much wealth they create, but what sorts of people they make us and how they relate us to others.[1]

In effect, Thoreau saw economics as a branch of applied virtue ethics, as it was for Aristotle and St. Thomas Aquinas. He argued the primacy of ethical over economic considerations, principles over pleasure, final or higher ends over proximate ends or mere means. But Thoreau did not rest content with a screed against materialism. Instead, he extended his arguments for subordinating economic activity to self-development into an analysis of all aspects of economic life: consumption and production, spending and saving, enterprise and leisure. Always the goal was to specify the best life he could live and how these activities might move him toward that life, whether as means or as constituent ends.

While virtue ethics arguably provides the proper framework for considering our economic lives, the complexity of modern economic life works to obscure it. In response, Thoreau structured his personal economy so as to clarify this framework, primarily through simple living and a rejection of the division of labor. As far as possible he secured his own food, in the bean field and the pond. He built his own house, using local materials. Thoreau lingered over these experiments and then over their interpretation. He saw the effects of his economic actions, because he was looking and because they were written directly into the land around him.

In the end, Thoreau concluded that a good life involved both limiting his economic activities and carefully attending to them. Thus, they became means to know himself and his world, and a springboard for higher achievements. "Economy is a subject which admits of being treated with levity," he wrote, "but it cannot so be disposed of" (20).

First Things First

In *Walden*, "Economy" comes first. It is the first and longest of eighteen chapters. Before serious "Reading" or entertaining "Visitors," before considering "Higher Laws" or visiting "The Ponds," Thoreau treats "Economy."

Economy must come first, for two reasons. First, insofar as "economy" is defined as that personal economy that consists in a correct matching of means to ends, an "industrious" and "enterprising" temperament and a keen desire to "improve one's opportunities," such economy is the key to all practical effectiveness. "I have always endeavored to acquire strict business habits," Thoreau writes, "they are indispensable to every man"—but especially to one pursuing difficult goals which are neither well regarded nor well rewarded by society (20).

Second, we are all tasked, transcendentalists no less than tradesmen, with supporting ourselves. Economic activity will thus be a part of our lives: how large a part is a key question. No matter what our overall goals in life, we must ask whether our economic activities further these directly or provide the means to engage in other activities that do so. Such questions demand answers, because "The Economy" has its own logic and its own answers, which can easily become ours by default. We also have a tendency to lose ourselves in our proximate economic purposes. Our economic forethought, valuable and necessary, can end by narrowing our lives.

Within the first half-dozen pages of this first chapter, Thoreau sets up a framework that will allow a careful analysis of his own and his neighbors' economic lives. His first words concerning these are meant to jolt us and stir our imaginations, preparatory to reseeing:

I have travelled a good deal in Concord; and every where, in shops, and offices, and fields, the inhabitants have appeared to me to be doing penance in a thousand remarkable ways. What I have heard of Brahmins sitting

exposed to four fires and looking in the face of the sun; or hanging suspended, with their heads downward, over flames; or looking at the heavens
over their shoulders "until it becomes impossible for them to resume their
natural position, while from the twist of the neck nothing but liquids can
pass into the stomach;" or dwelling, chained for life at the foot of a tree; or
measuring with their bodies, like caterpillars, the breadth of vast empires; or
standing on one leg on the tops of pillars,—even these forms of conscious
penance are hardly more incredible and astonishing than the scenes which I
daily witness. (4)

The rhetoric here is sly and well considered. To his largely Protestant
audience in mid-1850s America, the religious form of "penance" would
have seemed outlandish enough—another odd and wrong custom
brought in by the Irish Catholics streaming into their midst—doubly
odd when presented in connection with Indian brahmins. Yet in the
standard biblical account work *is* a penance: God's punishment for
humanity's sin and disobedience at the Fall. For many Christians this
hard, work-filled life is itself something to be endured, in hope of a better life to come. Perhaps these ideas, too, are outlandish. In fact, Thoreau
believes life-denying Christian otherworldliness is a main obstacle to
philosophical discussion of the nature of the good life and to its practical pursuit (72–80, 314–16). The passage invites readers to deny Thoreau's
charge, challenging each of us to specify the point of our economic
lives—thus opening up discussion.

Taken most simply, this hyperbolic description claims that most of
the work performed by Thoreau's neighbors is experienced by them as
unpleasant, unfulfilling drudgery. Thoreau's reader must ask himself or
herself: is this my experience? Crucially, there is no mention here of
money, implying that the enjoyment we get out of work and its effect on
us—not pay—should be the primary factors in our deciding where,
whether, and how much to work. When Thoreau later describes his own
work (farming, building, surveying, teaching, reading, writing) he
repeatedly returns to this point (42, 162).

The passage also suggests that his neighbors' work deforms their
characters and lives rather than improving them. This is most clearly
implied by the brahmins' twisted, paralyzed necks and is emphasized by
the images of immobility and stasis ("hanging suspended," "chained for
life," "standing . . . on the tops of pillars"). Thoreau writes near the beginning of New England's industrialization, with eyewitness knowledge of
the sorts of ailments and deformities to which factory life could lead:

limbs lost to machines, lungs ruined from stoking furnaces in unventilated rooms.[2] These are the extreme cases. But *Walden* focuses on those who are comparatively luckier and hence perhaps less aware of their peril: people whose work lives fail to allow them to develop as human beings. "Most men," Thoreau writes, "are so occupied with the factitious cares and superfluously course labors of life that its finer fruits cannot be plucked by them. Their fingers, from excessive toil, are too clumsy and tremble too much for that" (6).

Thoreau means, in these general and metaphorical remarks, to get us to feel or admit dissatisfaction. He thus pushes us in the direction of asking more from our economic lives. Thoreau's views show strong affinities with Nobel Prize–winning economist Amartya Sen's "capabilities-based" conception of human well-being, particularly in their shared emphasis on the active nature of the good life. According to Sen, we have capacities or capabilities whose use and development constitute human well-being.[3] According to Thoreau, our work should be an occasion for such development, because for most of us it takes up the best part of our day. The office worker sitting immobile in a chair for forty or fifty hours a week will likely become soft and flabby. The same is true for someone who, by choice or chance, is stuck in a monotonous, repetitive job that does not engage her mental capabilities.

The invocation of *nature* and *the natural* will be a part of any ethics based on capabilities: recall the brahmins' necks twisted out of their natural position and the inhuman, wormlike wriggling of some of the other "penitents." But their use is problematic. We can speak of both capabilities and their development as natural, meaning simply that most people in our society and others like it have these capabilities and develop them to a certain extent. But the mere existence of some capability cannot justify its positive evaluation: "natural" is not a synonym for "good." Nor does its *typical* use fully specify how a capability is best developed. The higher and more rarefied the use to which a capability is put, the less natural, in the sense of normal, it becomes.[4]

The best the ethicist can do is point out that people typically have certain capabilities that can be developed in a variety of ways, and argue further that some ways are better than others. The word "natural" here does no direct justificatory work but rather represents the claim that the capability or the potential for its higher development is widely present. So, for example, young children have the capacity to learn about wild nature and develop a great curiosity about it. Most adults lose this curiosity as they get older, but some, such as scientists and naturalists, keep it, improving their capacity to learn and increasing their knowledge. This can be seen as nurturing a natural capability and putting it to a better use than normal. But that this use *is* better must still be argued.[5]

According to Thoreau, then, we should judge our work and economic activities generally by whether they are enjoyable and whether they further our self-development. Instead, we often pursue money or possessions and neglect those further ends that they may support. Even worse, we sometimes just run in the ruts and act for no conscious purpose. The brahmins' efforts as Thoreau presents them hang in the air, unexplained, standing for the undirected economic lives of his neighbors. He continues: "The twelve labors of Hercules were trifling in comparison with those which my neighbors have undertaken; for they were only twelve, and had an end; but I could never see that these men slew or captured any monster or finished any labor" (4). If we cannot identify their purpose, then we cannot know when our efforts have succeeded. We cannot have the satisfaction of saying "This is a job well done." Or "That job is finished, I can rest now." Or "I have enough of what I was pursuing," either money or the things that money can buy. To be able to do so, we must consider our economic efforts as they relate to more than economic ends. Even the prodigious drudgery of Hercules compares favorably with the labors of those who cannot do so.[6]

Means/ends analysis—economy—is thus essential to virtue ethics, as Aristotle recognized long ago.[7] Not surprisingly, it is central to ethical discussion in *Walden*. Virtually every page comments on the goodness of some putative ends or the suitableness of particular means to attain them. Thoreau's analysis of means and ends occurs at various levels of generality, includes both detailed discussions and short, seemingly offhand remarks, and shifts from earnestness to irony and back again. But the main analytic moves are (somewhat schematically) the following:

Point out pointless action (4, 104–5, 164).
Challenge overwrought means to fairly simple ends (33–36, 65, 91–93).
Deny the goodness of certain widely pursued ends (65–66, 74–75, 195–96).
Suggest new means to accepted ends (53, 131–32).
Contest or more fully specify the meaning of accepted ends (97–101).
Argue for greater emphasis on our higher ends (21, 89–90, 323–24).
Define our "chief end" (16–18, 90–91, 328–29).

I present these in no particular order, as Thoreau shifts freely from one to the other in *Walden*. Such a procedure accurately portrays our ordinary ethical reasoning. I believe it also reflects the true situation of the ethical theorist, who cannot settle questions at the most general level and then read off the particulars of how individuals should live, but who must continually revisit general assumptions and particular judgments, revising both as he goes along.[8] Thoreau's attention to the full spectrum of means/ends reasoning and his attempts to tie general principles to particular ethical judgments are strengths of his ethical philosophy. Ironically, however, this comprehensiveness and specificity make it harder for most academic philosophers to recognize *Walden* as a genuine work in ethical philosophy, since contemporary ethical philosophy usually remains at a high level of generality and theoretical abstractness.

Key to Thoreau pursuing a comprehensive means/ends analysis is his rejection of two basic postulates of modern economic theory: that our ultimate goals in life are arbitrary, mere "preferences" beyond the range of rational debate, and that human beings have infinite desires for wealth, ownership, and consumption whose pursuit is limited only by scarcity of resources. We must reject these views, Thoreau believes, in favor of the classical beliefs that some goals are ignoble and childish, and that reason may convince us that we have consumed enough or garnered enough material wealth. These are old, simple, and very necessary ethical themes.

Thoreau asserts that economic anxiety is a common affliction in his busy, commercial society (11). Both the wealthy speculator monitoring her investments and the poor laborer who cannot get out of debt can find themselves obsessed with money, possessions, and the status they provide. But is such anxiety widespread, and is Thoreau propounding a reasonable alternative to this anxious life? Critics often note that Thoreau did not need to worry about supporting a wife and children, and that his superior abilities and education made it relatively easy for him to support himself. These factors certainly increased his economic choices and helped alleviate the anxiety he might have felt in undertaking his economic experiment at the pond. Still, Thoreau's situation was probably not essentially different from many of his readers today, both young, single ones and older ones with families but with relatively secure, well-paid jobs. Indeed, the immense increase in education and per capita wealth in the United States between Thoreau's time and our own should have made an easy economic sufficiency more widely available. Perhaps it *is* more widely available, and Americans remain chained to high-consumption, high-anxiety lifestyles less by choice than through inertia.

Interestingly, empirical studies have repeatedly shown that most people value *security* of income more highly than *increases* in income. Studies in the United States show that beyond the poorest 10 percent to 15 percent of the population, happiness and contentment do not correlate with some absolute level of wealth or some particular level relative to one's neighbors.[9] Rather, the evidence is clear that for most people, happiness depends on their assurance that they will have enough. A dynamic capitalist economy offers natural risktakers great scope for testing their luck and abilities. A few succeed spectacularly and many more enjoy the game. But most of us are not entrepreneurs or speculators and would rather have a sufficiency. To this majority, Thoreau says we *can* have enough, but most easily and certainly by scaling back our material wants and finding inexpensive paths to personal fulfillment.[10]

One half of saying "enough" involves recognizing happiness and such higher goals as self-development, an enriched experience, or increased knowledge as the ultimate purposes of our economic activities. The other half means seeing the limited value of money and possessions for achieving these goals. "I see young men, my townsmen," Thoreau continues his introductory remarks, "whose misfortune it is to have inherited farms, houses, barns, cattle, and farming tools; for these are more easily acquired than got rid of" (5). From a commonsense perspective it could hardly be a "misfortune" to be given the start on an economically productive life, which inheriting a farm still meant throughout mid-nineteenth-century America. Nor, from the perspective of the market, can it ever be disadvantageous to be given something for free that has substantial market value. Such a thing can be translated into money, which can then buy something that we *do* want.

But the abstraction of the market is no defense against an overconcern with money, while possessions may cause great harm without their disciplined use. If they are too numerous, we are forced to attend to them; if they are too valuable, we worry about theft and loss. The pursuit of money and possessions can lead us into careers that do not support our higher aspirations. This possibility, that men and women may become "the tools of their tools," that "when the farmer has got his house, he may not be the richer but the poorer for it, and it be the house that has got him," is a recurring theme in *Walden* (33, 37, 65–66).

Our inheritance, which includes old things and old ways of looking at things, may not be the start of our fortune, but rather a misfortune. Often, Thoreau believes, "men labor under a mistake. The better part of the man is soon ploughed into the soil for compost. By a seeming fate, commonly called necessity, they are employed, as it says in an old book, laying up treasures which moth and rust will corrupt and thieves break through and steal. It is a fool's life, as they will find when they get to the end of it, if not before" (5). That there is a "better part" of ourselves, which it is our duty to cultivate and not "plough into the soil" to fertilize the projects of others or our own unthinking, vegetable life, must be a basic tenet of any virtue ethics. So must be the denial of "fate," opening up the possibility that through increased self-knowledge, we may recognize that we "labor under a mistake" and change our lives accordingly.

This toil is *not* fated. We may organize our lives in new ways, ones more consonant with our ideals and happiness. Our present lives only seem fated, because the grooves have worn so deep. We must try new ways and, just as important, *imagine* new ways of living. For "what a man thinks of himself, that it is which determines, or rather indicates, his fate" (7). Earlier, Thoreau had invoked the naturalistic, foundational side of virtue ethics. Here he expresses its romantic, idealistic side, which recognizes that while no account of human nature can unshakably ground or fully specify our ethics, the freedom this opens up for self-creation and enacting our ideals is valuable recompense. The key to exploring these possibilities, Thoreau believes, is *economy*, defined now as "simplicity of life and elevation of purpose" (92).

Thoreau needs one more set of categories to support his economic/ ethical analysis: necessities, comforts, and luxuries. Of the many things that our money can buy, we want to ask whether they are indispensable (necessities), are superfluous (luxuries), or truly serve to make our lives more pleasurable (comforts). Thoreau's definitions of these are straight-forward, the key term being the first: "By the words, *necessary of life,* I mean whatever, of all that man obtains by his own exertions, has been from the first, or from long use has become, so important to human life that few, if any, whether from savageness, or poverty, or philosophy, ever attempt to do without it" (12). Although history and anthropology give us hints, the true necessities of life can be found only in experience. This is one reason Thoreau went to the pond. As for the rest, "most of the luxuries, and many of the so-called comforts of life, are not only not indispensable, but positive hindrances to the elevation of mankind" (14). Indulging in them might please us but rarely improves us, Thoreau believes.

Thoreau's position here is too simplistic, however, perhaps because he sees Americans so sunk in materialism that he does not want to confuse the issue. To note one important complication: he divides possessions into necessities, luxuries, and the intermediate term "comforts." But given his own ethical position, he needs a fourth intermediate category, "aids":

things that genuinely further self-development, just as comforts genuinely further pleasure. Judging by Thoreau's own life, he would have included books, musical instruments, hand lenses, and field glasses within this category. What *we* include within it remains to be seen, and we must remember that aids may no longer aid and comforts may no longer bring pleasure when used unwisely or excessively. Complicating Thoreau's position in this way only strengthens it, I believe.

Likening the provision of economic necessities to stoking a furnace, Thoreau asks his readers:

> When a man is warmed by the several modes which I have described, what does he want next? Surely not more warmth of the same kind, as more and richer food, larger and more splendid houses, finer and more abundant clothing, more numerous incessant and hotter fires, and the like. When he has obtained those things which are necessary to life, there is another alternative than to obtain the superfluities; and that is, to adventure on life now, his vacation from humbler toil having commenced. The soil, it appears, is suited to the seed, for it has sent its radicle downward, and it may now send its shoot upward also with confidence. Why has man rooted himself thus firmly in the earth, but that he may rise in the same proportion into the heavens above? (15)

This may sound grandiose, but the question is: do you believe it? And if not: what do you believe instead? All our other judgments upon our economic lives depend on our answers here: all our calculations of profit and loss, of lives well or ill spent.

We need not follow Thoreau so far as to see merely an instrumental value in "stoking the furnace." We may believe that pleasure is a necessary part of a good human life and still agree that achievements besides maximizing pleasure are also important. First in importance is the creation of ourselves: the development of personal characters and lives of which we can be proud. But also important are such achievements as raising happy children, learning about the world, and building professional careers that support us and are genuinely useful to society. These are the things for which we strive and on which serious people judge the success of their lives. The healthy side to all asceticism is its recognition of higher goals and its fostering of the discipline necessary to achieve them.

The relative value of pleasure, self-development, and personal achievement in a good human life is perhaps the most vexing question in virtue ethics. We may strive to further all these, while recognizing that sometimes we must choose between them. Each of us answers this question within his or her own life. Whatever our answers, our economic lives should support them. This is not necessarily to put on a hair shirt. To the extent that wealth or possessions further our true goals, they should be pursued. But no further. For "there is no more fatal blunderer than he who consumes the greater part of his life getting his living."[11]

Economy as Method and Metaphor

For Thoreau "economy" is both a key method and a key metaphor for ethics. Thoreau's method may be quickly summarized. First, he attempted to simplify his life. From his furniture to the number of dishes he cooked for dinner, the refrain is "simplicity, simplicity, simplicity!" (91). Second, he carefully attended to his economic experience: the quantifiable and the nonquantifiable aspects; the money earned and the economic processes themselves; the effects on him and the effects radiating out from him. Third, he frequently returned to the question of the final or true ends of his efforts and whether in fact his economic activities were furthering them. These three moves—simplification, attentiveness, preserving the full means/ends spectrum—supported one another. Thoreau applied them to numerous activities in *Walden*, from eating huckleberries to building his house.

Several points should be made about this method. For one thing, it personalizes ethics. The focus is on *my* economy and on what I should do in particular instances, not on *the* Economy and on what, ideally, we should be doing collectively. For another, it is flexible, clarifying the purposes and relative success of people who may have quite varied goals. Finally, the method works. Follow it and you will live more consciously, successfully, and happily.

Despite this last, crucial fact—that the method works, that it worked for Thoreau and can work for you or me—it has its limitations. Economy is not a substitute for effort but makes our efforts more effective. Thoreau's method, like Aristotle's practical reason, combines thought and action, and the thinking part is worthless by itself. In fact, ethical thought leads to pointless hairsplitting, bootless system building, aimless fantasizing, and plain hypocrisy, if not vitalized by action.

Furthermore, the method recognizes the limits of rationality, as both comprehensiveness and certainty elude our economic judgments. Thoreau has several nice ways of indicating this: for example, the mix of seriousness and whimsy with which he treats figures for income and expenditures at the pond (49, 55, 59–60). Thoreau keeps a complete list of the materials used to make his house and their cost, telling us: "I give the details because very few are able to tell exactly what their houses cost, and fewer still, if any, the separate cost of the various materials which compose them" (48–49). Thus we know that he paid two dollars and forty-three cents for "two second hand windows with glass," thirty-one cents for horsehair to mix with his plaster, and ten cents for a latch for his door. We learn *exactly* what he paid the town grocers for his food over the course of a year and *exactly* what the produce from his fields earned. "These statistics," he concludes, "however accidental and therefore uninstructive they may appear, as they have a certain completeness, have a certain value also. Nothing was given me of which I have not rendered some account" (60).

What is this "certain value"? Well, if you can specify income and expenditures clearly, you can limit your use of resources and direct them to where they will do the most good. The price of horsehair or second-hand windows varies "accidentally," with supply and demand, but we must track these accidents and act accordingly, if we wish to build and live economically. Still, such monetary metrics cannot capture the higher value of our activities or achievements. During his own lifetime, Thoreau earned more for his bushels of beans, little as that was, than for *A Week on the Concord and Merrimack Rivers*, the wonderful book he wrote while living at Walden Pond. Even if the public had paid more, much more, for the book, that would not have shown its true worth relative to the beans. It would not have captured the relative worth of hoeing beans and writing the book for Thoreau. Nor can the figures express or explain the value of Thoreau's faithfulness to the moral, artistic, and spiritual imperatives suggested by the notion of "rendering some account" of all we are given.

This suggests that if we follow the figures too slavishly, we will make mistakes. It may be a false economy, for example, to pay someone to plant your garden while you work overtime at the office, even though you earn more money than the gardener costs. "Where is this division of labor to end?" Thoreau asks, "and what object does it finally serve? No doubt another *may* also think for me; but it is not therefore desirable that he should do so to the exclusion of my thinking for myself" (46). Some essential faculties cannot be exercised by proxy. Some valuable experiences are more enjoyable than profitable.

Careful accounting helps Thoreau construct a sturdy, comfortable house for under thirty dollars and feed himself on "about twenty-seven cents a week" (60–61). More important, it helps him devote time to other things besides food and shelter. For the purpose of life is to live well, and "the cost of a thing is the amount of what I will call life which is required to be exchanged for it, immediately or in the long run" (31). This suggests that the part of our valuing that we can express in a monetary metric must be folded in to a larger ethical reasoning, and that this in turn must be folded in to a life where we make choices and deal with the "accidental" truths of our particular lives. Close figuring has tremendous value within this context, but it is badly misleading beyond it.[12]

Thoreau also reminds us that efficient reasoning and efficient action can be carried too far. We do not want our lives completely organized. *Walden* contains plenty of fishing, loafing, and woolgathering. Appealing characters such as Alek Therien, the careless French-Canadian woodchopper, make a nice contrast to the striving Thoreau and suggest other ethical options. Once again, the method should not be allowed to take over. It is valuable solely in service to a rich life. Maximal efficiency is not a legitimate goal, even though philosophical speculation, moralistic hectoring, or market pressures might push us in that direction.

But if method and order have their limits, so do genius and idealism. Without discipline and calculation, without specific skills and abilities, we cannot instantiate our ideals. We fail just as surely as those without ideals or with base ideals. There is a nice anecdote from Thoreau's years at the pond that shows this.

One of Thoreau's and Emerson's Concord neighbors was Amos Bronson Alcott, praised in *Walden* as "one of the last of the philosophers" and "the man of the most faith of any alive" (268). Alcott was a true idealist. He always had a new project or plan to reform society. His ideas in education, in particular, were revolutionary. Unfortunately Alcott was impractical, running off to pursue new projects without seeing old ones through, often out of money, sometimes unable to support his family.

To help him through a lean season, Emerson commissioned Alcott to design and build a "summer house" on his Walden property, perhaps stimulated by Thoreau's accounts of his life at the pond. Originally it was to be relatively simple and utilitarian, but under Alcott's guidance the summerhouse developed into an elaborate structure, whose floor plan changed with the designer's moods and inspirations. Since he wished to mimic nature, Alcott eschewed straight lines, and the house grew more complicated and rickety. Since it was not to cut its inhabitants off from the woods, Alcott left much of the structure open, and it quickly suffered wind and rain damage. Thoreau helped Alcott build the summerhouse, and his and Emerson's journals are filled with hilarious accounts of it.[13] Emerson first named it "Tumble-down Hall." His family, who never actually used it, came to call it "the Ruin."

Concord's residents had never seen a building quite like it. Throughout the summer of 1847, they came to laugh at this transcendentalist architecture. Alcott didn't mind. He just kept on building, taking Emerson's money for what was really part sculpture, part charity. "The Ruin" played with some interesting ideas—some of the same ideas that Thoreau was experimenting with in *his* building program at Walden. But while his neighbors might scratch their heads at Henry living out in the woods, they didn't laugh at his house. For more than one of them put it to good use when an unexpected storm cut short an afternoon's fishing, and anyone could see it was well built and suited to its purpose, which was not merely an artistic but an economic one. Like Thoreau's life, his house challenged his neighbors in a way Alcott's never could.

Thoreau repeatedly uses the word "economy" as a synonym for right living, and *Walden* employs economy as one of its main ethical metaphors. Stanley Cavell, in his influential study *The Senses of* Walden, notes the centrality of economic terms in the book's first chapter. "'Economy' turns into a nightmare maze of terms about money and possessions and work, each turning toward and joining the others," he writes. No summary of this chapter will capture the number of economic terms the writer sets in motion in it. There is profit and loss, rich and poor, cost and expense, borrow and pay, owe and own, business, commerce, enterprises, ventures, affairs, capital, price, amount, improvement, bargain, employment, inheritance, bankruptcy, work, trade, labor, idle, spend, waste, allowance, fortune, gain, earn, afford, possession, change, settling, living, interest, prospects, means, terms."[14] By "setting these terms in motion," Thoreau forces us to think about them. In place of our previously settled judgments about our enterprises, we now have question marks and unsettling comparisons. Thoreau will deliver a chesty maxim that appropriates the hard, no-nonsense language of business—but with a catch. For example, the bland "I have always endeavored to acquire strict business habits; they are indispensable to every man," followed by the fantastically extended metaphor of "trading with the Celestial Empire," which clearly calls us to higher ventures (20). Or again: "Who would not be early to rise, and rise earlier and earlier every successive day of his life, till he became unspeakably healthy, wealthy, and wise?" (127). This little bit of literary larceny simultaneously advocates and pokes fun at "method," provides an utterly practical piece of advice, and suggests higher goals and endless, heroic striving.

I think Cavell takes too negative a view of this "unsettling" of our economic terms. "What we call the Protestant Ethic, the use of worldly loss and gain to symbolize heavenly standing," he writes, "appears in *Walden* as some last suffocation of the soul. America and its Christianity have become perfect, dreamlike literalizations or parodies of themselves."[15] But using monetary or commercial metaphors to express higher values is not necessarily wrong or perverse. Like using physical metaphors to "picture" the mental or spiritual realms, it is useful and deeply ingrained in our thinking.[16] Just as physical metaphors can suggest the *reality* of the spiritual realm, so economic metaphors can suggest the *possibility* of instantiating higher values. The prevailing tone of *Walden* is one of hope, not suffocating despair, largely because Thoreau believes in the practical possibility of self-improvement. Rather than picturing a "nightmare," "Economy" moves on from his despairing neighbors and the immobile brahmins to discuss the concrete ways Thoreau improved his life at the pond. By implication, such improvements are also open to his neighbors and his readers.

Thoreau's appropriation of business discourse, like his appropriation of Christian ethical categories and rhetoric, involves both earnestness and irony. Modern commentators, who tend to be intellectuals and English professors, not businesspeople, are apt to catch the irony and miss the earnestness. But Thoreau really does believe that strict business habits are indispensable. He really does think people have a responsibility to make their own living, rather than sponging off their neighbors. Thoreau challenges the business culture's aims but also hopes to harness its drive (119). He tries to meet people where they live, ethically, and for many in Thoreau's time as in ours, that meant the worlds of business and commerce.

In effect, Thoreau's playfulness with economic terms—his use of irony, his multiple meanings, his straightforward denials of conventional economic judgments alongside examples of them—invites the reader to reconsider his economic life and his life in general. Just as the cut-and-dried nature of economic calculation can be used to serve this greater good, so too can the inherent ambiguity and uncertainty of language. For the upshot is a rich, flexible language of means and ends, profit and loss, which allows us to make decisions and choices but also forces us to question them. We can never rest in our judgments because we can never rest in our language. Just as idealists cannot escape economic realities, so economic "realists" cannot ignore the reality that they are making moral choices in their economic lives. Both must reckon with a larger view of freedom.

Like Cavell, Leonard Neufeldt notes Thoreau's "manipulations of [economic] language" and semantic playfulness, in his *The Economist: Henry Thoreau and Enterprise*.[17] But Neufeldt's excellent study puts these linguistic matters in a wider social and historical context, pointing out that during Thoreau's short lifetime New England industrialized, California boomed, large areas of the West were settled, and both absolute wealth and the gap between rich and poor increased dramatically in the United States. Antebellum American thinkers grappled with the consequences of tremendous economic change, both in their writings and in experimental communities such as Fruitlands and New Harmony.

Along with these economic changes, our modern economic vocabulary was being forged. Terms such as "profit" and "career," "wealth" and "success," which previously had strong moral overtones or supported both economic and non-economic meanings, were coming to be used in a "purely economic" sense, by economic theorists and the educated general public. Neufeldt documents these changes through study of the changing rhetoric of political speeches and self-help books (or "success manuals") in the first half of the nineteenth century. For example, according to Neufeldt, "industry," "in the early nineteenth century a synonym for [individual] diligence, self-discipline, concentrated effort, and perseverance," became associated with manufacturing, "shedding much of its moral meaning." "Profit," which was "both a moral and economic term" earlier in the century, "came to signify simply financial profit." Similarly, "by the 1840s [the term] *enterprise* had pretty much disengaged itself from its much earlier associations with moral discipline, courage, and self-sacrifice, characteristics that might be summed up as a conflation of the Greek *oikonomia*, the Latin *virtus*, and the late Latin *interprendere*. . . . By Thoreau's time . . . the term referred to an admirable risk taking, a venturesome spirit, the shrewdness and diligence to conceive a design and follow through with it." And the use of "enterprise" was more and more restricted to business contexts.[18]

In *Walden*, Thoreau moves in the opposite direction, *remoralizing* such terms. He asks whether a successful businessman is really "doing a good job," questions the role of material "wealth" in helping us live "rich" lives, denies that dams and swamp drainage are genuine "improvements" on the land, treats his own attempts to know the local landscape as a divine sort of "trading" between grand principalities. Both his early, famous essay "Resistance to Civil Government" and the later "Life without Principle" ask readers the perennial question: "What shall it profit a man to gain the world and lose his own soul?" All this, of course, was not just clever wordplay. It was part of Thoreau's attempt to preserve individual choice and question the direction in which his country was headed. Thoreau's attempt to remoralize America's economic discourse was tied to his attempt to moralize his own economic life and the lives of his readers.

Neufeldt points out that in the years following *Walden*'s publication, Thoreau and his fellow moralists decisively lost the battle for economic terms and for a moral economy. In the Gilded Age, "it was difficult for the new generation of Americans to imagine the debate in the 1840s and 50s over the astonishing growth of business enterprise and wealth. It was even more difficult to find pertinence in Thoreau's case for a system of valuation other than that of the gold standard."[19] Business boomed, and capitalists called the shots. The Fourteenth Amendment to the U.S. Constitution, as interpreted by the Supreme Court, did not protect the political rights of former slaves. It did, the justices ruled, protect the "persons" of corporations and the economic interests of their shareholders.

Still, *Walden* remained, helping subsequent generations imagine something better. Thoreau's words provoked ever more readers over the next hundred and fifty years as he questioned their success or dared them to pursue their true vocations. Those words still irk and inspire students today, as anyone who teaches *Walden* can attest. Not just because Thoreau continues to speak our language, and undermine it, but because there is a life behind the words. It is Thoreau's reflective practice, the combination of earnest living and clear thinking, that continues to move readers. "Economy" works as a metaphor because it is also a method.

The Train to Fitchburg

Thoreau wasn't the most systematic or influential economic thinker of the nineteenth century, but he might have been the funniest. Putting down a breathless account of the latest construction on the information superhighway, I pick up *Walden* and read the following: "We are in great haste to construct a magnetic telegraph from Maine to Texas; but Maine and Texas, it may be, have nothing important to communicate. . . . As if the main object were to talk fast and not to talk sensibly. We are eager to tunnel under the Atlantic and bring the old world some weeks nearer to the new; but perchance the first news that will leak through into the broad, flapping American ear will be that the Princess Adelaide has the whooping cough" (52). Or that the Duchess of York has a new boyfriend.

This passage is funny, but it also expresses the attitudes and makes the distinctions on which any useful theory of "appropriate technology" must rest: a broad skepticism concerning progress, a focus on the point of the technology in question and whether it in fact fosters its intended goals, a consideration of possible unintended side effects, and a recognition that technology helps to form *us*, its makers. What sets Thoreau apart from most of today's writers on appropriate technology is his insistence on analyzing technology at the individual, not the social, level and the high, almost rarefied goals he posits for individuals. The point of communication technology, the passage says, should be mutual enlightenment—not diversion, profit, or the spread of ever more information. Thoreau asks his readers to consider the proper ends of communication technology and to use it—or *not* use it—accordingly. He discusses the telegraph and the penny press, innovations of the day, but his ideas apply just as well to television and the internet.

Writing at a time of great technological innovation, Thoreau is skeptical of new technologies and consumer products: "Our inventions are wont to be pretty toys, which distract our attention from serious things. They are but improved means to an unimproved end, an end which it was already but too easy to arrive at; as railroads lead to Boston or New York" (52). Still, such skepticism does not preclude the recognition that technology may improve people's lives. Thoreau's journal contains passages applauding useful, appropriate technology: window glass, for example.[20] The point is to evaluate new technologies consciously and use them selectively, rather than blindly praising or rejecting "the latest thing." Thoreau himself developed a new pencil-making process that revived his father's flagging business. He also attached little leather booties to Mrs. Emerson's chickens, when she asked him to stop their digging in her garden. Clearly the search for appropriate technology involves ingenuity and a sense of humor (as well as limits to our attempts to change, control, or "booty-fy" nature).

One danger of technological improvements is that they tend to distance us from wild nature and from our immediate environment. This theme is explored in one of *Walden*'s most famous passages. Though it focuses on transportation, its argument has wide applicability to our technology and consumer decisions:

One says to me, "I wonder that you do not lay up money; you love to travel; you might take the cars and go to Fitchburg today and see the country." But I am wiser than that. I have learned that the swiftest traveller is he that goes afoot. I say to my friend, Suppose we try who will get there first. The distance is thirty miles; the fare ninety cents. That is almost a day's wages. I remember when wages were sixty cents a day for laborers on this very road. Well, I start now on foot, and get there before night; I have travelled at that rate by the week together. You will in the mean while have earned your fare, and arrive there some time tomorrow, or possibly this evening, if you are lucky enough to get a job in season. Instead of going to Fitchburg, you will be working here the greater part of the day. And so, if the railroad reached round the world, I think that I should keep ahead of you; and as for seeing the country and getting experience of that kind, I should have to cut your acquaintance altogether. (53)

The original suggestion, reasonable on its face, is that Thoreau or indeed anyone would be better off using the most modern, efficient means of transportation available. Thoreau denies this by making explicit his true purposes and by considering the full costs of the various means that might be used to achieve them.

The suggested goals are "to travel" and "to see the country," broadened slightly at the end of the passage to "seeing the country and getting experience." But the fastest and most efficient means of transportation are not the best ones for these purposes, for there is a world of sights worth seeing along the country roads to Fitchburg. Thoreau wants to look closely, find new plants, sample the huckleberries, note the colors shining in a pond at dusk, compare the ways people talk or farm in different townships. He wants not merely to see, but to see, hear, smell, taste, touch. He wants not merely to see, but to understand. This takes time. For this sort of seeing, covering less ground more slowly is better.

Thoreau the traveler wants to "get experience," but the experiences of walking the roads and riding the rails to Fitchburg are completely different. In walking, you experience changes in the weather (not always pleasant) and hear birds calling and people working. You feel changes in the topography in your bones and muscles, while the train's bed has been graded and smoothed. You might have to walk up to a farmhouse and ask for directions, food and lodging—and who knows whether they will be forthcoming? On the train, these matters are largely settled beforehand, and the people you interact with are being paid to serve you. This has its positive side, but also its limits. People usually disclose more of themselves when encountered in situ and sometimes offer genuine hospitality, one of life's greatest gifts. If it is chiefly these experiences that we value in travel, then slower means are better. If we simply want to get to Fitchburg as quickly as possible and we have the fare in our pocket, then perhaps the train is better. But then we must recognize that we are giving up "experiencing" or more deeply "seeing" the countryside. There is a trade-off.

The other major factor to consider along with the purpose of any purchase is its cost. We must pay for these things, both in money and in the time needed to earn the money. This is a truism, but how we judge the price of things is crucial. The professional economist notes, correctly, that greater wealth gives one prima facie the ability to utilize more goods and services. Thoreau notes, correctly, that our time is limited and that out of that time most of us must both earn whatever money we feel is sufficient *and* live and enjoy life. The Fitchburg example reminds us that we may maximize money earning or free time. Depending on our overall goals, the one or the other will more likely help us achieve them and live more satisfying lives.

Now Thoreau certainly took advantage of the railroad he railed against. He rode it to Boston, New York, and, yes, Fitchburg to give lectures and to Maine, New Hampshire, and Cape Cod for longer trips to wilder landscapes. But he could take it or leave it as this suited his needs and interests. Given technology's importance in our lives, such a wary, conscious use is well worth emulating.

How many of us, for example, might benefit from riding a bicycle to work rather than driving a car? Bicycling can help keep us active and fit. Some amount of physical exertion is necessary for our health and comfort, and incorporating daily exercise into our schedules keeps us at it on days when we might shirk a trip to the health club. Bicycling can also save us money, provide new experiences, and increase our knowledge of the places we live. None of this proves that most people should bicycle to work, much less that everyone should. There is no one right answer here for all of us. Still, there are better or worse answers for each of us, which we are free to pursue. Often, mere inertia and lack of imagination keep us from doing so.

Thoreau reminds us that our economic actions affect us in complex ways. Transportation does not just take us from point A to point B, more or less efficiently. It also relates us to everything in between—or it can do so. Transportation changes *us:* helps make us flabby or fit, for example. Transportation changes the landscape itself, and in the modern world that too often means choking it on pollution or destroying it by paving it over. It isn't clear that this is in our best interests, comprehensively defined, for this world we are rushing through is also the world we and our progeny must live in. Here, of course, the discussion must be broadened to evaluate the effects of different transportation systems on whole societies. When we do so, these new considerations may well argue for communal action and mutual restraint.

Thoreau, though, would remind us that as individuals we cannot wait for society to choose wisely. We must choose "appropriate technology" in our own lives. Society's choices may constrain ours, but they do not determine them. In fact, we have much greater choice concerning how, when, and whether to use various technologies than we commonly believe. If we allow ourselves, in Emerson's words, to "become the tools of our tools," we have no one to blame but ourselves.

Similar points may be made about "appropriate consumption." Many writers in the ancient virtue ethics tradition argued that human lives could be improved through decreasing consumption and indeed through decreasing economic activity generally: consuming less food, avoiding ostentatious building or entertaining, thinking less about money. For Plato and Aristotle, Epicurus and Seneca, the good life was equally a life devoted to right thinking and a life *not* devoted to wealth getting or sybaritism. These two positions supported each other and were held to be key to achieving happiness.[21]

A leading issue in ancient ethical debate was whether the pursuit of the good life entailed limiting consumption and harshly disciplining our natural desires or providing for their moderate fulfillment. This question in turn was related to the role that pleasure and physical satisfaction were thought to play in a good life: whether defining of it, irrelevant to it, or a more or less important part of it. A wide variety of positions were staked out on these issues, which I will not attempt to summarize here. The main point is that almost all of the ancient writers argued for limiting material acquisition and limiting our attempts to satisfy our physical desires through consumption. This was true for those who thought pleasure the greatest human good and for those who declared physical pleasure irrelevant to questions of how people should live their lives. It was true for those who argued that individuals should set moderate goals and accept moderate successes in life, and for those who advocated the pursuit of perfection. The major philosophical schools all accepted the idea that proper levels of consumption depended on the role of consumption in a good human life.

Walden recapitulates this ancient, inconclusive debate. Early in the book, Thoreau strikes a strong ascetic pose, writing: "None can be an impartial or wise observer of human life but from the vantage ground of what *we* should call voluntary poverty" (14). This asserts more than that "voluntary poverty" is a necessary *effect* of the wise person's concentrating on higher things. There is a further, positive value to such freely chosen poverty. Money, things, and their pursuit distract us from what is truly important. They warp our sense of justice (our "impartiality"). Their possession makes us soft. Wealth and the things that wealth can buy are positive hindrances to wisdom and a good life. Often, particularly in *Walden*'s first chapter, Thoreau suggests an absolute correlation: the more wealth and consumption, the less virtue, wisdom, and striving for higher things.

Elsewhere, though, Thoreau takes a more moderate, reformist tone. *Walden* portrays many simple, graceful acts of consumption: Thoreau eating bread that he has baked himself or burning wood that he has cut and split. These are pleasant, enjoyable acts. They manifest nature's bounty, which, he says, we should enjoy to the fullest. In his later manuscript *Wild Fruits,* Thoreau gives free rein to such enjoyable consumption. For example, he mentions a variety of huckleberries—"large, often pear-shaped, sweet blue ones"—which tend to sprout in cut-over woods. "They have not borne there before for a century, being over-shadowed and stinted by the forest, but they have the more concentrated their juices, and profited by the new recipes which Nature has given them, and now they offer to you fruit of the very finest flavor, like wine of the oldest vintage."[22] Thoreau as gourmand! But reading *Wild Fruits,* we see that making distinctions through a discriminating palate helps Thoreau know nature's variety. Not just different kinds of berries, but also variations in habitat, rainfall, and season, all affect the quality of this wild produce.

Thoreau's emphasis on moral principle, his natural genius for asceticism, and his belief that we often fail to do right due to greed and gluttony lead him to denigrate sensuality and the consumption that it occasions. But his keen senses, his naturalist's interest in the world around him, and his joy at connecting to nature lead him back to his senses and to praising a reasonable consumption. *Walden* is clearly the work of a sensualist as well as an ascetic. A reasonable consumption, kept within bounds by principles and higher goals, adds to Thoreau's sensual delight in nature.[23]

Whether he is strictly limiting or tastefully refining his consumption, Thoreau takes a strong stand against thoughtless gluttony. In "Higher

Laws," a chapter of *Walden* largely devoted to discussing food consumption, he bluntly restates this position: "The abdomen under the wings of the butterfly still represents the larva. This is the tid-bit which tempts his insectivorous fate. The gross feeder is a man in the larva state" (215). Here we find the idea, familiar in ancient ethics, that a life devoted to physical consumption is ignoble or infantile. The reference to larvae neatly combines these two thoughts, for a larva is both the infant butterfly and metaphorically less noble than the adult, grubbing along the ground while the adult flies freely through the air. The grub chews indiscriminately and voraciously, while the butterfly sips the nectar of a few, select plants. Both consume, but the grub only takes, while the butterfly also pollinates plants, manifesting a creative role. Just so, Thoreau believes physical consumption should be subordinate to self-development and artistic creation. When "gross feeding" replaces personal development, our "vast abdomens" then become both the cause and the sign of our downfall.

Clearly and emphatically, Thoreau argues against overconsumption. Our consumption should further our lives. To the extent that it does so without harming others, it is good. To the extent that it substitutes for living well or actually impedes it, consumption is bad. Whether discussing food, furniture, or numerous other possessions and consumables, *Walden* repeats that there is a limit to their usefulness. We should make particular consumption decisions accordingly. More generally, we must ask: "Shall we always study to obtain more of these things, and not sometimes to be content with less?" (36).

The Bean Field

As with consumption, so with production: our work should improve our lives and the lives of those around us. This, not some fanciful attempt at full economic autarky, lies behind Thoreau's self-bestowed commission as a "jack of all trades." It underlies all his "work" at the pond—physical, intellectual, and spiritual—and his repeated criticisms of our modern division of labor. Thoreau's chief quarrel with economic specialization is that it robs people of experience. In building his house, for example, he is by turns architect, carpenter, and bricklayer. There is a pleasure in this variety, Thoreau believes. It keeps our work from becoming boring and our thoughts agile and engaged (40–45). Thoreau adds that work may also further knowledge of the natural world. His chimney taught him which clays made the best bricks and whether shells or limestone made the best mortar. He learned the feel of these materials and where they could be found locally (240–46).

Just as important, in making a chimney or a table, we attend to its purpose—thus to how it can best fulfill its purpose and to whether it is necessary at all. In this way, Thoreau discovered that he didn't need yeast to leaven his bread and never again bothered with it. In this way, he discovered that he only needed a one-room house, and was saved the trouble and expense of building something grander.

Of course, there are losses to balance against the gains of such autarky: losses in efficiency and productivity and, for those who aren't as handy as Thoreau, a loss in the quality of the products of our labor. Is the knowledge and experience gained worth the trade-off? For Thoreau it often was, if only to get closer to certain elemental aspects of human life.

One important example of this is recounted in the chapter titled "The Bean-Field": "Before I finished my house, wishing to earn ten or twelve dollars by some honest and agreeable method, in order to meet my unusual expenses, I planted about two acres and a half of light and sandy soil near it chiefly with beans. . . . Removing the weeds, putting fresh soil about the bean stems, and encouraging this weed which I had sown, making the yellow soil express its summer thought in bean leaves and blossoms rather than in wormwood and piper and millet grass, making the earth say beans instead of grass,—this was my daily work" (54, 156–57). Despite his pursuit of a limited autarky, the need to function within a market society dictates that Thoreau earn some money. But in deciding to earn it in this particular way, through farming, Thoreau doubly resists allowing market forces supremacy. First, he could have earned the money with less effort by surveying or working as a day laborer, as he well knew. Such work paid a dollar or two a day, while his total profits for a season of relatively hard work added up to less than ten dollars (55). Still, he chose to farm. Second, unlike the "gentlemen farmers" and agricultural reformers to whom he compares his efforts, his innovations aim neither at a greater crop yield or a greater monetary profit. He makes a point of doing most of the work himself, rather than contracting it out to more productive specialists with more elaborate tools. He does not, he tells us, bother with "imported" fertilizers. These moves would increase his productivity, but he refuses to allow that to dictate how he will farm.

What did Thoreau's determination to farm, and to farm in his own way, teach him? "As I had little aid from horses or cattle," he writes, "or hired men or boys, or improved implements of husbandry, I was much slower, and became much more intimate with my beans than usual. But labor of the hands, even when pursued to the verge of drudgery, is perhaps never the worst form of idleness. It has a constant and imperishable moral, and to the scholar it yields a classic result" (157). All was not pastoral bliss in the bean field. Thoreau was up most days at dawn and worked long forenoons tending his beans. True, he did hear brown thrashers as he worked his rows and saw nighthawks circling overhead as he rested on his hoe. Not being in a hurry, he had plenty of time to watch the wildlife at the margins of his field, strengthening his ties to his "brute neighbors" and adding to his knowledge of the landscape. To a poet-naturalist, opportunities for such encounters, even opportunities to feel changes in the weather and mark the natural course of the day, are strengthening and vivifying. Thoreau contrasts this work with factory and office work, suggesting again that the experience lost is not made up in increased pay or productivity.

Still, he tells us that the genial sun blistered his feet, and his account makes it clear that he sometimes pursued this work not merely to the verge of drudgery, but beyond it. Summing up the experience, he writes that "it was on the whole a rare amusement, which, continued too long, might have become a dissipation" (162), the dissipation, that is, of which Thoreau accuses his fellow townsmen: a surrender to drudgery.

But negative results are as valuable as positive ones; they also convey information. What is the "constant and imperishable moral," the "classic result" of which Thoreau speaks? First, I think, there is a real appreciation of the value of leisure, such as a wealthy or pampered person cannot know. Also, confirmation that some human activities really are "higher," through direct comparison with drudgery. Also, the valuable knowledge that some work fails to allow him to develop his capacities, that it is deadening—and this irrespective of how well that work pays. But these lessons are yielded only to "scholars," those who bring a questioning attitude to bear on their work, and only if they pursue such labor to *the verge* of drudgery, not if they continue it indefinitely. To do so risks allowing our higher capacities to atrophy, so that we cease feeling their lack of fulfillment. Drudgery can turn us into drudges.

The scholar—taking the word now in a different sense, as one like Thoreau who belongs to the learned class—also learns that this drudge work exists and that someone must do it. This opens up further questions concerning the division of labor. Will we let the more clever among us avoid all this dirty and unpleasant work and monopolize the most fulfilling employment? How is the scholar to justify, or truly earn, his privileged position? Is it through performing his share of the necessary drudge work of society? Or through a commitment to teaching his fellow citizens? Or through the indirect effects of his knowledge, filtering down to the general public through the popular media and technological change (a sort of academic trickle-down effect)?

Such questions hardly make sense on a standard economic view. One does not *justify* one's economic position; one *competes* for it. One need not earn a place in society; one earns the money that shows that some people value one's contributions enough to pay for them. But Thoreau wonders: "if the civilized man's pursuits are no worthier than the savage's, if he is employed the greater part of his life in obtaining gross necessaries and comforts merely, why should he have a better dwelling than the former?" (34). Under the spell of the standard economic view, such ethical questions are easily forgotten as we intellectuals type away in our offices and someone else empties the wastebaskets. But this attitude and this Economy, with its great disparities in wealth and status, tend to undermine egalitarian morality and democratic government. This should be cause for concern.

In the end, Thoreau's very lack of productivity helped clarify the results of his experiment at the pond. Because as unremunerative as his farming was, it proved sufficient to his needs. After summarizing his first year's expenses and income, and toting up his profits—$8.71 1/2—he remarks: "The next year I did better still, for I spaded up all the land which I required [rather than hiring a team and plowman], about a third of an acre, and I learned from the experience of both years . . . that if one would live simply and eat only the crop which he raised, and raise no more than he ate, and not exchange it for an insufficient quantity of more luxurious and expensive things, he would need to cultivate only a few rods of ground . . . and he could do all his necessary farm work as it were with his left hand at odd hours in the summer" (55–56). The most important question that Thoreau asked concerning both production and consumption was how little of these he could get by with, the goal being to meet his economic needs as efficiently as possible. In later years he preferred to earn what little money he required primarily by land surveying, which like farming kept him out in the open air, and which paid better. But either way, the main point was proved. And because so many of his fellow townsmen were farmers, Thoreau's experiment allowed him to speak directly to their lives.

The move beyond pay and profit to the experience of work is necessary, then, to order our own personal economy most efficiently. We must move beyond economic abstractions to further our true goals: happiness, self-development, and flourishing. But such attentiveness also opens us to deep economic issues concerning the meaning of work and the proper relation between our human economy and the economy of nature. Early in "The Bean-Field," Thoreau asks: "What was the meaning of this so steady and self-respecting, this small Herculean labor, I knew not. I came to love my rows, my beans, though so many more than I wanted. They attached me to the earth, and so I got strength like Antaeus. But why should I raise them? Only Heaven knows. This was my curious labor all summer" (155). What is the meaning of work? "The Market" gives one answer: "*your* work is worth eight dollars and seventy-one and one half cents, or its equivalent in goods and services." Thoreau believes that through his personal economy, he has earned the right to see this answer as unimportant.

The remark "only Heaven knows" refers obliquely to another answer, given in the Bible's story of humanity's fall from grace. In this view, you will recall, work is a misfortune, a punishment for disobeying God and eating of the tree of knowledge:

And the LORD God said unto Adam . . . Because thou hast hearkened unto the voice of thy wife, and hast eaten of the tree, of which I commanded thee, saying, Thou shalt not eat of it: cursed is the ground for thy sake; in sorrow shalt thou eat of it all the days of thy life; Thorns also and thistles shall it bring forth to thee; and thou shalt eat the herb of the field; In the sweat of thy face shalt thou eat bread, till thou return unto the ground.[24]

"In sorrow shalt thou eat"—work is bad. "Cursed is the ground"—nature is no longer supremely bountiful, supplying a surfeit of fruit, but now brings forth "thorns and thistles." The harmony between man and nature is broken, and nature provides for us only through our own efforts. These misfortunes have come about through the desire to understand the world and obtain the divine power that comes with knowledge.

The only part of the biblical account that Thoreau accepts is the connection between knowledge and divinity. He believes that the search for knowledge, rightly undertaken, manifests not human disobedience but a true reverence. Nor need it be the occasion for a rift between humanity and nature. The pursuit of knowledge is rather the best hope for our reconciliation. In a practical inversion of the biblical attitude toward work, Thoreau seeks to use his work, as we have seen, as a means to better know nature. And he denies the Fall, as applied to nature or humanity. Nature is still bountiful, he insists: "Nature does her best to feed her children."[25] He believes his experiment has proven that "it is not necessary that a man should earn his living by the sweat of his brow, unless he sweats easier than I do" (71).

Modern societies have in one sense turned away from the Bible's fatalistic attitude toward work, pursuing scientific knowledge of nature and applying it to increase economic productivity. Yet this alone, Thoreau insists, cannot remove the curse of work. It cannot dry the sweating brow of humanity, nor alleviate the "anxiety and strain" that blight our lives, nor end the struggle against nature that our economy has become. But a different sort of knowledge—self-knowledge concerning the limits of our material needs—can allow us to turn our work into "a pastime." If there is some limit to the yields that we demand, then farming may appear as cooperation between a bountiful nature and a resourceful humanity (absent this, it can be nothing but struggle). This, in turn, may give us the time needed to explore the Garden, from which we are barred by our own greed and inattentiveness, not by divine decree.

Against the biblical account, Thoreau juxtaposes the legend of Antaeus. According to Greek myth, Antaeus was the son of a mortal consort and Demeter, the goddess of the earth. He wrestled with Hercules (himself of mixed human and divine parentage). Hercules found that every time he pinned him to the ground, Antaeus's strength was renewed, and he sprang up stronger than ever. Hercules eventually defeated Antaeus by holding him above the Earth, thus completing one of the twelve tasks necessary to gain his place in heaven.

Thoreau here likens himself to Antaeus, who got strength from touching his mother the Earth. How? Above all, through the physical sustenance he obtained. Here again, we see the value of simplicity in forcing us to reckon with the obvious. Most of us work at least part of the time to provide basic sustenance for ourselves and our loved ones. But we forget this. Our work can then seem pointless, and we may forget our dependence on the good earth in achieving this basic goal.

Thoreau found strength, too, he suggests, through the discipline demanded by his "steady" and "self-respecting" labor. Work develops discipline, which may then be put in the service of whatever goals we choose. Disciplined, useful work also gives the average citizen a legitimate claim to the respect of his fellow citizens. Thoreau as transcendentalist believes he is stronger for wrestling with the problem of how to sustain himself. He associates himself both with Antaeus, the son of the Earth, and Hercules, the son of the sky god Zeus: recall his reference to "this small Herculean labor" of tending beans and the earlier juxtaposition of the pointless labors of the Indian brahmins with the labors of Hercules. Thoreau sees himself and all human beings as partly divine. Like Hercules, we perform our feats on Earth in order to gain a place in heaven (or, to find a heaven right here). The implication is that our economic strivings should lead us toward something more, but also that they make this "something more" possible and are not to be sneered at or avoided. Like Antaeus, when we no longer touch the Earth, we weaken. All our efforts depend on earthly sustenance. Our abstract thought must be regularly fertilized by experience. Our ethical ideals must be tried in life.[26]

There is still more, although it is difficult to describe: a feeling of gratitude for Earth's gifts, a belief in the rightness of nature's cycles of work and rest, growth and harvest. Finally, there is happiness and even joy at playing one's part within these cycles:

> Husbandry was once a sacred art; but it is pursued with irreverent haste and heedlessness by us, our object being to have large farms and large crops merely. . . . We are wont to forget that the sun looks on our cultivated fields and on the prairies and forests without distinction. They all reflect and absorb his rays alike, and the former make but a small part of the glorious picture which he beholds in his daily course. In his view the earth is all equally cultivated like a garden. Therefore we should receive the benefit of his light and heat with a corresponding trust and magnanimity. What though I value the seed of these beans, and harvest that in the fall of the year? . . . These beans have results which are not harvested by me. Do they not grow for woodchucks partly? . . . Shall I not rejoice also at the abundance of the weeds whose seeds are the granary of the birds? (165–66)

Such acceptance and rejoicing are rare in modern societies. Most of us are too busy about our beans. The places and practices where such words resonate are fast disappearing.

Yet the hope remains that agriculture and all our works may be pious undertakings, tying us closer to our native Earth. A genuine gratitude for our lives and sustenance can occur, though, only in the pause from grasping, calculating, and desiring. It occurs when we look up from our toil and notice a hawk cutting the air, or in a simple prayer of thanks before a meal. In such acts Thanksgiving becomes, not a once-a-year formality, but a remembrance of the goodness and fecundity of our place. We then accept our portion both of work and of the fruits of nature's bounty, without striving to alter or engross more than our share. Once we realize our proper place within nature, we can then appreciate not just our own good fortune but the blessings given to all nature's creatures.

Within the Western ethical tradition, lives of greed or sybaritism have generally been condemned. Still, they have remained live options, and succeeding moralists have felt obliged to repeat the introductory lessons. It is not just that our economic lives provide occasions that tempt us away from doing good. There is something about economic life that causes us to set it up as an independent realm, beyond or beneath ethics. For one thing, this is convenient. For another, economic activities themselves naturally focus our attention on the efficient use of means and away from the sharp questioning of ends.

Twentieth-century ethicists' near exclusive focus on rights and duties and their neglect of human excellence have unwittingly played into this tendency to exempt our economic lives from ethical scrutiny. For while many of our economic decisions do escape the narrow compass of strict obligation, only the truly trivial ones fail to make us better or worse people, if only marginally so. I do not have a duty to quit my dead-end job, perhaps, but it may be making me stupider with each passing day.[27] I do not have a duty to stop eating fried food, but it may be clogging my arteries and making me fatter. And if I am less intelligent and less healthy, then I am a worse person. Still a person, of course, with all a person's rights—but a worse person. Once again: "Our whole life is startlingly moral. There is never an instant's truce between virtue and vice" (218). This holds true as much for our economic decisions as for any others.

Ethics thus provides the proper framework for considering our economic lives, and this is one area where we moderns should move beyond the ancients. Ancient virtue ethicists often took a supercilious view of common economic activities. This was only to be expected from members of aristocratic, slaveholding societies, where the flourishing of the few was the primary concern. Modern ethicists should not take such a dismissive attitude, recognizing the substantial possibilities economic life holds for furthering happiness and self-development and committed as we should be to promoting the excellence of all members of society. We should also remember that self-improvement and social reform are hard work and that discipline and "economy" are necessary in order to achieve them.

Despite a certain amount of romantic moonshine, Thoreau attempted to live a life at Walden Pond and write a story in *Walden* that explored these possibilities and shared them with others. As is typically the case with heroic exemplars in the virtue ethics tradition, his account provides material for both perfectionist and reformist arguments. True believers sharing his ultimate goals may deepen their insight into those ideals and find practical strategies for attaining them. Those attached to more conventional lives or holding less rigorous views of the good life may nevertheless be reminded of the many benefits to be found in living consciously and methodically, avoiding the pitfalls of greed and consumerism, and furthering our ties to nature.

Walden provides both practical suggestions and parables. In either case, it takes imagination and effort to apply Thoreau's message in our various situations. He hopes he is enlarging our range of alternatives, but exasperated undergraduates have been known to complain: "Does he really expect us all to move to a pond and grow beans?" Not exactly. But Thoreau obviously expects a lot from his neighbors and readers, as he does from himself. He is right to do so. And regardless of the correctness or replicability of his answers, he leaves us struggling with the right questions and provides an economic method that will help us answer them.

Solitude and Society

"My dear Henry, A frog was made to live in a swamp, but a man was not made to live in a swamp. Yours ever, R." So wrote an exasperated Ralph Waldo Emerson in his journal, after yet another contentious, unsatisfying discussion with his protégé. The charge made by Emerson and others was that Thoreau was cold and asocial; interesting and challenging, perhaps, but lacking in the milk of human kindness; in short, a poor friend. As Emerson wrote in another journal entry: "As for taking Thoreau's arm, I should as soon take the arm of an elm tree."[1] Thoreau himself sometimes worried about his asocial tendencies. In a journal entry during the winter of 1852, he wrote: "Everywhere snow—gathered into sloping drifts about the walls & fences—beneath the snow the frozen ground. . . . Life is reduced to its lowest terms. . . . There is a similar crust over my heart."[2]

We might well wonder whether a hermit can tell us anything much about ethics, which treats the question of how we should live with other people. As Aristotle wrote, human beings are *zōa politika,* social animals who cannot flourish alone. Even if we accept that Thoreau had the right to go to the woods and cultivate his own excellence in private, we may doubt whether doing so was good for him, or whether the reflections growing out of such solitude provide guidance for more normal people.

I believe they do, but it must be admitted from the start that Thoreau's perspective on human sociability is limited in important ways. He had a genius for both solitude and social criticism, but apparently not for social intercourse. No one can teach us more about the uses of solitude and the dangers of society, and such knowledge is valuable for all of us—regardless of our relative inclination to solitude or society. Concerning the joys of human relationships Thoreau has less to offer. Here, more than in any other area of life, his accomplishments fell short of his ideals. Here too, perhaps, the rigor of his ideals betrayed him and undermined his own happiness.

Not that Thoreau was friendless. We should remember that *Walden* recounts a period in Thoreau's life when he deliberately pursued solitary tasks and that the book exaggerates the solitude of that period. Even in *Walden* there are many references to visitors to the cabin, trips into town to gossip, social rambles, shared fishing idylls, and other pleasant social interactions. Thoreau's house was only one and one-half miles from downtown Concord, and he only stayed there for two years before returning to "sojourn in civilized life" once again (3). During the fifteen years left to him after he returned from the pond, he remained a beloved member of his family and an increasingly valued and respected member of his community, performing useful duties as town surveyor and keeping his neighbors alert and a degree or two more self-aware and honest with his sharp tongue. On the day of Thoreau's funeral, classes were let out early so that the schoolchildren of Concord could attend.

Yet the melancholy tone of that phrase "sojourner in civilized life" is undeniable. To be a traveler, a stranger, while living in the bosom of one's family and the town one grew up in! Does this acknowledge the space opened up whenever a person strives more, sees more, or achieves more than those around him? Or is Thoreau pointing to a gulf that separates all human beings from one another, if we would be attentive and honest enough to acknowledge it? Or again, does the phrase suggest a defect in Thoreau's character, or a failure in his life? Perhaps these possibilities are not mutually exclusive. Taking them as such may make reading *Walden* too easy for us.

Having taught *Walden* to many classes of college students, I can attest to Thoreau's remarkable ability to get under people's skins. Many readers rush to write him off as a hermit, a hypocrite, or both. "I could never live all alone in the woods like that," they say, and all his suggestions, condemnations, questions, and ideals can be conveniently shrugged off. "Besides, didn't he drop his laundry off at home, and stop by regularly for Sunday dinners at the Emersons?"

Yes, he did. The fact remains that each of us must make what we can of our opportunities for solitude and society. Each of us must strike a balance between them. Thoreau's wary procedure suggests that opening up a physical and intellectual space between ourselves and others is one key to a proper society, allowing us to meet our friends, neighbors, and fellow citizens on a higher, more demanding plane. This most asocial of books thus opens up the fundamental political question: what are the proper goals of human society? And it resoundingly rejects the modern answer—material prosperity and a fair distribution of goods—as insufficient and ignoble, a partial answer at best. *Walden* hints at a better answer than this to the puzzle of human society, even if it does not spell this out and even if Thoreau himself never succeeded in living this answer fully to his own satisfaction.

The Virtues of Solitude

Hermits often feel compelled to defend their solitary lives. To the common charge that they are shirking moral duties or social responsibilities, they may respond: "I've got a right! As long as I'm not harming others, I have a right to live alone and pursue projects I consider worthwhile, regardless of whether other people believe I could be spending my time more sensibly or productively." The aptness of this response depends on your view of how far our social responsibilities extend. We have already considered Thoreau's arguments, in "Resistance to Civil Government," for a limited view of our social duties and his arguments in *Walden* that individuals possess a legitimate space to pursue private projects and personal virtue.

But by itself, this would be a poor defense of solitude, or at least an incomplete one. You may have a right to take off your pants and sit on a hot plate, but that does not make it an intelligent or virtuous thing to do. Analogously, you may have a right to seclude yourself, but if doing so fails to contribute to your own good or the good of society, if it makes you unhappy or ignorant or socially maladroit, then arguably you should not indulge in it.

On the contrary, Thoreau believes solitude is essential to living a good life. In *Walden,* six key virtues are presented as particularly dependent on solitude: freedom, self-reliance, personal focus, self-knowledge, connection to nature, and philosophical reflectiveness.[3] To the extent that these virtues and their fruits are important components of a mature, intellectually vigorous and enjoyable life, and some measure of solitude furthers them—perhaps is even essential to their development—to that extent solitude's value stands as proven. Let us consider these virtues in turn.

As noted earlier, *freedom* is perhaps the most frequently praised virtue in *Walden*. For Thoreau, freedom means, most simply, doing what he wants to do during the course of his day. Solitude makes this possible, both by encouraging personal focus and by limiting the direct claims others make on us (if they aren't there, they can't make any claims). Solitude limits indirect claims as well. When we are with others our behavior changes, as we consciously or unconsciously gauge their responses to us. This is not all bad, but it does limit our freedom. Thoreau can swim naked at dawn, stop for twenty minutes and listen to the hootings of a pair of owls, dream away all the forenoon sitting in front of his cabin, or stand on his head to see what the ice-bound lake looks like from that position. If other people were present he would be interrupted, distracted, or too embarrassed to do these things. He would thus miss out on interesting experiences—and he would be less free.

Taking a larger view, solitude also allows us to escape, to some degree, the expectations and demands of family and society and to set the larger parameters of our lives. For Thoreau at the pond, this meant above all the freedom to write: to work on his craft without the distractions and premature judgments of others. Of course, contacts with Emerson and others were important in Thoreau's development as a writer. It is not the case that completely cutting himself off from others would have been ideal. But this just emphasizes the contextual, balanced value of solitude. Thoreau needed certain kinds, for a certain while. Like many of us, he struggled to find the right amounts and kinds of solitude at particular times in his life.

In Thoreau's view, true freedom also means being able to think for yourself. This too may be helped by solitude, which to some degree forces us to think our own thoughts as the external stimuli of gossip and friendly chatter are removed. Still, we may merely recycle past gossip and other people's thoughts. In order to do more, we must carefully interrogate our own lives, as Thoreau did his. This can cross over the line into minute and pointless self-obsession, but it can also lead to a kind of freedom, where one acts consciously on a deep understanding of what one wants to achieve in life. Free and focused activity will be a key desideratum for any virtue ethics. Such freedom does not depend on absolute solitude, but arguably it does demand a certain independence from others.

In addition to freedom, solitude helps further *self-reliance*. In his great essay of the same name, Emerson defines this as the strength to live your own life and think your own thoughts, regardless of society's responses or expectations. Self-reliance includes the ability to trust yourself and your judgments of the world's affairs. "These are the voices which we hear in solitude," Emerson writes, "but they grow faint and inaudible as we enter into the world." We strive to understand our own nature, to hear the voice of conscience, and to follow their lead in the choices of adult life. But "society everywhere is in conspiracy against the manhood of every one of its members. Society is a joint-stock company in which the members agree for the better securing of his bread to each shareholder, to surrender the liberty and culture of the eater. The virtue in most request is conformity. Self-reliance is its aversion."[4]

At Walden Pond, Thoreau attempted to find his own voice and to live up to it. Solitude gave him time to clarify his thoughts and space from the prying eyes and sometimes caustic comments of skeptics. It also allowed him to explore the practical aspects of Emerson's ideal: building his own house, raising and cooking his own food. These too are arguably an important part of self-reliance, albeit one that philosophers and other intellectuals tend to overlook. Characteristically, Thoreau insisted on fleshing out Emersonian generalities in practice and in detail.

Critics sometimes question the value of self-reliance, believing that a healthy society is the key to happiness and that the quest for self-reliance leads us to neglect our social relationships. Certainly if self-reliance is defined primarily as an ability to do without others and we court the greatest possible autarky, the social virtues may atrophy. Thoreau sometimes wondered if he had moved too far along this path.

But autarky—whether economic or emotional—is not primarily what Emerson or Thoreau has in mind. The goal is not to maximize the ability to do without others, but rather to maximize self-consciousness and the ability to *act*, regardless of other people's beliefs. If we are parching and shriveling our souls, then we have pushed self-reliance too far. Self-reliance should not be bought at the price of self-development or personal flourishing. The ideal is to build up our selves *and* a positive society. The stronger, more self-reliant we are, the more we will have to offer others, and the more diversity will exist in the world.

Compare Thoreau's and Emerson's efforts at economic self-reliance. Emerson clearly saw the dangers to self-reliance in conventional economic life. He sometimes chafed at having to peddle lectures in order to support his family in wealth and comfort, complaining of being "driven abroad by the necessity of paying my debts."[5] Nevertheless, his answer was to meet the economic world and succeed in standard terms. Thoreau, on the other hand, attempted greater independence from conventionally defined economic needs. He pursued a limited economic autarky, seeking to build up an economic cushion, not of money, à la Emerson, but of hardiness and indifference to wealth and possessions.

A similar story could be told about Thoreau's emotional autarky. For all Emerson's sometime aloofness, he shared his emotional life with others much more than Thoreau did. He married and had children, sharing the joys and sorrows of marriage with his wife. He wrote more, and more openly, to his friends. He found his voice more often in large lectures than Thoreau, who did little lecturing and preferred solitary communion with the page. It is not that Thoreau tried to cut himself off from people. But he both reveled in solitude and failed in society to a greater extent than Emerson.

Thoreau's solitary experiment thus presents a different path than Emerson's. Both men's lives and writings suggest possibilities within Emerson's ethics waiting to be actualized. We are the richer for having both of them. Thoreau's Walden experiment might also suggest limits to the value of self-reliance. Still, some degree of self-reliance is necessary to test ideals in this way, and some aptitude for solitude helps us achieve self-reliance.

How does solitude help Thoreau develop *personal focus?* Largely by limiting outside distractions. Although he says little about his literary efforts in *Walden,* Thoreau initially went to the pond to work on his writing. He made astonishing progress there, writing most of his first book and much else besides. Of course, solitude does not guarantee such focus and discipline, nor does it obviate the need for hard work and ever-renewed effort. But solitude helps, as all writers know.

At Walden, Thoreau comes to find such focus key not merely to writing but to *living* well: thinking clearly, attending fully to one's neighbors, experiencing all the world has to offer. "Let us spend one day as deliberately as Nature," he writes, "and not be thrown off the track by every nutshell and mosquito's wing that falls on the rails" (97). Attend fully to "the present moment," and all things are possible (17). It isn't always clear whether Thoreau is calling for a kind of Zen mindfulness or old-fashioned Yankee efficiency. Both will take us further into life and closer to reality, he insists.

Focus breeds focus—diving deeply into an activity makes it more interesting and enjoyable, and we can focus more intensely for longer periods of time. Discipline breeds discipline—well-directed efforts lead to success, and positive reinforcement kicks in. Isolating yourself and removing distractions facilitates this. With focus and discipline, the writer or naturalist, the runner or dancer, may reach a deep solitude even in the midst of crowds. Of course, for most people personal focus finds many of its most important applications in social activities. Solitude may find completion in society, a point I return to below.

Self-knowledge is a key virtue in *Walden,* upon which much else depends. This will be the case for any plausible virtue ethics, since we must understand the self if we hope to improve it. It is doubly the case for Thoreau with his romantic concern for authenticity, his skepticism concerning universal ethical prescriptions, and his strong belief in a moral imperative to pursue knowledge. "Every man is the lord of a realm beside which the earthly empire of the Czar is but a petty state, a hummock left by the ice," he thunders in *Walden*'s "Conclusion." "If you would travel farther than all travellers, be naturalized in all climes, and cause the Sphinx to dash her head against a stone, even obey the precept of the old philosopher, and Explore thyself" (321–22).

Thoreau pursues self-knowledge in a variety of ways in *Walden,* not all of which are complex or intellectual. His method of economy makes his actions and motivations more explicit. If in one sense "we are what we do," we may learn much about ourselves by bringing our actions fully to consciousness. Seeing how I build a chimney (slowly and well, or hastily and sloppily? with or without ornamentation?) tells me something about my personality. So does how I react when it topples over after I've been working on it for two days. Solitude, with its enforced simplicity of action and increased time for personal reflection, facilitates this.

Another path to self-knowledge is a more direct introspection: careful scrutiny of our thoughts, feelings, and the general contents of consciousness. But as Philip Koch, our premier contemporary philosopher of solitude, points out, such introspection depends, in the first instance, on a basic attentiveness or "self-attunement."[6] Prior to reflection, there must be a clear perception and sustained paying attention to the self. Solitude is extremely valuable for this. Free of distractions, our own thoughts and feelings become phenomena to us in a way that can hardly happen when we are with other people, paying attention to *their* actions and reactions to us.

Yet other paths to self-awareness and self-knowledge include meditation, imaginative identification with others, and reflection on the many stories of which we are parts. *Walden* explores all these various approaches. Consider Thoreau's mystical merging with the All, in solitary meditation at the start of "Brute Neighbors" (224). Or his extended identification with Walden in "The Ponds," suggesting an environmental, relational view of the self (a view currently being explored by "ecopsychologists," such as Theodore Roszak).[7] Or his retelling of a Hindu fable that recounts human forgetfulness of our true divinity: the fact that our soul is a part of Brahma, the Divine Principle in all things (96). Consider the reflections, in "Solitude," on the self as phenomena: a place of thoughts and emotions, focused on the world and other people, but also distanced from them: "I *may* be affected by a theatrical exhibition; on the other hand, I *may not* be affected by an actual event which appears to concern me much more. I only know myself as a human entity; the scene, so to speak, of thoughts and affections" (135). Or consider Thoreau's description of a self that stands apart from and above this phenomenal, or empirically given, self: "However intense my experience, I am conscious of the presence and criticism of a part of me, which, as it were, is not a part of me, but spectator, sharing no experience, but taking note of it; and that is no more I than it is you" (135). Here Thoreau, rather than identifying his (whole) self with the locus of the flux of personal experience, equates at least a portion of his self with an ability to get beyond all this and leave the empirical self behind. In part this is the moral self or Conscience (it "criticizes" what it beholds, presumably including our actions), in part the knowing self or Reason. Thoreau's explorations here are squarely within the mainstream Western philosophical tradition, when he both equates this Reason with what is truly us, or best in us, and when he insists that this is *not* us: not, that is, our particular personality ("it is no more I than you").

How, or whether, all these psychological perspectives fit into a coherent and comprehensive view of the self is unclear. Thoreau provides no account of how all the various selves at play in *Walden* relate to one another—unless it is in the unity of its narrative, or in the unity of the life behind the narrative. But *Walden* suggests that Thoreau's explorations and tentative formulations give him pieces of a more complex and complete picture of himself.

In some ways, no doubt, we define our selves through our interactions with other people, and *Walden* has little or nothing to say on this important topic. We may sometimes *legitimately* see ourselves through others' eyes or know ourselves through the roles we play in society. *Walden*'s psychology, like Thoreau's life, must be admitted to be somewhat incomplete on this side. Still, recognizing this should only strengthen our desire to get the whole psychological story—including that part best given in quiet seclusion.

To state that Henry Thoreau achieved a remarkable *connection to nature* and knowledge of the fields, forests, rivers, and ponds around Concord is to state the obvious. To assert that such empathy and knowledge are necessary components of a good human life is more controversial. Thoreau believed they were, as I discuss more fully in the next chapter. Here the important questions are: What role does solitude play in Thoreau's developing knowledge and attunement to nature? What role might it play in ours?

The first requisite for knowing nature is to go to her and be attentive. Not everyone who does so becomes a naturalist or nature lover, but no one becomes these without this. *Walden*'s beautiful descriptions of wild nature are based on hundreds of precise, painstaking journal entries and thousands of hours of careful observations. "How many mornings, summer and winter, before yet any neighbor was stirring about his business, have I been about mine!" Thoreau writes. "So many autumn, ay, and winter days, spent outside the town, trying to hear what was in the wind, to hear and carry it express!" (17)

But to observe nature, it helps to be alone. In company, we naturally attend to the people we are with. We react to them, even if only subconsciously. We talk to one another and thereby move in thought from this walk here to somewhere else. We talk to one another and move from a world of smells, sounds, and sights to a world of abstract concepts. In solitude, all this is reversed, and we notice things we had never noticed before: the sound of a wood thrush's wings as it flies, the different tones of water playing over the rocks as we rest by a stream. Even alone, it is true, we may engage in internal monologues and ignore everything around us. But this need not happen. We can also move in the other direction, finding ourselves more deeply in our senses, tuning in to the smells and snuffles, the sights and sounds that are all around us.

In his funeral eulogy, Emerson remarked of Thoreau that "his senses were acute" and praised his patience in observing nature: "He knew how to sit immovable, a part of the rock he rested on, until the bird, the reptile, the fish, which had retired from him, should come back, and resume its habits."[8] Whatever his natural abilities, though, these virtues were improved by Thoreau through long practice. They were cultivated in solitude, necessarily, and in turn fructified that solitude. How much focused, solitary looking—and hard work at the solitary writing bench—went into Thoreau's virtuoso descriptions of the many colors of Walden's waters (176–77), or wood partridge behavior (226–27), or the sand foliage in the railroad cut (304–9)!

Solitude, quietness, concentration, and close watching remain the keys to seeing and connecting to wild nature. "You only need sit still long enough in some attractive spot in the woods that all its inhabitants may exhibit themselves to you by turns," Thoreau writes in the chapter "Brute Neighbors" (229). From attendance and observation, all else follows. The deep, local knowledge of the naturalist. The theorizing and experimentation of the scientist.[9] The connection, communion, and dissolution of self of the mystic. *Walden* and Thoreau's whole career display all of these.

But more important than any knowledge or elevated experience, for Thoreau, is a personal connection and love of nature. In *Walden* he writes: "I experienced sometimes that the most sweet and tender, the most innocent and encouraging society may be found in any natural object, even for the poor misanthrope and melancholy man. There can be no very black melancholy to him who lives in the midst of Nature and has his senses still" (131). Sometimes this connection is with individual woodchucks, squirrels, loons, or beech trees; sometimes it comes as an all-encompassing sympathy (129). Living alone in nature, Thoreau says simply, toward the end of "Solitude," we "come to know that we are never alone" (136).

To reflect on what we observe, to pursue knowledge, to work up our scattered observations and theories into a coherent and comprehensive worldview—these are some of our highest human capabilities. Here I use the term *philosophical reflectiveness* for the virtue that broadly includes all of this. As Philip Koch writes, "the more given to reflection a person is, the more a philosopher."[10] Philosophers, at least, should agree that such reflectiveness is a good thing.

Walden is filled with examples of solitary observation or contemplation growing into reflection. Of course, these examples are literary creations, not exact reports. But we may assume that they build upon Thoreau's experiences, and we may find similar occasions in our own lives. Forced indoors by a long spring rain, for example, Thoreau reflects from his doorway: "The gentle rain which waters my beans and keeps me in the house today is not dreary and melancholy, but good for me too. Though it prevents my hoeing them, it is of far more worth than my hoeing" (131). This might be true, but the ethical insight is unlikely to come in the midst of work and business. It demands quiet and reflection. The passage seems to loop back on itself, suggesting that the rain is good for Thoreau not just because it waters his beans, but because it forces him to slow down, pause in his work, and reflect. The occasion and the reflection open up the question of the relative importance of human work and nature's work. He pushes the thought: "If it should continue so long as to cause the seed to rot in the ground and destroy the potatoes in the lowlands, it would still be good for the grass on the uplands, and, being good for the grass, it would be good for me." Few will be willing to follow Thoreau this far in theory, and fewer still will embrace such non-anthropocentrism in practice. But solitary reflection opens us up to the question of the human place in nature in a way that human social interactions cannot.

Solitude provides occasions for metaphysical as well as ethical reflection. In his life at Walden Pond and again in the words of *Walden*, Thoreau moved away from Emerson's transcendental idealism, the philosophy of his youth, and toward a more unstable mix of idealism and naturalistic realism. This is the grand trajectory of Thoreau's intellectual career, with ramifications throughout his philosophy, from ethics to epistemology to metaphysics. In seeking ways to describe this philosophy, he develops metaphors in which nature transcends itself (the sand bank in "Spring") and in which nature and thought interpenetrate one another (the intellect as "cleaver" and "burrowing organ," at the end of "Where I Lived, and What I Lived For"). I believe Thoreau is describing his attempt to work out this post-Emersonian philosophy in another of *Walden*'s well-known passages of solitary reflection:

> Sometimes, after staying in a village parlor [Emerson's?] till the family had all retired, I have returned to the woods and . . . spent the hours of midnight fishing from a boat by moonlight, serenaded by owls and foxes, and hearing, from time to time, the creaking note of some unknown bird close at hand. These experiences were very memorable and valuable to me. . . . It was very queer, especially in dark nights, when your thoughts had wandered to vast and cosmogonal themes in other spheres, to feel this faint jerk, which came to interrupt your dreams and link you to Nature again. (174–75)

The final line may refer obliquely to Emerson's essay *Nature*, perhaps suggesting the need to link grand, abstract speculations more closely to nature's particulars than Emerson had been able to do. This passage, like others in *Walden*, reminds us of a wild, dark nature beyond all human ties and institutions, with which any serious philosophy must reckon. Thoreau continues: "It seemed as if I might next cast my line upward into the air, as well as downward into this element which was scarcely more dense. Thus I caught two fishes as it were with one hook."

Here a solitary experience gives Thoreau a key symbol to articulate his developing philosophy: both his own uneasy relationship to transcendentalism (later, again, he will ask: "shall I go to heaven or a-fishing?" [224]) and his hopes to explore the realms of spirit and matter, ideals and realities, and relate the two in a comprehensive philosophy. As a true philosopher, revising his methods and restating his conclusions was the work of a lifetime. It was not solely a solitary life, of course; Thoreau's philosophical starting point was an Emersonian transcendentalism, borrowed, like the ax with which he chopped down the trees to make his cabin (40–41). But much of Thoreau's subsequent philosophical development was indeed the product of solitary reflection.

If "philosophy begins in wonder," as Aristotle famously said, wonder often enough begins in solitude, where nature's beauty and the respite from everyday society conspire to awaken us. In *Walden*, Thoreau repeatedly describes himself as a philosopher or a would-be philosopher. This may mean many things, but for Thoreau two are paramount:

ethically, someone who strives to live a life of great virtue; intellectually, someone who seeks a comprehensive, coherent, and true conception of the universe. In *Walden,* we see Thoreau trying to live up to both halves of this demanding philosophical ideal. We see a commitment to the pursuit of personal excellence, in particular activities and in his general goals. And we see philosophical reflection growing out of common experiences: sometimes in short asides that speak to the moment; sometimes in grand set pieces like the flowing sand bank or the battle of the ants, which move toward more general, perhaps even universal, truths. Solitude aids these efforts of focused action and thoughtful reflection.

Freedom, self-reliance, personal focus, self-knowledge, connection to nature, and philosophical reflectiveness. These are genuine virtues. They do not sum up all of human virtue, but they are important enough—and solitude is important enough to them—to suggest that the best lives will include a good deal of solitude.

However, cultivating solitude need not preclude society. Philip Koch makes the key point that the virtues of solitude "find completions in propitious moments of engaged encounter."[11] This does not mean that solitude only has meaning as an interlude between our more important social interactions, rather that periods of solitude and society can work together, drawing out our full human potential.

For example, we have seen how important knowing nature was for Thoreau and the role solitude played in this. At the same time, numerous social interactions facilitated this developing knowledge. Thoreau's mother was an early influence, taking him and his siblings on walks in the woods to identify flowers. Thoreau was a voracious, lifelong reader of natural history books. He discussed rare and unusual sightings of plants and animals with local hunters and fishermen. He was a contributing member of the Boston Society of Natural History, one of the premier scientific groups in America at the time.

In sharing his knowledge of nature, Thoreau once again connected with society. He was renowned among local children for knowing the names of all the flowers and for showing them the best huckleberry patches and fishing holes. He became a sort of unofficial town naturalist in Concord, collecting and dispensing information to all. Throughout the 1850s, he gave talks to the Concord lyceum based on his observations of nature (some of which were published posthumously as "Walking," "Autumnal Tints," "Wild Apples," and parts of *The Maine Woods*).

So it is with all the virtues of solitude. They often find improvement or perfection in social engagement; they may be put to work for the good of society. "We meet at very short intervals," Thoreau writes, "and give each other a new taste of that old musty cheese that we are" (136). But the solitary may bring back something new that benefits his neighbors, as Thoreau brought a better self back from the pond and in due time brought forth *Walden*.

Neighbors

From its first sentence, *Walden* announces Thoreau's concern with his neighbors: he proposes to crow, remember, "in order to wake my neighbors up." He would not write so much about himself and his experience at the pond, he claims, "if very particular inquiries had not been made by my townsmen concerning my mode of life" (3). It is his "travels in Concord" (4) and the "misfortunes" of "his townsmen" (5) that prompt his first economic speculations. As this supposedly most asocial of books proceeds, we actually find a fair amount of visiting back and forth between the pond and the village, to vary Thoreau's solitude and communion with nature. And we sense, despite Thoreau's portrait of self-reliance and contentment, an urgent need to communicate: "to speak . . . like a man in a waking moment, to men in their waking moments" (324).

In place of the typical abstractions of moral philosophy, *Walden* provides concrete consideration of Thoreau's actual neighbors. Contemporary moralists have much to say about our duties to people in general, but little to say about neighbors. Yet neighbors are an important moral category, because they may challenge our egalitarian ideals, compel us to specify particular duties to others, or make explicit our own generosity or stinginess. We have already seen how the woodchopper Therien suggests possible limitations and uncertainties in Thoreau's ethical philosophy. When we look at the briefer appearances of Thoreau's other neighbors in *Walden,* we find that each in his or her own way serves to challenge or confirm that philosophy. They test it, and Thoreau too, to some extent. Thoreau believes that this is an important part of what neighbors can do for one another. "I do not wish to flatter my townsmen," he writes, "nor to be flattered by them, for that will not advance either of us. We need to be provoked,—goaded like oxen, as we are, into a trot" (108).

One of *Walden*'s most extensive neighborly passages, in the chapter "Baker Farm," describes Thoreau's chance visit to the Field family, living a few miles off in the woods (204–9). As with Therien, the parallels between Thoreau's and the recent immigrant family's situations are obvious. Both inhabit shacks adjacent to ponds, where the family breadwinner occasionally fishes. Both are poor. Most important, both are making new lives in a new world. As he sets the scene, Thoreau describes the family's lot as hard and hand to mouth. The father, John Field, works day jobs to bring in a little money, while the mother tends her growing family. Thoreau learns that Field has made a bad bargain and is being cheated by a neighboring farmer for his work "bogging." But rather than dwell on this fact or argue for fairness toward the poor Irish generally, he lectures the couple on how to live better lives by reducing their wants: eating less meat, doing without coffee, and the like. Frugality and a proper economy, such as Thoreau himself follows, are their best hopes for more pleasant and leisurely lives. "I tried to help him with my experience," Thoreau writes, "telling him that he was one of my nearest neighbors" (205).

In my experience, many readers are put off by this encounter. Thoreau's advice seems condescending, and his account of the meeting emphasizes his superior knowledge, self-control, and even hygiene: "An honest, hard-working, but shiftless man plainly was John Field; and his wife, she too was brave to cook so many successive dinners in the recesses of that lofty stove; with round greasy face and bare breast, still thinking to improve her condition one day; with the never absent mop in one hand, and yet no effects of it visible any where" (204). This may seem downright insulting, to modern eyes. Yet Thoreau clearly believes he is giving his neighbors advice well suited to their condition. In suggesting that higher goals and radically different ways of life are real possibilities, he believes he is speaking up, not down, to John Field. "For I purposely talked to him as if he were a philosopher," Thoreau writes, "or desired to be one" (205).

Rather than demanding fair or equal treatment from the world, it is usually better to set about making the best of things. This does not deny or excuse unfairness: Thoreau mentions the neighboring farmer's sharp dealings with Field, just as he obliquely mentions the reading public's failure to support his own literary work in the parable of the Indian basket maker (19). But the important question is what to focus on. Rather than waste time arguing that other people should become more just or generous, or improve their literary taste, it is better to practice economy and self-reliance ourselves. This is the surest way to improve our lives. As we become more experienced and learn to calculate better, we will learn to make better bargains with our neighbors, as a matter of course. But part of making better bargains is being able to hold ourselves off the market for a time.

The best he can do for others, Thoreau believes, is to challenge them to live better lives and educate them about how to achieve this. To do so is to assert that they *can* do better: no racial, cultural, or intellectual barriers prevent it. Their self-improvement will depend on *thinking* their way toward better lives, since "what a man thinks of himself, that it is which determines, or rather indicates, his fate" (7). Self-improvement must include not merely discontent with our circumstances, but with ourselves. John Field has the former but not the latter, and this marks a key difference between his and Thoreau's experiments by the ponds.

Another, of course, is that Field has a family, including a "wrinkled, sibyl-like, cone-headed infant that sat upon its father's knee as in the palaces of nobles, and looked out from its home in the midst of wet and hunger inquisitively upon the stranger, with the privilege of infancy, not knowing but it was the last of a noble line, and the hope and cynosure of the world, instead of John Field's poor starveling brat" (204). If *Walden* ponders America's past, with its Puritans and Indians, it also looks to the future. The Irish had only recently come to Concord in great numbers, to help build the railroad. Many of Thoreau's respectable neighbors had little to do with them, although some contributed to immigrant aid societies or gave charity to individuals. Of course, they would have doubtless affirmed their possession of immortal souls—the equivalent, in Thoreau's time, of our own secular morality of equal rights. Such affirmations cost little, after all. But Thoreau recognizes that the Irish are now an important part of America: the "sibyl-like" infant foretells the future. Happily it is an open-ended prophecy, for unlike its parents this infant is not yet weighed down by low expectations or a poor opinion of itself. It may in fact live a "noble" life, if it can grow into a noble view of itself and its rightful place in the world.

This brief scene shows us once again the demandingness of virtue ethics and some of its tensions with egalitarian morality. If he wants to hold his neighbors to such demanding standards, Thoreau cannot help but portray himself as superior to them. He cannot ask less of them and still accept them as fully human. Granted that Thoreau is a better neighbor than the farmer who cheats John Field out of his fair wages: is he being a good neighbor here? I believe he is. To make a neighbor of another person means linking your life to his, and Thoreau suggests that Yankees and Irish are now so linked in America. It means caring about the choices our neighbors make without interfering unduly in them and recognizing that in many ways we are choosing together for a shared future.

Interestingly, Thoreau's initial account of this meeting, in his journal, contained an additional clause, when he mentioned "the wrinkled & Sybil like—crone-like infant. . . . The young creature not knowing but it might be the last of a line of kings instead of John Fields poor starveling brat—*or I should rather say still knowing* that it was the last of a noble line and the hope and cynosure of the world."[12] Why did Thoreau, when he came to write *Walden,* edit out these final words expressing his own unambiguous belief in the child's value and potential? Perhaps because of a natural prickliness or refusal to engage in sentimentality. More important, the final version better dramatizes how much is at stake in how we think about ourselves and those around us. Pious sentiments about the value of each and every human life cannot save us from our own low expectations or bad habits. Whether that child grew up to a divine life or to drudgery was an open question, as Thoreau's final account indicated. "Poor John Field! . . . not to rise in this world, he nor his posterity, till their wading webbed bog-trotting feet get *talaria* to their heels" (208–9).

In this case, as in others, reviewing his journal indicates a more humane and compassionate Thoreau. "They showed me Johnny Ruyaden [Riordan] today," he writes in another entry, "with one thickness of ragged cloth over his little shirt for all this cold weather—with shoes with large holes in the toes into which the snow got as he said—Without a an outer garment—to walk a mile to school every day over the bleakest of causeways. . . . O I should rather hear that Americas first born were all slain than that his little fingers and toes should feel cold while I am warm." Noting that the child's clothes were patched cast-offs from his wealthier neighbors—perhaps even from the Thoreau family—he exclaims: "Our charitable institutions are an insult to humanity. A charity which dispenses the crumbs that fall from its overloaded tables. which are left after its feasts."[13]

This is a very different criticism of philanthropy than that found in *Walden,* where Thoreau had written: "Be sure that you give the poor the aid they most need, though it be your example which leaves them far behind. If you give money, spend yourself with it, and do not merely abandon it to them" (75). Thoreau apparently took his own advice in this case; his journal entry ten days later adds: "Carried a new cloak to Johnny Riaden? I found that the shanty was warmed by the simple social relations of the Irish. On sunday they come from the town & stand in the door way and so keep out the cold. One is not cold among his brothers and sisters [we remember that Thoreau lived almost all his life in his parental home]. What if there is less fire on the hearth, there is more in the heart." There is no condescension here, but rather gratitude that the boy is faring well and real concern for his whole family. "These Irish are not succeeding so ill after all," Thoreau thinks: "The little boy goes to the primary school and proves a forward boy there—And the mothers brother who has let himself in the village tells me that he takes the Flag of our Union—(if that is the paper edited by an Irishman). It is musical news to hear that Johnny does not love to be kept at home from school in deep snows."[14] In its relative concern for body and soul, and in the direct, personal way he takes action to address a real need, this anecdote well illustrates Thoreau's views about proper charity.

A good neighbor provides compassion as well as criticism, accepts and enjoys his neighbors as well as challenging their laziness and faults. It is in his journal, several million words written over the course of twenty-five years, that we often find this more accepting Thoreau: recounting an afternoon trying to find and catch a stray pig; bragging that, once again, his melon crop was the best in the village; chatting with an old farmer about muskrats and the weather for half an hour; telling the story of a crazy neighbor who tried to dig to the other side of the world, and who carefully placed a stone in the bottom of the hole at night, so that no one would fall through. The journal contains hundreds of such vignettes, adding up to an affectionate portrait of village life and clearly showing how important that life was to Thoreau.

Even his communion with nature takes on a more social cast in the journal. As Mary Elkins Moller remarks in her valuable study *Thoreau in the Human Community,* Thoreau's natural history notes often record his debts to his neighbors and their shared interest in what they were discussing: "Only rarely did [Thoreau] write, 'Someone told me . . .' or 'I heard . . .' Almost always the report is specifically credited: 'RWE told me,' 'Channing saw,' 'Minott heard,' 'Rice says,' 'Bigelow showed me'; 'Miss Caroline Pratt saw the white bobolink yesterday where Channing saw it the day before, in the midst of a large flock.'"[15] Often neighbors came to Thoreau with questions about what they had seen, or Thoreau went to them, realizing that Concord's older inhabitants were a store of natural lore. When Thoreau parades through the center of town to show off a giant mushroom he has found or the rarely seen flowers of the white pine, we catch glimpses of the respect and interest at least some of his townsmen took in his discoveries.[16]

Turning to the reminiscences gathered in Walter Harding's *Thoreau as Seen by His Contemporaries*, we find a similar picture. It is pleasant to read that Concord's jailor, Sam Staples, before locking his neighbor up for civil disobedience, offered: "I'll pay your tax, Henry, if you're hard up" (only to learn, in Staples's words, that "'Twas nothin' but principle").[17] It is pleasant, after reading about Thoreau's solitary gardening and abstemious dinners in *Walden*, to read this neighborly gossip, in a recently discovered letter:

> David [Henry Thoreau] had a party of gentlemen, Thursday evening, to eat melons. I went in to see the table, which was adorned with sunflowers, cornstalks, beet leaves & squash blossoms. There were forty-six melons, fifteen different kinds; & apples, all the production of his own garden. This is the only thing of interest that has happened in town this week. When we went in to see the tables, Mrs. Thoreau felt called upon to apologize for Henry having a party, it having been spread abroad by her that such customs met with his contempt & entire disapprobation.[18]

Most touching are the memories of children, now grown, who portray Thoreau as a kindly uncle or elder brother. We see boat trips on the river, where Thoreau enthralled the youngsters by catching bream with his bare hands.[19] Other accounts show him dropping by of an evening to pop corn, tell stories, juggle, or "swallow his knife and produce it again from our ears or noses."[20] Most numerous are the reports of huckleberry parties, organized and led by Thoreau, who, "when he found fine berries during his walks, he always remembered us, and came to arrange a huckleberrying for us."[21] Harding records some demurrers, who found Thoreau standoffish or cold; one, who read his writings subsequently, remarked: "There was a great intermediate class between Emerson and the Canadian wood chopper who would have gladly aided Thoreau if he had been a little more human in his dealings with them."[22] Emerson's son Edward, on the other hand, reminiscing fifty-five years after Thoreau's death, wrote warmly: "Our woods and waters will always be different because of this man. Something of him abides and truly 'for good' in his town. Here he was born, and within its borders he found a wealth of beauty and interest—all that he asked—and shared it with us all."[23]

When we turn back to *Walden*, we find some of this relaxed sociability, as Thoreau portrays himself sharing an afternoon's fishing (173–74) or chatting amiably with Alcott, Channing, or a neighboring farmer (267–70). Mostly though, Thoreau's neighbors serve as warnings, from the grasping, philistine farmer Flint (195–96) to the drunken Colonel Quoil (262). His neighbors show him how *not* to live, from their endless, "Herculean" business labors (4) to their slavish devotion to tradition (8–10); from the "shams and delusions" they "esteem for soundest truths" (95) to their reading, conversation, and thinking, "all on a very low level, worthy only of pygmies and manikins" (107). "The greater part of what my neighbors call good I believe in my soul to be bad," Thoreau states bluntly (10). Often, social forms are presented as a threat to the integrity of the self; Thoreau charges his neighbors with "contracting yourselves into a nutshell of civility, or dilating into an atmosphere of thin and vaporous generosity, that you may persuade your neighbor to let you make his shoes, or his hat" (7). Often, this prophet of alert wakefulness associates society with sleepiness and illusion (93–98, 325). "The Village" (*Walden's* shortest chapter by far, as if he could not wait to get clear of it) portrays Concord as a place to gossip, sell one's neighbors useless goods, or get arrested. Thoreau "escapes" from the village, back into the sanity of nature, as quickly as possible (169).

But we cannot take *Walden* as Thoreau's final word on human sociability, if only because he returned to town, where he lived out the rest of his life, productive and largely content (if still sometimes disgusted with his neighbors). Given Thoreau's position that we *live* as well as write our philosophies, we are justified in looking at his life in Concord to round out his social philosophy. Given the fact that he spent two years living by the pond and twenty adult years living in the village, we should probably view those two years as a season of solitude, valuable for learning what he needed to learn at that time in his life; arguably necessary, so that he could return to town, strike a proper balance between solitude and society, and fully appreciate nature *and* culture.

For again, we must remember that the solitary, wary procedure portrayed in *Walden* doesn't just close doors; it also opens them. Absent people, we may form new sorts of connections. In *Walden*, Thoreau finds that rabbits are neighbors (83), ponds are neighbors (86), woodchucks are neighbors (155), trees are neighbors (201)—or can be. "I found myself suddenly neighbor to the birds," Thoreau writes, "not by having imprisoned one, but having caged myself near them" (85). Here solitude takes Thoreau in an interesting new direction that challenges conventional morality. Contrary to the typical belief that nonhuman beings are unimportant, Thoreau finds himself surrounded by "brute neighbors" with their own lives and stories, demanding respect (see the following chapter).

In a similar way, solitude seems to have opened Thoreau's imagination to people displaced and largely forgotten in American history. Native Americans are a recurrent, ghostly presence in *Walden;* they are our predecessors every bit as much as the pilgrims and revolutionary heroes to whom we tend to look to find the meaning of our history. Thoreau also reflects deeply on those black and poor white "Former Inhabitants" who lived in the woods around Walden in the decades before he took up residence there (256–64). Their stories aren't usually found in New England's official town histories, but they are chronicled in some detail in *Walden,* which largely ignores Concord's official worthies. Other scholars have discussed this "alternative history," showing how astonishingly far ahead of his time Thoreau was in this.[24] Here I want to emphasize that, as with his environmental ethics, a certain distance from social engagement and social convention seems to have been necessary to achieve a more inclusive and accurate historical vision. "For many weeks I met no one in my walks," he wrote: "For human society I was obliged to conjure up the former occupants of these woods" (256).

Thoreau took these new ethical values and historical views back with him to the village. Integrating them with what remained of value in more traditional perspectives then became his task (as it remains ours). Similarly, combining "infinite demands" with an appreciation of his actual neighbors, so as to encourage them and sustain himself, tasked Thoreau—sometimes beyond his abilities. It is interesting to watch Thoreau struggling with this issue in his journal. "Let us not have a rabid virtue that will be revenged on society," he reminds himself: "that falls on it not like the morning dew but like the fervid noonday sun to wither it."[25] And again: "We must have infinite faith in each other, if we have not we must never let it leak out that we have not. . . . When I hear a grown man or woman say—Once I had faith in men—now I have not— I am inclined to ask Who are you—whom the world has disappointed— Have not you rather disappointed the world. There is the same ground for faith now that ever there was—It needs only a little love in you who complain to ground it on."[26] The journal documents Thoreau's efforts to *live* his demanding social philosophy. His uncertainties, his self-exhortations and self-criticisms, his obvious happiness with neighborly successes and unhappiness with neighborly failures, all serve to humanize him. This messy, incomplete struggle, too, is philosophy, as impressive in its own way as *Walden's* grand synthesis.

Friendship

As with neighboring, so with friendship: Thoreau tries to realize what is best in it and widen our sense of possibility. Readers who know Thoreau primarily through *Walden* may be surprised to learn that human friendship was an important issue for him. His journal during the 1840s is filled with reflections on this theme, evincing a deep need and desire for fulfilling relationships. *A Week on the Concord and Merrimack Rivers* contains an extended essay on friendship. Remembering Thoreau's caution there that "all that can be said of Friendship, is like botany to flowers," let us briefly consider this essay.[27]

Two themes that recur throughout Thoreau's reflections in *A Week* are friendship's importance and its transience and uncertainty. "Friendship is evanescent in every man's experience," Thoreau writes. "The heart is forever inexperienced" and friendship liable to many failures and reversals. We yearn for friendship, yet we cannot guarantee its occurrence or continuance, since friendships have their own dynamics, which are beyond the ability of friends to control. Still, "who would not sail through mutiny and storm even over Atlantic waves, to reach the fabulous retreating shores of some continent man?"[28]

Here in a book dedicated to the memory of John, his brother and best friend, Thoreau affirms our need for friendship. It is striking to read *Walden*'s solitary admit that "our fates at least are social. Our courses do not diverge.... Men naturally, though feebly, seek this alliance." We seek friends to share our experiences and thoughts and to call into being the sweetness of social intercourse itself. When we find a friend, we naturally seek to bridge any and all gaps between us. As Thoreau puts it, "we are dreaming that our Friends are our *Friends*, and that we are our Friends' *Friends*."[29] Here, in contrast to *Walden*, he asks for more human society—a better, richer human society.

Given the frequent charges of coldness and aloofness, it is also striking that Thoreau flags just this emotional condition as most to be avoided. He quotes the Chinese philosopher Mencius: "If one loses a fowl or a dog, he knows well how to seek them again; if one loses the sentiments of his heart, he does not know how to seek them again.... The duties of practical philosophy consist only in seeking after those sentiments of the heart which we have lost; that is all."[30] Cultivate proper sentiments, a true love for your friends, and those feelings will overcome any obstacles to friendship that *can* be overcome. Cultivate proper sentiments toward your fellow human beings, and this will obviate the need for a more detailed account of your moral obligations, since you will fulfill them spontaneously and gladly and indeed go beyond them in helping others.

Alongside this high valuation of friendship, however, Thoreau upholds a very demanding ideal of such relationships. As in *Walden*, he asks that common, everyday occurrences raise us beyond the common and everyday. Looking at what typically passes for friendship in his society, he finds it wanting. "Men do not, after all, *love* their Friends greatly," he charges: "I do not often see the farmers made seers and wise to the verge of insanity by their Friendship for one another. They are not often transfigured and translated by love in each other's presence. I do not observe them purified, refined, and elevated by the love of a man. If one abates a little the price of his wood, or gives a neighbor his vote at townmeeting, or a barrel of apples, or lends him his wagon frequently, it is esteemed a rare instance of Friendship."[31] Our friendships, of course, provide utility, enjoyment, comfort, and security in many ways. But if they do not make us better people, they do not provide all that friendship can and should provide.

This view follows logically from Thoreau's general ethical position that virtue, wisdom, and a rich experience are our proper goals in life, not pleasure and comfort. It is also squarely in the virtue ethics tradition. Aristotle, for example, whose *Nicomachean Ethics* devotes twice as much space to friendship as to justice, defines three main categories of friendship: friendships for pleasure, friendships for utility, and friendships for the cultivation of virtue. While he is less dismissive of the first two kinds than Thoreau, Aristotle clearly sees the cultivation of virtue as the highest use to which human relationships can be put.[32]

"In our daily intercourse with men," Thoreau complains, "our nobler faculties are dormant and suffered to rust. None will pay us the compliment to expect nobleness of us." The problem is that we are too accepting of one another, even making such acceptance the key to friendship. We all have much that is ignoble within us: deceit, meanness, selfishness. To accept someone as is, or to demand of her only common courtesy and that she break no explicit laws, is to ask very little. To calculate on her and use her to our advantage, as she uses us, is similarly undemanding. But much of what we call friendship or relationship is precisely this. In fact, it can become the whole of it: "A man may have *good* neighbors, so called, and acquaintances, and even companions, wife, parents, brothers, sisters, children, who meet himself and one another on this ground [of acceptance] only. . . . What is commonly called Friendship even is only a little more honor among rogues."[33] Call the last sentence hyperbole. Still, who can deny that the passage describes many of our daily interactions, as we help each other in trivial ways, exchange stale jokes, perhaps nuzzle together for warmth. Say, with Aristotle, that some amount of such routine or comforting social intercourse is necessary. Still, we ought to ask for more from our friendships.

To do so, however, we must ask more of ourselves. "A Friend is one who incessantly pays us the compliment of expecting from us all the virtues, and who can appreciate them in us," Thoreau writes.[34] But if he appreciates our virtues, he will also be dismayed by our vices. Thoreau remarks in a letter to his friend H. G. O. Blake: "As you suggest, we would fain value one another for what we are absolutely, rather than relatively. How will this do for a symbol of sympathy?"[35]

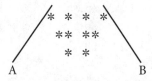

But this noble ideal will be difficult to live up to. For it both dismisses the common comforts of friendship and demands much of the beloved friend. It makes human relationships an arduous but glorious challenge, with potentially great rewards. It also brings the possibility of new sorts of failure: failure to live up to our own ideals or the ideals of our friends; failure to agree on those ideals.

It is easier to ask less of ourselves and to seek from others simple confirmation of our own goodness. Plato's *Symposium*, Western philosophy's greatest meditation on love and friendship, suggests that there is an unbridgeable divide between the accepting and the demanding sorts of love. Socrates' account of the true lovers' "ascent" from the love of beautiful bodies to beautiful deeds and character, and from particular examples of virtue, beauty, and goodness to direct comprehension of the forms or essences of these things, has inspired idealists and perfectionists for twenty-three centuries. For just as long, skeptics have echoed Alcibiades' complaint that such a vision leaves out all love of real individuals, making love an arid abstraction, and that it fails to capture what humans find most valuable in love ("I thought that what he wanted was *me*," the jilted Alcibiades complains, describing his feelings after Socrates had rejected his advances). As Plato presents the scene, the symposiasts applaud Socrates and award him the crown for the best speech in praise of love.

Yet Plato also suggests that few of them could live up to such a demanding vision. The casual, accepting view of love and friendship carries the twin dangers of stagnation and acceptance of our own weaknesses. Yet how many of us pursue the higher course, or listen as eagerly to the hard truths told to us by our friends as we listen to their compliments?

Although Plato perhaps expresses this idealistic and agonistic view of human relationships most eloquently, it is found throughout the ancient virtue ethics tradition, East as well as West. In addition to Mencius, Thoreau approvingly quotes Confucius on this theme: "To contract ties of Friendship with any one, is to contract Friendship with his virtue. There ought not to be any other motive in Friendship." "But men wish us to contract Friendship with their vice also," Thoreau continues. Like Alcibiades, they wish to put comfort over truth and acceptance over moral striving:

> I have a Friend who wishes me to see that to be right which I know to be wrong. But if Friendship is to rob me of my eyes, if it is to darken the day, I will have none of it. . . . A want of discernment cannot be an ingredient in it. If I can see my Friend's virtues more distinctly than another's, his faults too are made more conspicuous by contrast. We have not so good a right to hate any as our Friend. Faults are no less faults because they are inevitably balanced by corresponding virtues, and for a fault there is no excuse. . . . I have never known one who could bear criticism, who could not be flattered, who would not bribe his judge, or was content that the truth should be loved always better than himself.[36]

In Athens, Beijing, or Concord, the idealism is the same. Our goal should be excellence, not a slack comfort. No one—including Thoreau himself, presumably—can live up to this ideal all the time. We naturally seek comfort and the assurance that we are loved for who we are. Still, Thoreau insists, only a *hatred* of vice and weakness wherever they occur shows a love of virtue. Only a willingness to sacrifice those parts of our selves that harbor vice and weakness shows a true commitment to excellence. And only this commitment proves our worthiness for friendship.

Clearly, Thoreau is not writing about friendship as it typically exists, but about Friendship: an ideal that our particular friendships may more or less approximate. As in Plato, this idealization extends to an idealized view of the friend and of oneself: "our actual friends are but distant relations of those to whom we are pledged." We may and should sacrifice the real individual to the superior idealization. In proportion as we have a true love for another, "our lives are divine and miraculous, and answer to our ideal. There are passages of affection in our intercourse with mortal men and women, such as no prophecy had taught us to expect, which transcend our earthly life, and anticipate heaven for us."[37]

Successes are possible: Thoreau's is a practical idealism, after all. But all successes set the stage for further striving, in Thoreau's view, so there will be no surcease from our efforts. And the more demanding we are of our friends, the more disappointments we will have. Hence Thoreau's frequent remarks about friendship's necessary limitations and failures. "It is impossible to say all that we think, even to our truest Friend." And again: "friendship's drama is always a tragedy."[38]

Thoreau's answer to the inevitable failure of friendship is twofold. First, there is the classic idealist's answer that the ideal is a higher reality and that even when particular friendships suffer, the love of principles and virtue remains and can be shared, nurtured, and cherished by friends. Second, there is a willingness to try friendship again, with this friend or with another. For after all deductions, we cannot do without friendship: "ignorance and bungling with love are better than wisdom and skill without." We can achieve enough of the ideal here in our earthly lives to continue to believe in both the ideal and our imperfect instantiations of it. As we must acknowledge our insufficiencies, so we must appreciate our possibilities. For all its disappointments, friendship offers perennial hope and intimations of immortality. "Surely my Friend shall forever be my Friend," Thoreau concluded his essay, "and reflect a ray of God to me, and time shall foster and adorn and consecrate our Friendship, no less than the ruins of temples. As I love nature, as I love singing birds, and gleaming stubble, and flowing rivers, and morning and evening, and summer and winter, I love thee my Friend."[39]

Emerson and Thoreau

Thoreau believed in the demanding view of friendship described in *A Week* and tried to live up to it. Can real friendships survive and thrive under such a conception? Thoreau's friendship with his fellow idealist Emerson provides an ambiguous answer.[40]

Thoreau and Emerson's friendship blossomed during the autumn after Thoreau returned home from college in 1837. Emerson was then at the height of his intellectual and creative powers. He was writing or had recently written his most powerful pieces. His philosophy of striving and self-reliance strongly attracted Thoreau, who had the good fortune to be granted the society of America's leading progressive thinker just as he began his own intellectual career.

Emerson for his part enjoyed Thoreau's intellectual acuity and daring. "I delight much in my young friend, who seems to have as free & erect a mind as any I have ever met," he wrote in his journal shortly after Thoreau's return to Concord.[41] And again, only a few months later: "My good Henry Thoreau made this else solitary afternoon sunny with his simplicity and clear perception. . . . Everything that boy says makes merry with society, though nothing can be graver than his meaning."[42] Henry was "a noble manly youth full of melodies & inventions . . . a scholar & a poet & as full of buds of promise as a young apple tree."[43]

Thoreau and Emerson stimulated one another intellectually. Their friendship was not just intellectual, however, but emotional and personal. Thoreau, usually so emotionally reticent, overcame this to some extent early in his friendship with Emerson. Robert Richardson Jr., Thoreau's and Emerson's biographer, writes that "Thoreau's admiration for Emerson was, this winter [their first together as friends] literally without bounds." In Thoreau's journal entries, according to Richardson, "he is entirely without his usual armor of bristling objection and defensive quirk, and is content for once to use the plain language of master and pupil. He refers to 'my recent growth' and to how he is always having to 'reach up' in order to take the good things offered by 'my friend.'" "Early in February," Richardson writes, "Thoreau noted with wonder that 'the world has never learned what men can build each other up to be—when both master and pupil work in love.'"[44] Emerson, more emotionally open than Thoreau in any case, reciprocated these feelings. Recounting a river excursion, Emerson wrote in his journal: "The good river-god has taken the form of my valiant Henry Thoreau here & introduced me to the riches of his shadowy, starlit moonlit stream, a lovely new world lying as close & yet as unknown to this vulgar trite one of streets & shops as death to life or poetry to prose. . . . Take care, good friend! I said, as I looked west into the sunset overhead & underneath, & he with his face toward me rowed towards it,—take care; you know not what you do, dipping your wooden oar into this enchanted liquid, painted with all reds & purples and yellows which glows under & behind you."[45]

Over the next few years, Thoreau became a trusted and intimate member of the Emerson family. He lived with them for extended periods in 1841–43 and 1847–48, the second time looking after Emerson's family during the master's European lecture tour. For much of the 1840s Thoreau and Emerson sustained a close personal friendship, with an intimacy closer to ancient philosophical traditions than to modern academic philosophical training.

Clearly, in this relationship Emerson was the mentor. Emerson suggested that Thoreau keep a journal. He recommended themes, including a review article of several natural history works that became Thoreau's first published nature writing. He critiqued his articles and peddled them to various editors, with mixed results. He provided the site for Thoreau's experiment at Walden Pond. At the same time that Emerson was stating his mature philosophy, Thoreau was struggling to develop his own message, learn the craft of writing, and simply find a career in which he could support himself.

Given Thoreau's strong independent streak, this relationship of dependence was bound to cause friction. There were the tensions that inevitably arise when people live with one another and interact much, and there were differences between the two men's personalities. In conversation Emerson was more conciliatory, Thoreau more contentious. Emerson was the more social, Thoreau the more solitary. Emerson, the property owner and family man, was somewhat more deferential toward social forms, while Thoreau was more radically critical of what he took to be hypocrisy, triviality, and the nuzzling together of the herd. Such personality differences shaded off into serious intellectual differences: one of their first recorded quarrels occurred during an afternoon walk when Thoreau, noting the proliferation of fences along the road, declared that he would not abide them, as he had as much right to "God's earth" as anyone. Emerson responded with a defense of the institution of private property. Harmon Smith, who has written a valuable book on their friendship, suggests that Emerson's subsequent essay, "The Protest," was directed toward Thoreau.[46] In it, Emerson warns aspiring youths of the dangers of letting their frustrations at society's shortcomings consume their time and talents.

New strains were put on their relationship as Thoreau came into his own as a thinker. Emerson was a generous and open-minded man, but as Thoreau moved away from his earlier idealism toward a more complex mixture of idealism and naturalism, Emerson found his views less congenial. While Emerson extolled engagement with nature, Thoreau's immersion in and love for actual nature was much greater. This inevitably colored his philosophy. Early on and persistently, Thoreau questioned the transcendental tendency to look past nature in search of higher truths. In a journal entry in 1840, he wrote: "The poet does not need to see how meadows are something else than earth—grass, and water, but how they are thus much." Thoreau's naturalism eventually led him to appreciate and defend nature's intrinsic value and to explore immanent conceptions of deity—positions far removed from Emerson and most transcendentalists. As Thoreau once succinctly put his differences with Emerson: "We do not believe in the same God."[47]

The move from Emerson's "Nature" to Thoreau's "wildness" encompassed the full trajectory of Thoreau's intellectual career. It involved recognition of nature's fundamental, life-giving spontaneity and a consequent de-emphasis on regularity and law; an appreciation of nature's sensuous particularities and less hankering after abstract truths. Thoreau's naturalistic outlook also demanded an earthier lifestyle than Emerson's idealism. Thoreau's journal during the 1850s, unlike Emerson's, is filled with natural history observations. It also contains the tart observation: "I doubt if Emerson could trundle a wheel barrow through the streets—because it would be out of character."[48] The contrast between the two men's philosophies and lives can be overstated. But Thoreau's acceptance of Emerson's challenge to "take up an original relation to the universe" eventually led to a very different kind of transcendentalism.

Intellectual stimulation depends on frank talk: on hashing out disagreements as well as sharing and celebrating agreements. Thoreau and Emerson seem to have struck a good balance for a long time, but two such independent minds were bound to clash. In 1849 they had a serious falling out, which appears to have been precipitated by Emerson's reaction to Thoreau's first book. Emerson had done much to see *A Week* into print, but in the end it seems to have disappointed him, and he shared this disappointment with Thoreau. Thoreau took his mentor's rejection hard, writing in his journal: "I had a friend, I wrote a book, I asked my friend's criticism, I never got but praise for what was good in it—my friend became estranged from me and then I got blame for all that was bad,—& so I at last got the criticism which I wanted."[49] It is sad as well as ironic that disagreement over this book, with its obvious intellectual debts to Emerson and its paean to true friendship, should have been the cause of their falling out.

We do not know what Emerson said. Perhaps he objected to *A Week*'s obvious criticism of a symbolic or "correspondential" attitude toward nature, expressed in a number of passages:

> Better that the primrose by the river's brim be a yellow primrose, and nothing more, than that it be something less.

> May we not *see* God? Are we to be put off and amused in this life, as it were with a mere allegory? Is not Nature, rightly read, that of which she is commonly taken to be the symbol merely?[50]

Perhaps Emerson, like many subsequent critics, objected to *A Week's* unevenness: the disproportion between the charming riverside descriptions and the ponderous philosophical and literary digressions arbitrarily strung out along the way. Ideally, such criticisms could be made and discussed without harming a friendship, but the reality proved more painful and difficult.

In discussing this, Thoreau struggles to hold on to the ideal. He refuses to assume that his friends should say only nice things about his writings. Rather, like Emerson in his own essay on "Friendship," Thoreau insists that commitment to truth is a key to true friendship. He writes in the same journal passage quoted earlier: "No one appreciates our virtues like our friend, yet methinks that I do not receive from my friend that criticism which is most valuable & indispensable to me until he is estranged from me. He who knows best what we are, knows what we are not. He will never tell me the fatal truth which it concerns me most to know until he is estranged from me." Here is that Platonic idealism that insists we must so love virtue that we are willing to cut away all imperfections from ourselves or our friends (Thoreau is discussing criticism of his book and not his person, but for a true writer these cannot be separated). Here is that tragic dimension of friendship that he had noted in *A Week*, in his suggestion that we cannot get what we most need from our friends without estrangement and pain.

This journal passage is complex and conflicted, written as Thoreau wrestles with his emotions and his ideal. Emerson had in fact written that *two* things are the necessary requisites for true friendship: "truth" and "tenderness."[51] A part of Thoreau wants to suggest that it is Emerson who has fallen short in keeping these two necessary components together. *He* could have heard the truth about his writing earlier, Thoreau suggests, but Emerson would not give it to him until they had fallen into enmity. Yet Thoreau also wonders if that is right. Perhaps in the tragic nature of things, conflict and loss are necessary to get the whole benefit of friendship.

Despite all, Thoreau strives to uphold the ideal. He accepts the justness and "value" of Emerson's criticism, as he must as a lover of truth above personal comfort. But he also suggests that such acceptance of truth can be combined with tenderness, continuing in his journal entry: "When we are such friends & have such for our friends that our love is not partiality, that truth is not crowded out or postponed—or delayed there will be *Friendship*. . . . When two can treat each other with absolute truth, then there will be but those two in the world. Then men will no longer be divided but be one as God is."[52] In the *Symposium,* Plato suggests that as our love matures and becomes less partial, love of individuals and "tenderness" must drop away. Still feeling keenly the loss of Emerson's friendship, Thoreau is not here prepared to accept this. In his willingness to probe the painful phenomena of his tattered friendship, while still trying to affirm something better, we see Thoreau's true idealism.

Both men made efforts over the next few years to heal the breach between them. After a time, they re-established friendly relations, if not at the high pitch of past years. Perhaps such a break was necessary in order for Thoreau to assert his independence. Perhaps, too, they had largely exhausted the stimulation they provided one another. Thoreau, inspired by Emerson's transcendental idealism, had developed it in new and valuable ways. What greater gift could a student give to his teacher? Emerson and Thoreau were important thinkers, and perhaps we should not so much lament the feelings they lost as value the insight they gained. Finally, perhaps we should appreciate the friendship they had, rather than lament its passing. A lessening of the heat of love and friendship seems all but inevitable in human relationships. Thoreau wrote in later years: "It may be enough that we have met *some time,* and now can never forget it."[53]

Nevertheless, Emerson and Thoreau felt their break keenly and struggled to understand it. Emerson blamed Thoreau's coldness and contentiousness for much of their trouble. Looking back on two decades of friendship with Henry, he wrote in his journal for 1856: "If I knew only Thoreau, I should think cooperation of good men impossible. Must we always talk for victory, and never once for truth, for comfort, and joy?"[54] It is significant that Emerson should associate truth with comfort and joy, while in *Walden* Thoreau emphasized solitude and struggle in the pursuit of truth. Emerson continues: "Centrality he has, and penetration, strong understanding, and the higher gifts,—the insight of the real, or from the real, and the moral rectitude that belongs to it; but all this and all his resources of wit and invention are lost to me, in every experiment, year after year, that I make, to hold intercourse with his mind. Always some weary captious paradox to fight you with, and the time and temper wasted." Here again we see a basic philosophical difference, along with a difference in temperament and style. For Emerson, Thoreau's frequent paradoxical statements manifest only perverseness. But arguably, Thoreau does not simply indulge in paradoxes to annoy Emerson and his other readers, but to point toward the complexity of phenomena and insufficiencies in our views of those phenomena. His paradoxes challenge our conventional beliefs.

For example, Emerson had earlier criticized a piece of Thoreau's writing, for its "old fault of unlimited contradiction. The trick of his rhetoric is soon learned: it consists in substituting for the obvious word and thought its diametrical antagonist. He praises wild mountains and winter forests for their domestic air; snow and ice for their warmth; villagers and wood-choppers for their urbanity.... With the constant inclination to disprise cities and civilization, he yet can find no way to know woods and woodmen except by paralleling them with towns and townsmen. Channing declared the piece is excellent, but it makes me nervous and wretched to read it, with all its merits."[55] But this particular "trick" of speaking of nature as "domestic" lies very close to the heart of Thoreau's naturalistic challenge to Emerson's idealism. Emerson might have been right that in 1843 this way of speaking masked Thoreau's limited ability to describe nature. But in due course this insight into nature's domesticity flowered into an environmental ethics that recognized our kinship with other species and the need for humans to live in harmony with nature, and into a proto-ecology that recognized the importance of nature's interconnections and the higher order to be found in patterns of landscape succession ("ecology," from *oikos,* the home). Perhaps Emerson's "nervousness and wretchedness" with Thoreau's paradoxes came from his inability to follow him into new realms of thought, or to reconsider the basic premises of his own philosophy.

Thoreau challenged Emerson in the practical as well as the intellectual realm. As Emerson wrote in his journal: "Thoreau gives me, in flesh and blood and pertinacious Saxon belief, my own ethics. He is far more real, and daily practically obeying them, than I."[56] It was a mark of Emerson's generosity to be able to say this. Yet it can't have been easy to live with such a perpetual challenge to oneself. If an ethics of self-reliance led Thoreau to chafe at having a mentor, it was also demanding enough for its promulgator to feel threatened by his most successful and uncompromising pupil.

Both the intellectual and ethical challenges came together in Emerson's response to Thoreau's night in jail. Clearly, this act of civil disobedience bothered Emerson. In conversation with Bronson Alcott, he criticized it as "mean and skulking, and in bad taste." Seeing Thoreau afterward, he reportedly asked him why he had gone to jail, only to meet the reply: "Why did you not?"[57] In his first journal entry on the matter, Emerson fulminates and sputters, casting doubt on the justice and the effectiveness of Thoreau's course. But in a later entry that puts Thoreau's actions in the larger perspective of possible political responses to the Mexican War, he finds more merit in them: "Mr. Webster told [the proponents of war] how much the war cost, that was his protest, but voted the war, and sends his son to it. They calculated rightly on Mr. Webster. My friend Mr. Thoreau has gone to jail rather than pay his tax. On him they could not calculate."[58] Here Emerson seems to approve of such deeds, as means to radically challenge a rotten status quo. I want to suggest that this fruitful uncertainty was valuable for Emerson—if not completely comfortable. We see in his uncertainty and reconsideration the same effects Thoreau's action reportedly had on some of his other neighbors. A few years later, Emerson himself publicly advocated civil disobedience, in defiance of the Fugitive Slave Law of 1850. Score a point, then, for agonistic idealism in personal relations.

At the same time, we can be contentious to no purpose. We can be intolerant of one another's faults. We can simply be cold and unfeeling. These criticisms and more Emerson leveled at Thoreau, who had to accept that there was some truth in them. Interestingly, both he and Emerson associated this coldness in his human relations with the strength of his connection to nature. Thoreau journalized: "By my intimacy with nature I find myself withdrawn from man. My interest in the sun & the moon—in the morning & the evening compels me to solitude. . . . In your higher moods what man is there to meet? You are of necessity isolated. The mind that perceives clearly any natural beauty is in that instant withdrawn from human society. My desire for society is infinitely increased—my fitness for any actual society is diminished."[59] Here again Thoreau suggests a tragic dimension to our relationships, as unfulfillable desires are created by the genuine good of connection to wild nature.

Emerson tended to see this dilemma as mere perverseness, as if Thoreau need not choose between nature and human society, or as if he *could* choose to step back from his ever deeper natural relationships. While he had once praised Thoreau's interest in natural history and gladly rowed further out into wild nature with him, he now focused on the insufficiencies and dangers of this path: "Henry Thoreau is like the wood god who solicits the wandering poet and draws him into antres [caverns] vast and deserts idle, and bereaves him of his memory, and leaves him naked, plaiting vine and with twigs in his hand. Very seductive are the first steps from the town to the woods, but the end is want and madness."[60] Thoreau was less optimistic that he could change his fundamental nature and less pessimistic about his own possibilities for happiness. "If I am too cold for human friendship," he wrote, "I trust I shall not soon be too cold for natural influences. It appears to be a law that you cannot have a deep sympathy with both man & nature. Those qualities which bring you near to the one estrange you from the other."[61]

In looking at this friendship, we may wonder whether Emerson and Thoreau each failed to fully profit from one another. Thoreau might have learned from Emerson how to sweeten his intercourse with others and find lasting warmth and joy in a wider circle of friends and family. He perhaps relied overly much on Emerson to meet people; had he widened his own circle of acquaintances, this might have facilitated his intellectual development and subsequent public reception. Emerson, for his part, might have developed his philosophy further, beyond vague generalities about duty and nature, through considering the concrete particularities that Thoreau dealt with more directly and effectively.[62] He might have reconsidered old positions and explored new complexities, rather than having his work trail off into repetition and decay in the years after Thoreau's death.

But this is mere speculation. In any case, Thoreau and Emerson made much of one another. The more pressing question, for each of us, is what *we* should make of our own friendships. We would do well to get as much from them as Emerson and Thoreau apparently got from theirs. Toward the end of his life, Emerson recalled Thoreau as his "best friend." Not his easiest or most congenial perhaps, but his best.

Friendship, neighboring, and solitude provide different pleasures and opportunities for personal development. Before discussing the amount of solitude or society that are ideal—for us as individuals or for people generally—we should perhaps explore both realms more thoroughly. Through his rich, positive account of solitude, his now expansive, now selective account of neighboring, and his demanding account of friendship, Thoreau suggests new possibilities that we too can try. In the end, *Walden*'s hopefulness and experimentalism might prove more valuable than Thoreau's arguments or his particular example, as we seek to learn how to live well in solitude and society.

Nature

Environmental ethics asks how people should treat the rest of nature. In the words of a leading environmental philosopher, it seeks to specify "duties to and values in the natural world."[1] Over the past few decades, environmental ethics has emerged as an important field within academic philosophy, its growth spurred by our immense environmental problems and the sense that a change in values will be needed to successfully address them.

As we strive to develop a strong and effective environmental ethics, I believe no thinker has more to offer than Henry Thoreau. He was one of the earliest and remains one of the strongest critics of anthropocentrism: the view that only human beings have rights or "intrinsic value," and that other creatures may be used in any way we see fit. Perhaps even more important, Thoreau shows us how to lead flourishing lives while still treating nature with respect.

There is a great practical need to develop positive arguments for environmental protection. The recognition of nature's intrinsic value is sometimes seen as intolerably limiting, spawning an endless string of environmental "thou shalt nots." Often, the general public views environmentalists as killjoys, willing to countenance any trade-offs of human freedom or happiness in pursuit of our aims. Partly this is unavoidable. In defending nature, environmentalists are necessarily proscriptive. Recognizing intrinsic values in nature *does* limit its morally permissible use. Yet the writings of the great naturalists—and our own experiences—tell a story of joyful relationship with nature. The artist, the scientist, the poet, the hunter and the fisherman, all pay attention to nature and "capture values" that enrich their lives. This suggests that a recognition of nature's intrinsic value brings rewards to go with its proscriptions.

As we have seen, in *Walden* Thoreau writes as a virtue ethicist. I contend that *Walden* provides a fully developed and inspiring *environmental* virtue ethics, which links environmental protection to human happiness, excellence, and flourishing.[2] Thoreau thus points the way toward a comprehensive, life-affirming environmental ethics. By recognizing nature's value, we enrich our own lives. By restraining our gross physical consumption, we are more likely to lead healthy and enjoyable lives and promote conditions in which future generations can do the same. By devoting ourselves to higher pursuits than moneymaking, we act in our *enlightened* self-interest—with great benefits for the many other species with whom we share the Earth. These arguments need to be made—along with intrinsic value arguments—if we are to convince people to take the steps necessary to protect the natural world.

Fishy Virtue

Thoreau challenges conventional ethics in many ways. One of his most important challenges involves locating value directly in the nonhuman world, a theme already made explicit in *A Week on the Concord and Merrimack Rivers*. Early in *A Week,* Thoreau gives a detailed account of the various species of fish in the Concord River. This is one of those digressions that have annoyed so many readers. "We come upon them like snags," wrote James Russell Lowell, "jolting us headforemost out of our places as we are rowing placidly up stream or drifting down."[3] Thoreau might have integrated this account more smoothly into the narrative, of course, but another alternative would have been to ignore the fish entirely: to glide downstream without noticing them, or to carelessly populate the deeps and shallows with generic or imaginary fish. This is the way of most boaters and most writers. This Thoreau will not do.

Instead, he describes the fish, accurately and in detail: their appearance, behavior (nesting, feeding, migrations), habitat preferences, relative abundance, and more. These fish have many fine qualities: the bream "assiduously" guards its nest; the pickerel is "swift and wary." Thoreau plays up both their otherness and their closeness to us: the fish are at once "fabulous inhabitant[s] of another element, a thing heard of but not seen" and "our finny contemporaries in the Concord waters."[4] These wonderful creatures are part of the same landscape as ourselves. We may know them if we will but look.

Much of this section has little explicit ethical content. At first there are no ethical arguments, just descriptions continually bubbling up into little assertions of goodness: the "grace" of the bream, the "scholastic and classical" beauty of the chivin. Finally, however, Thoreau comes to the plight of the shad and other anadromous, migratory fishes. Formerly found in great numbers in New England's rivers, they are now often blocked by dams. Here the definite "ought" of moral concern flows out:

Poor shad! where is thy redress? When Nature gave thee instinct, gave she thee the heart to bear thy fate? Still wandering the sea in thy scaly armor to inquire humbly at the mouths of rivers if man has perchance left them free for thee to enter. By countless shoals loitering uncertain meanwhile, merely stemming the tide there, in danger from sea foes in spite of thy bright armor, awaiting new instructions, until the sands, until the water itself, tell thee if it be so or not. Thus by whole migrating nations, full of instinct, which is thy faith, in this backward spring, turned adrift, and perchance knowest not where men do *not* dwell, where there are *not* factories, in these days. Armed with no sword, no electric shock, but mere Shad, armed only with innocence and a just cause, with tender dumb mouth only forward, and scales easy to be detached. I for one am with thee, and who knows what may avail a crow bar against that Billerica dam?[5]

Our treatment of the shad is unjust. The fish obviously cannot "petition for redress," but they would be justified in doing so. The dams are not merely inconvenient or inexpedient for fishermen, downstream farmers, or other human beings—they are wrong, immoral, because of their effects on "mere Shad." One hundred and thirty years before EarthFirst! Thoreau suggests that the injustice is grave enough to justify a new kind of civil disobedience. We have here not the monstrous injustice of making a mere tool out of a man or woman, but the (equally?) monstrous injustice of extirpating whole species, whole forms of life, from the landscape.

Thoreau goes on to provide one of the earliest explicit calls for a non-anthropocentric ethics. The passage quoted above continues: "Away with the superficial and selfish phil-*anthropy* of men,—who knows what admirable virtue of fishes may be below low-water mark, bearing up against a hard destiny, not admired by that fellow creature who alone can appreciate it!" Reserving all love and concern for humans—phil-*anthropy*, emphasis in the original—is both superficial, based on ignorance of what is below the surface, and selfish, an excuse for unjustified self-partiality. Thoreau neatly brings his point home with the "fish" puns.

Only here, in attempting to nail down these charges, does Thoreau use the word "virtue," making explicit what had been implicit in his earlier descriptions. Thoreau clearly employs the ancient conception of virtue as excellence here. A fish cannot act morally, but it can flourish as a good of its kind. The traits Thoreau praises in the bream and shad arguably are virtues, because they are the characteristic qualities that make these species what they are and that help them succeed in the natural economy of the Concord River.[6]

Thoreau's suggestion that certain piscine qualities are genuine virtues parallels recent attempts by Holmes Rolston, Paul Taylor, and other environmental philosophers to justify the intrinsic value of nonhuman beings: to argue their basic goodness independent of their instrumental value to humans. These philosophers' arguments typically ground intrinsic value in various natural qualities, such as sentience (the ability to feel pleasure and pain), intelligence, goal directedness, complexity, or an ancient and unique genealogy. All beings who have these qualities, it is argued, are good in themselves, regardless of what further good they may be to us. Recognizing their intrinsic value does not preclude all human use of these nonhuman beings, but it does set moral limits to that use.[7] In the same way, Thoreau moves from facts to values, as a (mostly) descriptive section concludes with an explicit assertion of fish virtue and the demands of interspecific justice.

Does Thoreau undermine his case for fishy virtue by speaking of the "humility" and "bravery" of fish, qualities that we typically associate with some degree of intelligence and thus largely or exclusively with humans? Can fish be "innocent" if they cannot be guilty (can infants or saints)? Thoreau writes "perchance" the shad do not know where rivers still run unobstructed by humans, but of course they do not have conscious knowledge that may be formulated into propositional statements and delivered in scholarly lectures. If Thoreau's argument rests on an inaccurate picture of what shad actually are, it necessarily fails to justify their moral considerability or any after-hours crowbar work on the Billerica dam.

There are several ways a sympathetic expositor might respond here. One might argue that shad *do* possess literal, nonmetaphorical knowledge, perhaps as populations rather than as individuals. Through some combination of genetic programming and environmental cues (of which we are almost as ignorant as Thoreau) they do return to their native spawning grounds. They do "loiter uncertain" until some "intelligence" passes to them from the land or water, some cue that sends them up one particular river or another. They may fail to "know" of any undammed streams, if all the streams have been dammed, just as they "know" of home streams that have "proven" themselves good habitat in the past. The shad cannot be "in suspense" in our sense of conscious uncertainty as to probable outcomes, yet they are suspended in water and suspended between the fates of continued flourishing and utter destruction. Recall the ancient conception of the virtues: those qualities that foster success and flourishing. Perhaps a less individually based and conscious "knowledge" is the shad's equivalent of human practical reason, helping to further shad success as reason (ideally) furthers our own.

Alternately, we might question the notion that other beings have value only to the degree that they resemble us. Maybe we should value them for their own essential qualities, which might be very different from ours. Typically, those skeptical of nonhuman intrinsic value argue that rationality, or the related ability to act morally, defines and limits moral considerability. Thoreau's admonition that we are "fellow creatures" who "alone can appreciate" the varied diversity of nonhuman life suggests the following counterargument: if a true humanity involves the use of reason, that should lead to knowledge of the world around us, and thus to appreciation, and thus to restraint. If we truly value reason, it will show us a world where much besides reason has value. If we truly value diversity, we will have to jettison theories of value centered so firmly in our own nature. Those who argue that we are free to use the rest of nature any way we see fit because we are rational and able to restrain our natural selfishness show, ironically, their own poorly developed knowledge and capacity for altruism.

Yet a third alternative is to reject hierarchical morality altogether. Perhaps the notion that the lesser capabilities of some beings give them lesser value is mistaken. After all, despite the fact that we recognize that people have widely different capabilities, most of us see the gradual acceptance of equal rights among people as moral progress.[8]

Thoreau sees a genuine heroism in the shad's efforts to spawn. It is a great story, but different from human greatness. The shoals of fish do not come armed with lance, or consciousness, or the human sense of personal importance. The shad, the philosopher will tell you, do not *act* at all, since they do not have conscious purposes. Yet we may watch them migrating upstream or hold one gleaming in our hands, imagine the vast distances they have traveled, and marvel. They truly are "reserved for higher destinies": higher up New England's rivers and streams, to spawn.[9] The shad's whole destiny is here on Earth, in this life. The same may be true for us, of course. In *Walden*, Thoreau will suggest that this is no reason to despair, for "heaven is under our feet as well as over our heads" (283).

Thoreau's discussion here shows some of the difficulties of moving beyond an anthropocentric value system. One must steer the course between an uncritical anthropomorphism that gives other beings bogus honorific qualities, and a hypercritical reductionism that denies other beings all qualities that we cannot yet detect in them and undervalues those qualities that we do detect. Our ethics should be based on accurate knowledge of the world. Yet perhaps engagement is even more important than accuracy. Thoreau argues that we should work to know nature, however imperfectly, and thus move beyond the "superficial" views with which most people content themselves. Whatever lives of excellence—or mere complexity and strangeness—fish or other nonhuman beings can achieve, humans alone can fully appreciate them. We should do so, Thoreau says, for their sakes and ours. For if the Billerica dam and similar developments unjustly obstruct fish, they may also ruin the fishing and limit possibilities for human knowledge, poetry, and fulfilling contact with wild nature.

"Thou shalt ere long have thy way up the rivers," Thoreau cries, "up all the rivers of the globe, if I am not mistaken. Yea, even thy dull watery dream shall be more than realized. If it were not so, but thou wert to be overlooked at first and at last, then would I not take their heaven. Yes, I say so, who think I know better than thou canst."[10] Was this the passage that jerked James Russell Lowell out of his boat, rather than the long description of the Concord River's fish species or Thoreau's other digressions? Certainly it bears a marked resemblance to the passage Lowell, as editor of the *Atlantic Monthly,* later censored in "Chesuncook": "It [a pine tree] is as immortal as I am, and perchance will go to as high a heaven, there to tower above me still."[11]

It is ironic that Lowell fastened so thoroughly, early and late, on Thoreau's derivativeness in condemning his literary achievements, given his own public suppression of Thoreau's non-anthropocentrism, one of the more striking and original aspects of his work. Here was certainly one area where Thoreau pushed far ahead of his mentor Emerson. Here was a realm where, as he said, he looked toward the West and the wild, while Lowell and most of his civilized readers remained committed to the conventional anthropocentrism espoused on both sides of the Atlantic.

Higher Laws

Walden represents a more searching, sustained attempt to specify a non-anthropocentric ethics. Thoreau there repeatedly asserts the intrinsic value of nonhuman nature—whether in trees (201), woodchucks (166), or Walden Pond itself (192–93)—and tries to justify these assertions. But *Walden* also discusses the benefits to *people* of recognizing nature's value and living accordingly.

The chapter "Higher Laws" develops a detailed and sweeping critique of hunting, fishing, and meat eating generally. As in *A Week,* Thoreau's wordplay identifies a key issue: "No humane being, past the thoughtless age of boyhood, will wantonly murder any creature, which holds its life by the same tenure that he does. The hare in its extremity cries like a child. I warn you, mothers, that my sympathies do not always make the usual phil-*anthropic* distinctions" (212, emphasis in the original). The "usual distinctions," of course, are between human suffering and the suffering of other sentient beings, which we discount, and between the ending of a human and a nonhuman life. Here Thoreau equates a true humanity with greater sympathy for all nature's creatures and with a deep appreciation of their existence. If causing unnecessary suffering or ending a life unnecessarily are prima facie wrong, then we should avoid killing animals, since we arguably get no important benefits from killing them, or at least no benefits that outweigh their losses.

Contemporary briefs against meat eating, such as Peter Singer's animal welfare arguments or Tom Regan's animal rights arguments, can get quite complicated.[12] The precise nature of animals, the degree to which their experience resembles human experience (particularly different species' varied capacities to suffer), the demands of reason and consistency, the exact wording of general ethical principles, are all debated in sophisticated philosophical terms. Thoreau instead appeals directly to experience: "It may be vain to ask why the imagination will not be reconciled to flesh and fat. I am satisfied that it is not. Is it not a reproach that man is a carnivorous animal? True, he can and does live, in great measure, by preying on other animals; but this is a miserable way,—as any one who will go to snaring rabbits, or slaughtering lambs, may learn" (216). Such activities are literally miserable—they cause terror, pain, and suffering—and we can see this if we look. Here again we see Thoreau's ethical method: simplify your life and pay careful attention to the effects of your actions. If we do this, he believes, we will be much more likely to *see* right and wrong. At the very least, we will better understand the trade-offs our actions necessitate, for ourselves and others, and whether our actions conform to our principles.

There is a lot to be said for this method. No argument about general ethical principles, or the essential nature of pigs or chickens, can take the place of actually visiting a modern factory farm and seeing how cruelly the animals are raised. Thoreau's phrase "it may be vain to ask" perhaps suggests skepticism concerning reason's ability to fully answer our ethical questions. Alternatively, it might show Thoreau's faith in our ethical intuitions. Either of these reasons, or both, may help explain why Thoreau does not develop detailed moral arguments against meat eating.

Another reason is *Walden*'s general focus on personal flourishing, rather than on our duties to others. In line with this, Thoreau discusses carnivory's typical effects on our health and happiness. Meat eating is expensive, he asserts, and also filthy. It is much easier to clean up after a vegetarian meal. Once again, an appeal to experience is key: "Having been my own butcher and scullion and cook, as well as the gentleman for whom the dishes were served up, I can speak from an unusually complete experience" (214).

True, fishing and hunting do serve to introduce many children to the woods, furthering an interest in nature they might not otherwise develop. For this reason, these are beneficial activities for youth: "We cannot but pity the boy who has never fired a gun; he is no more humane, while his education has been sadly neglected. . . . Such is oftenest the young man's introduction to the forest, and the most original part of himself" (212). But our knowledge and acquaintance with nature's creatures should deepen over time. By directly participating in killing, a boy comes to understand what killing is. This allows him, for the first time, to act humanely by consciously deciding not to kill. And by the time he does this, he has better reasons to be in the woods. The hunter, Thoreau believes, should evolve into a poet or naturalist and put aside his gun (213).

Experience also teaches us that meat eating is not necessary. It isn't necessary for health, because we can sustain an active, healthy life on a vegetarian diet (9). It isn't necessary for dietary variety, because we can do without such variety; indeed, gourmandizing takes us away from life's more important goals. Here Thoreau segues into the more general theme that limiting and disciplining our appetites rather than giving in to them is conducive to the higher human pursuits: "I believe that every man who has ever been earnest to preserve his higher or poetic faculties in the best condition has been particularly inclined to abstain from animal food, and from much food of any kind. . . . The gross feeder is a man in the larva state; and there are whole nations in that condition, nations without fancy or imagination, whose vast abdomens betray them" (214–15).

Does Thoreau overstate his case here? Not *every* earnest man or woman has acted thus. Many writers and artists have indulged mightily in sensual pleasures; others believed that a moderate indulgence in these pleasures, not asceticism, was the proper way to enhance their higher faculties. Thoreau cannot prove either group wrong. Yet just as clearly, "gross feeding" (and even more, hard drinking) has undermined many talented men and women. Furthermore, many of us do fail to explore life's higher or more challenging activities due to our satisfaction with lower ones. We sacrifice the greater to the less. As Americans' waistlines expand and we sacrifice some of our most spectacular wilderness areas to oil and gas development, Thoreau's criticism of "nations whose vast abdomens betray them" rings true.

Still, one can argue against meat eating without embracing asceticism. An alternative position, not developed by Thoreau but readily defended, is that we may avoid causing unnecessary suffering by enjoying a varied and nutritious vegetarian diet. When we consider the health benefits, both self-interest and morality may support vegetarianism.

In "Higher Laws," Thoreau's discussion broadens out into a consideration of some of the most important and vexing issues in virtue ethics. What attitude should we take toward our appetites? Is reason properly "the slave of the passions" (Hume), their absolute master (Kant), or something in between? How should we balance the pursuit of pleasure, moral commitment, and the other components of a good human life? In "Higher Laws," the logic of Thoreau's argument for vegetarianism—his attempt to nail down its justification and strengthen its moral force—leads finally to a very ascetic, demanding, and moralistic position. Yet we cannot take this as his final word on these questions. For elsewhere in *Walden,* Thoreau speaks enthusiastically about physical pleasure and a sensual appreciation of the world. In youth, he writes, he lived "a purely sensual life" and "inhabited my body wholly." We must look at *Walden* as a whole in order to understand Thoreau's conception of the good life and the proper roles of pleasure and sensuality within it. We should also consider whether here, as elsewhere, he is more interested in opening up key virtue ethics questions and pressing his readers to *live* their particular answers, than he is with providing final answers to the questions themselves.

There are ethical dangers in taking too negative a view of our natural appetites, which we can see more clearly if we follow the argument in "Higher Laws" a little further. "I have found repeatedly, of late years, that I cannot fish without falling a little in self-respect," Thoreau writes. "There is unquestionably this instinct in me which belongs to the lower orders of creation" (213–14). Fishing teaches him about fish and the other living things in the pond, as well as about himself. It is sometimes an occasion for meditation or poetic vision. Yet the instinct, beneficial in these ways and perfectly natural, is a "lower" one. Similarly, meat eating is natural; done in moderation, it is pleasurable and does not harm our health. Still, we have ideals that point beyond what feels good to us, and we should follow them: "No man ever followed his genius till it misled him. Though the result were bodily weakness, yet perhaps no one can say that the consequences were to be regretted, for these were a life in conformity to higher principles" (216).

Faced with natural inclinations that he feels must be overcome, Thoreau decries appetite. This impulse finds its logical end in the hope of totally transcending desire: "Who has not sometimes derived an inexpressible satisfaction from his food in which appetite had no share? I have been thrilled to think that I owed a mental perception to the commonly gross sense of taste, that I have been inspired through the palate, that some berries which I had eaten on a hill-side had fed my genius" (218). Here we have the familiar idea of a life of pure thought and appreciation that does not partake of the grossly sensual. It involves a desire to make contact with the world with the finer sense of sight, perhaps, but not with touch. As nearly as possible the *mind* should touch the world, not the body. Thought is good, while appetite is unqualifiedly bad, an inferior (perhaps polluted) form of consciousness: "Not that food which entereth into the mouth defileth a man, but the appetite with which it is eaten. It is neither the quality nor the quantity, but the devotion to sensual savors; when that which is eaten is not a viand to sustain our animal, or inspire our spiritual life, but food for the worms that possess us. . . . The wonder is how . . . you and I, can live this slimy beastly life, eating and drinking" (218).

Precisely here is where Thoreau goes wrong, I think. Rejecting our own animal nature as "slimy and beastly" undermines attempts to locate intrinsic value in the beasts. And saying that "the food that entereth in" is not the point undermines arguments against meat eating based on animals' own intrinsic value. This overemphasizes the importance of our own purity versus the welfare of other beings and overemphasizes mental states at the expense of physical realities. Here, arguably, appetite should be disciplined in the name of morality and the effects of our actions on us should take a back seat to considering their effects on others.

Thoreau goes wrong here, too, in denying his sensual side, simply because it can lead him astray. This is an old mistake of philosophers, who often forget that reason can also lead us astray. Against such views we must remember, first, that it is possible to step back from pleasure and desire by making a reasonable place for them within our lives. Our sensuality need not lead us astray, even though it sometimes does. Second, the senses are important means to knowledge, working with reason to teach us about nature. So an extreme anti-sensualism will likely cohere badly with an environmental ethics, like Thoreau's, that seeks to connect with nature. Third, we should remember that sensual enjoyment is part of living a full and happy human life. Thoreau elsewhere acknowledges this while picking huckleberries, swimming in the pond, or enjoying his rest at the end of a long day hoeing beans.[13]

Thoreau is right to argue against gross sensuality and gluttony and right to ask us to moderate our appetites where appropriate. But we must not dilute moral arguments by making our appetites and not the things affected by them the sole objects of our concern. And we must remember that our nature is partly a physical nature, which is not intrinsically evil and which generates reasonable claims to use and enjoy the world. Like the mythical Antaeus, we too decline when we fail to touch the Earth, not just with our minds, but with our bodies (155). A position that recognizes these points will avoid the implausible otherworldliness of Thoreau's more extreme denials of physical desire and appetite. It is also more likely to win converts to environmentalism.

The Bean Field

The chapter "The Bean-Field" moves beyond a concern to avoid directly killing individual animals to a concern for preserving animal habitat and the wild landscape generally: in contemporary terms, from an animal rights ethics to a true environmental ethics. In order to earn a little cash, Thoreau planted two and a half acres of Emerson's lot in beans. "This was my curious labor all summer," he writes: "to make this portion of the earth's surface, which had yielded only cinquefoil, blackberries, johnswort, and the like, before, sweet wild fruits and pleasant flowers, produce instead this pulse" (155). Once again, as in "Higher Laws," simplification and attentiveness to his experience allow Thoreau to see ethical issues where others might see only questions of economic expediency. For he knows this landscape well, as a locus of beauty and value independent of his own uses. This complicates things.

"What shall I learn of beans or beans of me?" Thoreau continues (it was his *curious* labor all summer). For one thing, he learns the farmer's or gardener's common experience of dividing the world up morally based on its effects on whatever he is trying to grow. "My auxiliaries are the dews and rains which water this dry soil," Thoreau writes, "and what fertility is in the soil itself, which for the most part is lean and effete. My enemies are worms, cool days, and most of all woodchucks. The last have nibbled for me a quarter of an acre clean. But what right had I to oust johnswort and the rest, and break up their ancient herb garden?" (155). Just as "Higher Laws" begins with an anecdote about killing and eating a woodchuck, the first paragraph of "The Bean-Field" mentions conflicts with woodchuck "enemies." The chapter's point becomes clearer when we realize that Thoreau takes this "rights" question seriously—he believes that a woodchuck and a person can each have rights—and that he attempts to answer the question over the course of the chapter.

What justifies appropriating part of the landscape and displacing other intrinsically valuable beings? Perhaps the only convincing answer, once we have fully awakened to the moral issue, is necessity. Thoreau suggests this answer and the Bible's well-known story of how this necessity came about, when he asks early on: "But why should I raise them?" and immediately responds: "Only Heaven knows" (155). It is simply our human lot here on Earth. Thoreau must "produce this pulse" to keep his own pulse going. We are also intrinsically valuable beings, who need to eat to live. This justifies *some* displacement of nature, which can be minimized by taking only what we need.

For those who feel the force of nature's intrinsic value, this is the most important part of a responsible answer. Take what you need, but only what you need. Live simply, so that *nonhuman* others may simply live. Ecologists and conservation biologists have begun to quantify the price that other living beings pay for human consumption. According to one calculation, "humans now control 40 percent of the planet's land-based primary net productivity, that is, the basic plant growth that captures the energy on which everything else depends."[14] The directness of Thoreau's situation—clearing land to plant a crop, trapping out woodchucks he knew personally in order to protect his beans—forced him to confront the issue starkly. By fronting the problem on his own sacred ground, he was more likely to come up with a generous answer. And by attending to his own experience and distinguishing true needs from superfluous wants, he was *able* to answer generously.

"Only Heaven knows" why we must take life in order to live. But if it is natural to do this, it is also natural to put up our hoes sometimes and simply appreciate nature as it is. Working in his little field, Thoreau heard brown thrashers singing in the trees, saw nighthawks circling overhead on sunny afternoons, and disturbed "outlandish"-looking salamanders in their rocky hiding places. "When I paused to lean on my hoe," he writes, "these sounds and sights I heard and saw any where in the row, a part of the inexhaustible entertainment which the country offers" (159–60). This is the moment, when we pause in our own purposive work, when we can appreciate nature's intrinsic value. This is also the moment when we can recognize the higher uses of nature: those of the poet, the painter, the scientist, or any of the others who put aside economic activity for a time in order to know, create, or experience the world in a richer way.

If cultivation leads us to count our yields and value agricultural improvements, pausing in our cultivation may lead to a different sort of accounting: "And, by the way, who estimates the value of the crop which Nature yields in the still wilder fields unimproved by man? The crop of *English* hay is carefully weighed, the moisture calculated, the silicates and the potash; but in all dells and pond holes in the woods and pastures and swamps grows a rich and various crop only unreaped by man" (158). The answer is that very few people as yet appreciate wild nature's intrinsic value. We are too busy about our beans. If we can recognize value outside ourselves, we will be more likely to leave some of wild nature alone. Just as important, we will be able to "reap" this wild "crop" that we have hitherto let go to waste, through the appreciative methods modeled for us in *Walden*.

This suggests a further way in which some human appropriation of nature may be justified. We are the only creatures who can understand and celebrate what we see. Through poetry, art, natural history, and science, we can be nature's storytellers. We can also consciously choose to allow these stories to continue. Even at work in "The Bean-Field," Thoreau notes the plants and animals around him, and in other chapters they rightly take center stage. This, he suggests, justifies his own presence at Walden Pond. Rather than trying to justify the unlimited human appropriation of wild nature by appeal to our superior reason, Thoreau suggests that only such higher uses of reason justify its limited appropriation. Reason in service to unnecessary consumption is no longer a superior faculty and justifies nothing.

John Locke, in a famous attempt to justify the institution of private property, felt compelled to argue for the relative unimportance of nature's contribution to human wealth and sustenance:

> I think it will be but a very modest Computation to say, that of the *Products* of the earth useful to the Life of Man, nine-tenths are the *effects of labour:* nay, if we will rightly estimate things as they come to our use, and cast up the several Expenses about them, what in them is purely owing to *Nature,* and what to *labour,* we shall find, that in most of them ninety-nine hundredths are wholly to be put on the account of *labour.*[15]

This is hardly a "modest computation" and not just because it casually leaves nature's contribution vague by a factor of ten. But in its reliance on a particularly narrow criterion of use to define value, Locke's statement well reflects standard anthropocentric attitudes in his time and ours. We and our work are all-important.[16]

Thoreau, looking out the door of his house and across his bean field on a rainy day, comes to a different conclusion concerning the works of man and nature:

> While I enjoy the friendship of the seasons I trust that nothing can make life a burden to me. The gentle rain which waters my beans and keeps me in the house to-day is not drear and melancholy, but good for me too. Though it prevents my hoeing them, *it is of far more worth than my hoeing.* If it should continue so long as to cause the seeds to rot in the ground and destroy the potatoes in the low lands, it would still be good for the grass on the uplands, and, being good for the grass, it would be good for me. (131, emphasis added)

As our economic lives become more complex and specialized and our surroundings become more managed and humanized, Locke's attitude comes naturally, while Thoreau's recedes. Environmental ethicists may argue for nature's intrinsic value, but the experiential grounding for this belief fades. But when we eat food from our gardens, gather wood for the evening fire on a camping trip, or pick huckleberries, these actions both confirm and symbolize nature's goodness. We then know ourselves as inextricably dependent on nature, regardless of any calculations concerning relative contributions.

From this knowledge should come a belief in the rightness of nature's cycles of work and rest, growth and harvest, Thoreau believes, and happiness and even joy at playing one's part within these cycles. Finally, there should come a feeling of gratitude for the Earth's gifts and a willingness to share them: "We are wont to forget that the sun looks on our cultivated fields and on the prairies and forests without distinction. . . . These beans have results which are not harvested by me. Do they not grow for woodchucks partly? . . . Shall I not rejoice also at the abundance of the weeds whose seeds are the granary of the birds?" (166).

Between Thoreau's view of an intrinsically valuable landscape to be used lovingly and sparingly and a Lockean view of land ownership, with rights but no responsibilities toward the land, there is an unbridgeable gulf. Those holding the former attitude will have little interest in the "improved agriculture" that Thoreau mocks several times in "The Bean-Field" (158, 162); this attitude also leads naturally to efforts to protect some of the landscape from direct economic uses. Locke's more aggressive, entrepreneurial attitude finds its natural limit in a view of nature solely as economic resource, in which we may modify the landscape any way we see fit so as to maximize yields and profits. This purely economic view has been written across hundreds of millions of monocultural acres of America, from the sugarcane fields of Florida and the cornfields of Illinois to the wheat fields of Kansas and the rice fields of California. (Not coincidentally, this view is also writing the family farm out of existence.)

Walden's only sustained invective is Thoreau's remarkably harsh criticism of such greedy, life-denying land ownership. It comes near the end of the chapter "The Ponds," after Thoreau has described Walden and its surrounding ponds in loving detail:

> *Flint's Pond!* Such is the poverty of our nomenclature. What right had the unclean and stupid farmer, whose farm abutted on this sky water, whose shores he has ruthlessly laid bare, to give his name to it? Some skin-flint, who loved better the reflecting surface of a dollar . . . who never *saw* it, who never bathed in it, who never loved it, who never protected it, who never spoke a good word for it, nor thanked God that he had made it . . . who could show no title to it but the deed which a like-minded neighbor or legislature gave him,—him who thought only of its money value; whose presence perchance cursed all the shore. . . . I respect not his labours, his farm where every thing has its price; who would carry the landscape, who would carry his God, to market, if he could get any thing for him; who goes to market *for* his god as it is; on whose farm nothing grows free, whose fields bear no crops, whose meadows no flowers, whose trees no fruits, but dollars; who loves not the beauty of his fruits, whose fruits are not ripe for him till they are turned to dollars. (195–96)

Mr. Flint was not merely a character in *Walden* but a real person, one of Thoreau's neighbors.[17] The damage he did to the forests by his pond was real, too. In an enterprising America, Walden and the adjacent ponds and woods are threatened by just such destructive ownership: by the failure of Locke's descendants to *see* and appreciate nature, while they show a keen awareness of the land's utilitarian and monetary values.

Such examples lead to Thoreau's oracular commandment, "Enjoy the land, but own it not," which he kept throughout his life (208). But ownership itself is not necessarily the problem. After all, Thoreau squatted on Emerson's acreage at Walden Pond, part of which was bought to protect its forests from the ax. Thoreau also tells us that he considered buying the Hollowell Place, an old, rundown farmstead along the Sudbury

River, in order to forestall any "improvements" to it (82–83). Clearly, ownership can be a means to protect land. The key is the owner's attitude and his willingness to put nature's beauty and value above monetary gain. Such ownership is better for the land and better for us, Thoreau insists.

As Thoreau sets the scene, neither Walden Pond nor the surrounding woods have yet been irremediably harmed by his own or his neighbors' economic uses. Thoreau's little bean field itself represents a small, almost insignificant part of the more or less wild landscape adjacent to the pond.[18] His local wood gathering and berrying are even less of a transformative threat than his bean field. This is as it should be, Thoreau believes, for our human economy is but a part of the larger economy of nature. Thoreau shows his respect for this relative balance by setting up a small, benign personal economy in the shadow of life's greater one and by spending as much time studying the latter as sustaining the former. Thoreau's vision is one in which the human economy fits itself to nature's economy rather than vice versa. Both a speculative attitude toward land and wastefulness are equally wrong, in such a view. Thoreau castigates the farmer who shears off his woodlot purely for profit; *he* prefers gathering downed wood or grubbing up stumps to cutting live trees for firewood. Our necessary use of the land should not harm our home.

Because we do belong. In *Walden,* Thoreau emphasizes that he is a native, first by birth, then by conscious choice and genuine effort:

> When I was four years old, as I well remember, I was brought from Boston to this my native town, through these very woods and this field, to the pond. It is one of the oldest scenes stamped on my memory. And now tonight my flute has waked the echoes over that very water. The pines still stand here older than I; or, if some have fallen, I have cooked my supper with their stumps, and a new growth is rising all around, preparing another aspect for new infant eyes. Almost the same johnswort springs from the same perennial root. (155–56)

Thoreau does not say: I am a native, therefore I have a right to do whatever I choose here at the pond. He does not say: human beings are natural, so any way we treat the rest of nature is acceptable. Rather, he has grasped a valuable, living, more-than-human order, linking individual organisms and stretching across the generations. He will strive to remember this in his economic activities and to fit into the landscape rather than changing it to suit himself. That will mean more work for less yield, through not importing fertilizers or hired hands. It will mean resigning a certain number of his beans to the woodchucks. It will mean striving to keep Walden Pond beautiful so that future generations ("new infant eyes") can also enjoy the pond. It will mean taking only what he needs. If he does this, and only if he does this, he may hope that although trees may be cut, new forests will grow up to take their places. He may hope that none of the "original settlers" will be permanently displaced, that "almost the same johnswort" will continue to "spring from the same perennial root."

"The Bean-Field" represents something extraordinary in the history of philosophy. While there had been many discussions of vegetarianism and animal welfare in the Western ethical tradition, I know of no earlier attempt to set proper limits to the human appropriation of wild nature. Nor do I think the deepest of deep ecologists have bettered Thoreau's account of how to act on the recognition of nature's intrinsic value:

Satisfy necessities, avoid luxuries, and provide for a modest comfort in life.

Find happiness in knowing, experiencing, and being with nature, rather than in consuming, owning, or transforming it.

Tell nature's stories to celebrate them and to convince others to allow them to continue.

Here is an environmental ethics that forthrightly asserts values and rights within the nonhuman world. This goes beyond a concern for individual nonhuman animals—radical enough, in Thoreau's time—to a concern for endangered species (the shad), for how much of nature's productivity humans have a right to engross (the forests around Walden), and for preserving the wildness of the overall landscape. These concerns, in turn, are linked to Thoreau's grand goal of furthering genuine human flourishing.

The Ponds

It is striking how often Thoreau, in discussing the good life, specifies human flourishing and excellence in relation to nature. Some of this is quite basic. The simplest messages in *Walden* are to get outside, use your limbs, and delight in your senses. Run, walk, swim, sweat. Taste the sweetness of the year's first huckleberries and feel the juice dribble down your chin. It feels good to plunge into a pond first thing in the morning and WAKE UP, or to float lazily in a boat along its surface, wafted we know not where by the breeze, gazing up at the clouds. It feels good to trundle through the snow on a cold winter night and to warm up by a fire. *Walden* celebrates these simple, sensual experiences in nature (in addition to mining them for literary symbols or knowledge of deeper realities). Of course, "get out of the house" and "eat huckleberries" are not very profound messages. But then, who says ethics should be profound? What we need to know in order to live better lives may indeed by very simple.[19]

At the other end of the spectrum, we have seen how important an enriched experience, the pursuit of knowledge, creative expression, and other intellectual goals are in Thoreau's conception of the good life. Here again, he draws clear connections between knowing nature, cultivating virtue, and enjoying life. *Walden* and Thoreau's journals contain many examples of vivid, accurate observations, descriptions, explanations, and speculations in natural history. These passages show how cultivating the naturalist's virtues may enrich and intensify experience, and how knowledge of nature furthers personal expression. After describing the screech owls and great horned owls living near his cabin, accurately and in detail, Thoreau remarks: "I rejoice that there are owls. Let them do the idiotic and maniacal hooting for men" (125). And indeed they do, embodying moods or providing symbols for aspects of human experience that are difficult to express. Similarly, a playful loon helps him convey the elusive nature of our search for knowledge, while a crumbling sand bank illustrates nature's creativity. Just as nature gives us many new experiences to ponder, so she provides the means to understand them and convey them to others.

Like Emerson's *Nature*—but more practically and with greater emphasis on *wild* nature—*Walden* teaches that nature is our greatest resource. She provides all that humanity needs to flourish, if we will use her wisely.

These themes of love of nature, pursuit of knowledge, personal expression, and enriched experience all come together in *Walden*'s central chapter: "The Ponds." The plural title undoubtedly alludes to Walden's neighbors—Flint's, Goose, and White Ponds—which it also describes. But the title also refers to the many Waldens that Thoreau experiences and describes for us here. We are given the real pond with a certain depth and location, certain species of fish inhabiting it, particular bird species returning at particular times of the year. And we are given various imaginary ponds in the legends of Indians, settlers, Thoreau's contemporaries, and Thoreau himself. We are given the pond's varied inhabitants, from frogs and loons to fishermen and ice cutters. But also the pond as a harmonious whole, each ripple on its surface eventually smoothed out, no matter which unfortunate individual's end it speaks of. We are given the pond in time—personal, historical, mythological—and also a timeless Walden, symbol of nature's beauty, purity, and inexhaustible fecundity. "The Pond in Winter," in "Spring," and indeed in all seasons. The pond as phenomenon (recall the brilliant description of the varied colors of its water) and as thing-in-itself (or as near to this as Thoreau can get; how near is a philosophical puzzle the pond puts to him). The pond as described by the poet, the aesthete, and the scientist; the fisherman, the hunter, and the ice skater; the visitor and the resident; the ascetic, the sensualist, and the home economist.

It is because the pond can be all these things to Thoreau that it is so important to him. At the same time, if it were simply the scene of his own artistry and had no independent existence, it would have been much less important to him than it was. His recognition of this independent existence and his sustained efforts to know and appreciate it set Thoreau apart from the next half-century's flowery "nature fakers," on the one hand, and our own anemic postmodern literati, on the other.

Thoreau's journal recounts again and again his desire for a personal, fulfilling relationship with nature.[20] Walden documents his success in attaining it. "I experienced sometimes," he writes, "that the most sweet and tender, the most innocent and encouraging society may be found in any natural object" (131). Such personal, friendly, gentle acquaintance sustains him through his solitary days at the pond. "The poet," he had written earlier, "is that one who speaks civilly to Nature as a second person."[21]

At Walden, this personal affection and acquaintance broadens to include the river, the forests and fields, and the landscape generally. "The Ponds" gives Thoreau's respectful, loving, imaginative yet accurate description of Walden Pond, the second most fully developed character in Walden. Despite the many views taken and the variety of inhabitants described, Walden is portrayed as a coherent, harmonious whole and repeatedly personified. The central moment in the chapter is Thoreau's thrilled assertion of this personality: its goodness, their relationship, and finally his union with it:

Of all the characters I have known, perhaps Walden wears best, and best pre-serves its purity. . . . It is perennially young, and I may stand and see a swal-low dip apparently to pick an insect from its surface as of yore. It struck me again to-night, as if I had not seen it almost daily for more than twenty years,—Why, here is Walden, the same woodland lake that I discovered so many years ago; where a forest was cut down last winter another is springing up by its shore as lustily as ever; the same thought is welling up to its surface that was then; it is the same liquid joy and happiness to itself and its Maker, ay, and it may be to me. It is the work of a brave man surely, in whom there was no guile! He rounded this water with his hand, deepened and clarified it in his thought, and in his will bequeathed it to Concord. I see by its face that it is visited by the same reflection; and I can almost say, Walden, is it you? (192–93)

He may *almost* use the second person singular to address Walden. Why "almost"? First, because as a naturalist he must love accurately, and a pond is not a unity or a person in the same sense as a human being or a woodchuck. Thoreau, observing the complex interconnections between its individual inhabitants and the creative force "welling up" within it generating these individuals, sees an ecological unity. His per-sonification does justice to this insight and to the beauty he sees and the affection he feels. Yet insofar as the pond as an entity is less unified or integrated than an individual organism, or less singularly directed in its purposes than a conscious actor, its personification is misleading. If Thoreau wants to love *it*, then he must take this into account. Overly insistent personification manifests either ignorance or a failure to appre-ciate the pond for what it really is.[22]

Second, because as a true lover Thoreau recognizes the power and the elusiveness of the lovingly spoken "you." We may describe a pond or a person in any degree of detail we choose, but the loving "you" moves beyond such descriptions. It is a personal *act*. Speaking this loving "you" is never merely an accurate description of our feelings for the beloved, or this, combined with an accurate description of his or her various qualities. Rather it involves an affirmation of value and a taking on of responsibility. It is not something to be said lightly. The beauty of the beloved may call forth an effortless affirmation of our love. But to love well takes effort. Perhaps, then, Thoreau also means to say that he will not rest in a facile adoration of the pond and its myriad pro-ductions, but he will continue to work to know them and publish their glories.

Third, Thoreau hesitates to say "you," because when we love truly, we love the beloved himself or herself and not our own vision. The passage is followed and completed by this short poem:

It is no dream of mine,
To ornament a line;
I cannot come nearer to God and Heaven
Than I live to Walden even.
I am its stony shore,
And the breeze that passes o'er;
In the hollow of my hand
Are its water and its sand,
And its deepest resort
Lies high in my thought.

For all their lyricism, this poem and the preceding passage suggest skepticism concerning the extent to which we can truly know the beloved. The surface of the pond is "visited by the same reflection" as the writer; is this Thoreau's own face reflected in the water? He might wonder to what extent his "reflections" on the nature of the pond are in fact projections of his own interests and desires onto it. Thoreau has visited Walden nearly every day since he was a child, but the many stories of his own he now associates with it may prevent him from seeing *it* and appreciating *its* stories. Hesitation here marks an acceptance that our knowledge of the beloved is never complete or perfect, hence never does him or her full justice, hence can never take his or her place—unless, of course, we are in love with love, like Agathon in Plato's *Symposium*, and more concerned to cultivate our own romantic feelings than to know and do right by our beloved.[23]

These are the ineliminable dangers of love. They all come down, in one way or another, to putting ourselves above the beloved. The great danger for the lover of *nature* is that he will put his own systems and creations above her. The greater his success—in understanding nature or creating new symbolic worlds that move beyond her—the greater the temptation to do so. In the prose passage above, the imagined "Maker" of the pond, who may be God or a logos within nature, is mirrored in the companion poem by Thoreau himself, the author of *Walden*. Both authors "deepen and clarify" the pond "in thought" and "bequeath it to Concord," making it available to Thoreau's neighbors and readers. This juxtaposition proclaims Thoreau's godlike achievement. Knowledge of nature and nature's representation in a work such as *Walden* are divine: true second creations.

Three facts take the sting out of this presumptuous bragging and the anthropocentrism to which it might lead. First, Thoreau backs it up. He really does know Walden Pond and does create a great literary work. Second, as he says elsewhere, he is not bragging for himself but for humanity, and in order to wake up his neighbors. These are possibilities for all of us, which we should actualize and celebrate. Third, and by far the most important, Thoreau believes that the representation of nature may be great *because nature herself is great*. The key words in the poem are:

It is no dream of mine
To ornament a line.

Walden Pond is not the creation of his own fancy, but a glorious reality. This is the source of his own greatness, Thoreau says, even as he insists on that greatness.

Thoreau places these two lines at the heart of the heart of *Walden*, because we are perpetually forgetting them and taking our own physical artifacts and mental constructions for the whole of reality. In a similar way, the plural title "The Ponds" reminds us that we necessarily have two ponds: the pond in the ground and the pond in the book. Each of these fragment in their turn. The complex ecological system of the pond is imperfectly integrated; has uncertain, shifting, and overlapping boundaries; is the loci for many individual "personalities." The writer, strictly speaking, can never tell us *the* story of the pond, but only stories. New experiences and new experiencers create further stories, adding to the storied character of nature. The trick is to embrace this pluralism while remaining committed to the pursuit of truth and the goodness of nature.

Thoreau's position here is based on two axioms: first, that he does know Walden Pond, although that knowledge is incomplete, and second, that its stories are good ones that should be told and allowed to continue. Thoreau hesitates before saying "you" to Walden. But he does say it. He thus enriches his own life and (he may hope) helps preserve Walden's.

In getting to know Walden, Thoreau delved deeper into himself and swam further out into the great stream of life; articulated inchoate ideals and found his own voice; learned something of natural and human history and his own place within them. Thoreau's whole life—from his never-to-be-forgotten childhood exaltations to his mature artistic, scientific, and philosophical achievements—is thus intimately tied to Walden Pond and its environs. His goodness, such as it is, must be a function of *its* goodness. He went to the pond to pursue self-development and artistic achievement, but when he came to write a book about his experience he titled it *Walden*, not *I, Henry* or *A Portrait of the Artist as a Young Naturalist*. In an environmental virtue ethics, human excellence and nature's excellence are necessarily entwined.

Challenges

Walden provides an inspiring account of one man living well in nature. It argues that we will be better, happier people if we take the time to explore and enjoy our environment. The many activities through which we do this will give our lives diversity and interest; performing them will help us develop virtues we might not otherwise develop. In these ways *Walden* suggests the rudiments of an environmental virtue ethics that is noble and challenging, and that makes room for the rest of creation.

There are two main challenges to such an environmental ethics. First, there are those popular ideals that define happiness in terms of increased wealth and economic consumption. Modern life (and especially modern advertising) provides a variety of such ideals, from the crude to the refined. Here a Thoreauvian response is clear: a satisfactory conception of human well-being extends beyond economic consumption and gross physical pleasure to encompass nobler human activities. If we value such higher activities, we must limit those economic activities that undermine them, whether they do so by taking over our lives or by harming the environment that makes all human endeavor possible.

Thoreau's criticisms of gluttony and acquisitiveness, canvassed earlier, are very much in the ancient virtue ethics tradition. As he puts it: "The ancient philosophers, Chinese, Hindoo, Persian, and Greek, were a class than which none has been poorer in outward riches, none so rich in inward" (14). But these criticisms are also strikingly applicable to modern environmental issues. High levels of consumption deplete resources and generate excessive pollution, harming both wild nature and human beings. Americans' preference for gas-hogging suv's translates directly into more asthma attacks and lung cancer deaths and more wildlands sacrificed for petroleum extraction. Here, as elsewhere, "our vast abdomens betray us."

In Thoreau's view, an excessively economic orientation also warps our understanding of the world, literally cutting us off from reality. Farmer Flint cannot see his namesake pond and the many plants and animals inhabiting it—both because he isn't interested and because the pond and its inhabitants are so vividly apparent to him as resources to be used or sold. A wild goose may be a tasty meal in the oven, but not an animal with its own interesting habits or history, or a link with distant lands, or a symbol of spring. A wet meadow may be appreciated as the scene of two rich hay crops per year, but not as the site of dozens of plant species different from the adjacent uplands, or of interesting patterns of ecological succession. Flint does not know these stories and thus he cannot "interweave the thread of the pond's history with his own" (196). The idea wouldn't even occur to him. Rather, he would change the pond in any way that might prove profitable, wrenching its story abruptly out of past natural and cultural history and ending the stories of "old settlers" who do not fit his selfish economic regime.

"The Ponds'" juxtaposition of farmer Flint with naturalist Thoreau suggests a radical choice in how we will relate to nature. By focusing on the gross consumptive uses of nature, we miss out on the higher uses to which it can be put. By focusing on the landscape's monetary value, we miss out on the many other values it may exhibit or provide: aesthetic, spiritual, scientific, historical. Thoreau does not deny such economic values, any more than he seeks to avoid economic life itself. The point is to put economics in its proper, subordinate place, in our lives and on the landscape.

Thoreau revisits these themes in his late manuscript *Wild Fruits,* where the marketing of huckleberries is contrasted with an appreciation of their beauty, knowledge of their natural and cultural history, generosity in dividing them up, and gratitude for their abundance.[24] *Wild Fruits* and Thoreau's other late natural history writings work to specify the correct mix between scientific and experiential knowledge, and between knowledge of nature and its appreciation and celebration. They stick up for those experiences and attitudes toward nature that a market-oriented society is in danger of forgetting. While Thoreau remains as leery of the love of money as in *Walden,* in *Wild Fruits* he seems to take a more positive view of appetite and at least some kinds of consumption, especially compared to the discussion in "Higher Laws." Approached rightly, consumption may be an important avenue for knowledge and pleasant experience. Like *Walden, Wild Fruits* tries to specify a good economics: healthy and uplifting for us, relatively benign in its effects on nature. Such a proper economy must be part of any convincing environmental ethics.

We might call the second main challenge to an environmental virtue ethics the "artificial alternatives" challenge. A skeptic might argue that most if not all of what Thoreau finds in wild nature may also be found in the developed human environment; thus, we need not explore or preserve wild nature. A modern suburbanite can get his exercise by swimming at a health club or jogging around his neighborhood. He can improve his observational and descriptive abilities by painting still lifes or studying architecture. Finally, the critic might conclude, human beings are themselves interesting and diverse, and we should know and celebrate this diversity. Not only can we develop "the naturalist's virtues" without wild nature, but Thoreau and his modern followers may cut themselves off from essential human contact, fail to cultivate the social virtues, and foreclose important avenues for knowledge and happiness.

In answering this challenge, we must first admit that cultivating good personal relationships and appreciating human creativity are indeed essential to our flourishing. We may also admit that any ways we get exercise, uncover diversity, or hone our powers of observation, description, and analysis are better than nothing. Still, failing to know and experience wild nature is a genuine loss, just as a complete insensibility to the history and diversity of human cultures would be. The wild is essentially different from the tame. A person who does not explore wild nature misses out on whole realms of experience, just as a person who never travels or who has friends of only one race or gender misses out. Furthermore, wild nature is the crucible from which culture has emerged. As Thoreau puts it, "our ancestors were savages. The story of Romulus and Remus being suckled by a wolf is not a meaningless fable."[25] To know nothing of wild nature is thus necessarily to fail to properly contextualize human history and our own lives.

Hasty readers sometimes assert that *Walden* advocates a complete withdrawal from human society or the absolute superiority of nature over culture. But Thoreau's acts of settlement, the volumes of Homer, Plato, and Darwin by his bedside, and his return to the village at the end of his stay at the pond point to a different conclusion. Thoreau hopes that nature and culture may complement one another. He believes that the richest human life extracts from each sphere the best of what it offers. "In one direction from my house there was a colony of muskrats in the river meadows," Thoreau writes; "under the grove of elms and buttonwoods in the other horizon was a village of busy men" (167). Both are interesting and have much to teach him. Both deserve to be allowed to flourish. Drain the meadows and drive out the muskrats, and the men, too, will suffer: "A town is saved, not more by the righteous men in it than by the woods and swamps that surround it. A township where one primitive forest waves above while another primitive forest rots below,—such a town is fitted to raise not only corn and potatoes, but poets and philosophers for the coming ages."[26]

What does wild nature specifically have to offer that the human world does not? A larger context in which to put our lives, or to call them into question. New forms of beauty, mostly unseen and unappreciated by human beings. New stories and new kinds of stories, in which consciousness and individual control play a smaller part. Salutary reminders of our own unimportance (you will not break through the ice or get drenched by an unexpected thunderstorm at the mall). The revitalization of dead words and symbols. A sense of hope when our fellow human beings disappoint us.[27]

Just as *Wild Fruits* revisits important economic issues, the posthumously published "Walking" develops *Walden*'s claims for the high value of wild nature. "In Wildness is the preservation of the World," Thoreau crows there. "From the forest and wilderness come the tonics and barks which brace mankind." An ethical vision grounded on human flourishing and saying "yes" to life predisposes its adherents to enjoy—hence to value—vitality in all its manifestations. For "life consists with wildness. The most alive is the wildest. Not yet subdued to man, its presence refreshes him." For Thoreau this vital connection is literal, physical, sensual. "I think that I cannot preserve my health and spirits," he writes, "unless I spend four hours a day at least . . . sauntering through the woods and over the hills and fields." And, he claims, this physical contact with nature revitalizes the mind, stimulating that "uncivilized free and wild thinking" at the heart of all human creativity.[28]

"Walking" gives detailed advice for how to deepen our experience of nature. Yet it would be foolish to focus solely on improving the walker, while failing to preserve the landscape she walks through, just as it would be a mistake to locate all the value in human experience and none in wild nature itself. The magic comes when we bring a lively mind to a vital place. Thoreau made much of the Concord countryside; still, he reflected in his journal:

> I spend a considerable portion of my time observing the habits of the wild animals, my brute neighbors. . . . But when I consider the nobler animals have been exterminated here,—the cougar, panther, lynx, wolverene, wolf, bear, moose, deer, the beaver, the turkey, etc., etc.,—I cannot but feel as if I lived in a tamed, and, as it were, emasculated country. . . . I take infinite pains to know all the phenomena of the spring for instance, thinking that I have here the entire poem, and then, to my chagrin, I hear that it is but an imperfect

copy that I possess and have read, that my ancestors have torn out many of the first leaves and grandest passages, and mutilated it in many places.[29]

The poem is incomplete. Thoreau's efforts—and the efforts of future poets, historians, and scientists—cannot help but suffer. They too will "wish to know an entire heaven and an entire earth," rather than "a maimed and imperfect nature." Again, an environmental virtue ethics cannot separate our excellence and flourishing from nature's.

Similarly, when Thoreau states his wish to "speak a word" for "absolute freedom and wildness, as contrasted with a freedom and culture merely civil," he claims this freedom for himself *and for nature.* "I love even to see the domestic animals reassert their native rights,—any evidence that they have not wholly lost their original wild habits and vigor," he writes, describing with pleasure a neighbor's cow breaking out of its pasture and swimming the river, or a herd of cattle "running about and frisking in unwieldy sport, like huge rats."[30] When it comes to wild creatures, Thoreau realizes, genuine appreciation means suppressing the desire to control or interfere with them and allowing them to flourish in their own ways. But the human urge to control is strong. As Thoreau put it in another journal entry: "The unsympathizing man regards the wildness of some animals, their strangeness to him, as a sin; as if all their virtue consisted in their tamableness." This attitude cuts us off from the stimulating otherness of nature and from appreciating different kinds of order, for "what we call wildness is a civilization other than our own." A hen hawk isn't a chicken, Thoreau writes. "It will not consent to walk in the barn-yard, but it loves to soar above the clouds. It has its own way and is beautiful, when we would fain subject it to our will."[31] Just as a materialistic approach to life cuts us off from reality, so may a rigid, controlling approach. Just as *Walden* shows us how to live economically without economics taking over our lives, so "Walking" suggests ways to know, appreciate, and "saunter" through nature without overwhelming her.[32]

Thoreau's insight, explicitly stated in "Walking," is that human flourishing—at least in America in the second half of the nineteenth century—no longer requires the further taming of nature, but rather the preservation of what wildness remains. "I would not have every man nor every part of a man cultivated, any more than I would have every acre of earth cultivated," he writes. A "true culture" must respect spontaneity as well as order, creativity and daring, as well as safety and good behavior. And it must preserve wildness on the landscape if it hopes to preserve it in our hearts and minds. "To preserve wild animals implies generally the creation of a forest for them to dwell in or resort to. So it is with men."[33]

In the end, those who seek to protect wild nature do so for their own sakes as well as for Nature's:

> Our village life would stagnate if it were not for the unexplored forests and meadows which surround it. We need the tonic of wildness,—to wade sometimes in marshes where the bitterns and the meadow-hen lurk...and the mink crawls with its belly close to the ground. At the same time that we are earnest to explore and learn all things, we require that all things be mysterious and unexplorable, that land and sea be infinitely wild, unsurveyed and unfathomed by us because unfathomable. . . . We need to witness our own limits transgressed, and some life pasturing freely where we never wander. (317–18)

This passage captures the deep paradoxes involved in our attempts to know and experience the wild. Can we "witness...where we never wander"? Study nature without changing it? Move beyond our own concepts and categories to understand things in themselves? But crucially, it also asserts that we *can* draw back and limit our effects on the natural world, and that we can know *its* stories, rather than just projecting our own stories onto it.

Some critics of *Walden*—and of modern wilderness preservation efforts—assert that such judgments depend on specifying a single, sharp distinction between wild and civilized landscapes. Thoreau instead develops a nuanced understanding of this ambiguous yet necessary distinction, as in *Walden*'s description of his "half-civilized" bean field (158) or the comparison of native, cultivated, and naturalized trees in "Wild Apples." Similarly, critics often present a stark dichotomy: either we preserve the whole landscape completely with no human modification, or we use it in any way we see fit (the "do you want us all to live in caves?" argument). Thoreau instead suggests a flexible and contextual way of managing (and *not* managing) a diversity of landscapes. He argues for fully preserving parts of the remote Maine woods as wilderness, rather than settling or developing them (see next section). But he also advocates protecting semi-wild areas closer to home, and an important part of his experiment at the pond involves using the land while minimizing his displacement of wild nature. In short, Thoreau's environmental ethics demands both preservation of wild nature and (genuinely) wise use of natural resources. It is eminently practical.

The proper mix of wildness and culture in an individual or on a landscape are complex questions. One reason to keep some forests uncut and rivers running free is so that the questions themselves do not disappear, as they have for many human beings and many regions of the Earth. We may be comfortable in our villages, but there may be an excess of comfort. We need the physical and intellectual challenges that wild nature sets us. Nature may speak to us *piano* in individual flowers or birds: nonhuman beings who challenge us to know and appreciate them. Or she may thunder *fortissimo* with displays of power and vastness to overwhelm our understanding and destroy our sense of our own importance. Such experiences may lead to love, wonder, horror, awe, reverence—or to the renewed attempt to understand the order that we believe lies behind this complex world. These challenges to our intelligence and imagination strengthen them. Wild nature has been the source of great human achievements in science, poetry, religion, and philosophy. I share Thoreau's doubts that these highest human activities can thrive in its absence.[34]

Conservation

Walden says little about politics, arguing correctly that self-improvement cannot wait for the world to improve. However, any environmental ethics must give both personal and political guidance. I complete this analysis of Thoreau's environmental ethics by treating his conservation philosophy, as pieced together from his journal and later writings.

By Thoreau's time, little had been done in conservation in the United States, beyond some ineffective and haphazardly enforced state laws regulating hunting and fishing. National legislation to limit pollution, set aside land for wildlife, or support any other now-recognized environmental goals did not exist. Rules at any level of government to prevent dumping toxic chemicals in rivers or protect the lungs and limbs of factory workers were many decades in the future. Thoreau's journal entries and published writings show an interest in many of these issues, as John Broderick has documented in his article "Thoreau's Proposals for Legislation." For example, a trip along New Hampshire's dusty, unshaded roads led him to suggest that states landscape their highways and provide roadside parks for the comfort of travelers.[35] Several deaths at railroad crossings prompted him to propose state regulation. A deadly explosion at a nearby powder mill moved him to consider ways to make them safer, and references to the unhealthy and stultifying aspects of factory work are found both in *Walden* and in the journal.

However, Thoreau's greatest conservation concern was undoubtedly the protection of wild nature. He was an early, passionate voice for the preservation of native species and wild landscapes. In *Wild Fruits*, he writes: "What are the natural features which make a township handsome and worth going far to dwell in? A river with its water-falls, meadows, lakes, hills, cliffs, or individual rocks, a forest and single ancient trees. Such things are beautiful. They have a high use which dollars and cents never represent. If the inhabitants of a town were wise they would seek to preserve these things, though at a considerable expense. For such things educate far more than any hired teachers or preachers, or any at present recognized system of school education."[36] As in *Walden*, Thoreau goes on to speak of the role landscape can play in making human history come alive, the fascination and beauty to be found in studying flowers and wild animals, and the simple fun of cross-lot walks and berry-picking parties. "I [can] think of no natural feature which is a greater ornament and treasure to this town than the river," he continues, yet the town, foolishly, "has done nothing to preserve its natural beauty" or its citizens' access to it. Over the next hundred and fifty years, many cities and towns have realized the wisdom of river conservation and made "greenway" preservation the centerpiece of efforts to maintain livable communities.

Thoreau is clear that preserving the river and other natural features demands a public response. "They who laid out the town should have made the river available as a common possession forever," he writes. In the nature of things, private ownership cannot preserve these public goods, since it limits public access and provides no guarantee that the owner will preserve them. As we saw in *Walden*, Flint's Pond may be destroyed by falling into the hands of Flint. "It is for the very reason that some do not care for these things that we need to combine to protect all from the vandalism of a few."[37] As with the river, so the tops of any commanding hills should be held in common, Thoreau believes, both out of respect for nature and to provide the public continued opportunities to take "wider views of the universe."[38] "Think of a mountain top in the township, even to the Indians a sacred place, only accessible through private grounds. A temple, as it were, which you cannot enter without trespassing—nay, the temple itself private property and standing in a man's cow yard." Such areas "should be left unappropriated for modesty and reverence's sake."[39]

While some areas should remain public in perpetuity, Thoreau also advocates regulating private lands to prevent their degradation. Importantly, he would do this not merely for economic ends, but also to preserve beauty, deeming this even more important to human flourishing than preserving secure sources of wood. "It would be worth the while if in each town there were a committee appointed to see that the beauty of the town receive no detriment," Thoreau writes. "There are a few hopeful signs. There is the growing *library,* and then the town does set trees along the highways. But does not the broad landscape itself deserve attention?"[40]

While it might be important to preserve remote wilderness and stunning national parks, in *Wild Fruits* Thoreau focuses on the need to safeguard nature closer to home, in areas accessible to children and busy workers. "I think that each town should have a park, or rather a primitive forest," he writes, "of five hundred or a thousand acres, either in one body or several, where a stick should never be cut for fuel, nor for the navy, nor to make wagons, but stand and decay for higher uses—a common possession forever, for instruction and recreation."[41] Such parks would help preserve the "original settlers" of a township. Just as important, they could teach the inhabitants that not every acre of land should be devoted to economic purposes and that we can "create" beauty and value by leaving things alone—as Thoreau had recognized standing in his bean field.

"All Walden Wood might have been reserved," Thoreau continues, "with Walden in the midst of it, and the Easterbrooks country, an uncultivated area of some four square miles in the north of the town, might have been our huckleberry field," for common worship and enjoyment, rather than personal, pecuniary gain: "If any owners of these tracts are about to leave the world without natural heirs who need or deserve to be especially remembered, they will do wisely to abandon the possession to all mankind. . . . Forget the heathen in foreign parts, and remember the pagans and salvages here." Already in Thoreau's time, Emerson had taken the first steps in this direction, buying land along the pond to protect its trees. The next century and a half witnessed more individual efforts, the creation of Walden Pond State Reservation, and local efforts to set aside extensive adjoining woodlands. In our own time, the Walden Woods Project has stopped incompatible development near the pond, and attempts are ongoing to rehabilitate the adjacent Concord town dump. Those working on such campaigns, at Walden Pond and elsewhere, are Thoreau's true heirs. For as *Walden* reminds us, "to act collectively is according to the spirit of our institutions" (110). It is also the only way to preserve the many public environmental goods on which our happiness depends.

In his excellent summary of the subject, John Broderick states that "almost all" of Thoreau's legislative proposals, with their emphasis on conservation and education, may be described as "welfare proposals" aimed at furthering the culture of his fellow citizens. "Even conservation," Broderick asserts, "is government activity ultimately in behalf of human welfare, for to Thoreau the final importance of nature is in its effect on man. . . . Thoreau believed that government did have legitimate functions, and those functions were not dissimilar to those implied in Emerson's statement in 'Politics': 'the highest end of government is the culture of men.'"[42] This interpretation is plausible; since Thoreau was committed to a virtue ethics centered on self-culture, it makes sense that his political proposals should build on these well-developed, deeply held ethical beliefs. Thoreau's conservation proposals are not grounded on a narrow view of human welfare but on an expansive view, however, and on a comprehensive concern for the welfare of the natural world around him. This becomes clearer when we consider the full scope of his proposals for protecting nature.

Although Thoreau argues for preserving wild nature close to home, he does not make the mistake of assuming that preserving small parks and woodlots will fully preserve wild nature. "No one has yet described for me the difference between that wild forest which occupied our oldest townships, and the tame one which I find there to-day," Thoreau writes in *The Maine Woods*. "It is a difference which would be worth attending to" for what it tells us of natural and cultural history. Primitive "old-growth" forests have a different structure than regenerated second- and third-growth stands, he notes. They are darker and damper. They support a somewhat different understory flora. Some animals cannot survive outside large, relatively undisturbed wilderness areas, while long-settled areas tend to lose much of their native fauna. "Those Maine woods differ essentially from ours," Thoreau concludes. They are nature's creation, not man's, and fully preserve nature's beauty, diversity, and wildness.[43]

The Maine woods also give Thoreau a slight case of homesickness and remind him of what he values in Concord's tamer, pastoral landscape.[44] Still, he believes much will be lost if some fully wild areas are not preserved. Just as some species of wild orchids will not survive cultivation, so too with certain human experiences, moods, and artistic achievements: "Not only for strength, but for beauty, the poet must, from time to time, travel the logger's path and the Indian's trail, to drink at some new and more bracing fountain of the Muses, far in the recesses of the wilderness."[45] For nature's sake and for our own, true wilderness needs to be preserved.

Such reflections lead Thoreau to make one of the earliest calls for national parks, and still one of the most stirring:

> The kings of England formerly had their forests "to hold the king's game," for sport or food, sometimes destroying villages to create or extend them; and I think that they were impelled by a true instinct. Why should not we, who have renounced the king's authority, have our national preserves, where no villages need be destroyed, in which the bear and panther, and some even of the hunter race, may still exist, and not be "civilized off the face of the earth,"—our forests, not to hold the king's game merely, but to hold and preserve the king himself also, the lord of creation,—not for idle sport or food, but for inspiration and our own true recreation? or shall we, like villains, grub them all up, poaching on our own national domains?[46]

In Maine, Thoreau says, such a preserve would protect the full complement of native species and keep the land wild. For "these are not the artificial forests of an English king—a royal preserve merely. Here prevail no forest laws, but those of nature."[47] In some places, we should let nature, not people, write the stories on the land.

Once again, Thoreau was prescient. In the years following the Civil War, the United States designated Yellowstone and Yosemite as our first two national parks, with many more following in the twentieth century. In 1964, Congress passed the first Wilderness Act, ensuring that parts of our national parks, national forests, and other federal lands will remain wild and relatively unmodified. National parks have proven themselves to be one of America's best and most influential ideas, with the world's nations setting up parks and wilderness areas on all seven continents. Today, just as the Walden Woods Project works to preserve wild nature close to Thoreau's home, the environmental group RESTORE: The North Woods continues Thoreau's advocacy for New England wilderness. RESTORE proposes the creation of a 3.2 million-acre Maine Woods National Preserve, centered on Mount Katahdin and the lakes and rivers Thoreau traversed on his three visits to Maine. Other groups promote similar wilderness preservation and "rewilding" efforts throughout America and the world.

In addition to preserving wild areas, Thoreau also calls for a more enlightened management of rural landscapes used to produce fuel, fodder, and agricultural crops. Thoreau's late natural history writings draw out some of the management implications of his ecological studies.

Farmers commonly shoot squirrels as vermin, he notes in *The Dispersion of Seeds,* but his own observations show that squirrels are helping to plant future forests. They are valuable both to the calculating owner, who is saved the trouble and expense of planting an oak wood, and to those who can appreciate nature's economy in its own right. A wood-lot owner intent on maximizing profit may do best by "a judicious letting Nature alone," allowing the squirrels and winds to replant, rather than acting in ignorance of the likely effects of his actions. A wood-lot owner with an interest in natural history or with transcendentalist leanings may act with even greater restraint, cutting less, or not at all, in deference to these ongoing stories.[48]

Thoreau's discussion of proper forest management in his later writings is surprisingly hardheaded, accepting that some owners' primary interest is profit. He also discusses the active management of forests in positive terms. "Why not control our own woods and destiny more?" he asks, rather than blundering along in ignorance as we have been.[49] On the other hand, he is still convinced that beauty is the most valuable crop that human beings can take from a forest, although it is largely unreaped. He wants to leave some areas wild and unmanaged. He would not countenance a radical simplification of the landscape in order to increase productivity, since nature creates diversity and human beings thrive on it. Interestingly, Thoreau believes that even utilitarian forestry considerations argue for retaining a certain amount of diversity in the woods. One scholar notes that this position anticipated by nearly 150 years today's "New Forestry," which rejects single-species monocultures in favor of a more diverse and hence resilient forest.[50]

Thoreau's conservation ideal, as we might reconstruct it from these later writings, would perhaps be to work with nature to provide enough of what we need—wood for our fires, money to send the children to college—while ensuring that nature's diversity and beauty remain. If we don't cut some wood, we will freeze to death. But if we destroy our woods, then our children's education is useless. "Let me lead you back into your wood-lots again," Thoreau begins the essay "Succession of Forest Trees."[51] He wants his neighbors to walk into the woods with more insight and interest, knowing and appreciating their stories. He wants them to return to their woodlots, not to better calculate how many cords of wood they may get out of them, but to reap a harvest of knowledge and beauty. In the end, despite his high valuation of freedom, Thoreau is willing to curtail human independence in order to protect forests. His final words on management (and the final sentence of *The Dispersion of*

Seeds) are "forest wardens should be appointed by the town—overseers of poor husbandmen."[52]

Of course, preserving natural areas and regulating land use are only part of a comprehensive conservation philosophy. This must also include reining in industrial pollution, attending to the health and beauty of cities and towns, limiting population growth and economic consumption, and much more besides. Some of this Thoreau anticipated, some he did not. But in general, Thoreau's virtue ethics well supports a comprehensive environmentalism. Like most modern environmentalists, Thoreau believes more intelligent lifestyles will be better for us and better for the Earth.

Politics

Any ethics presupposes a politics. A conception of the good life for individuals presupposes notions of a good community: one that will allow, encourage, or force its citizens to live such lives. Thoreau as practical philosopher focuses on our individual choices; there is no political equivalent to *Walden*. However, we can recover elements of a vision of a just social order scattered throughout his writings. Part of this vision involves guaranteeing basic rights to all citizens. The great failure in this regard during Thoreau's lifetime, of course, was slavery, and this part of his ideal is argued for clearly and eloquently in his anti-slavery writings.

Thoreau's egalitarian commitment to basic political rights is undeniable. At the same time, he lectured and wrote on this topic only rarely, usually in response to some political crisis. Furthermore, Thoreau repeatedly expresses disgust with conventional politics and anger that politics has intruded into what he considers his proper affairs. Many commentators cannot stomach this contempt for politics. Thoreau—recognized in his own time as a strong abolitionist voice, acknowledged by Gandhi and King as an important influence on their political philosophies—has faired surprisingly badly at the hands of political scientists and political historians.[1] Arguably, however, Thoreau's disgust with the politics of his day was justified. In what follows, I discuss Thoreau's struggles to articulate a positive citizenship to complement his philosophy of personal flourishing. This effort may hold lessons for those engaged in similar struggles today.

If anti-slavery was one half of Thoreau's political message, the other half was anti-mammonism. Basic rights are necessary, but not sufficient, for a just political order. For once we have secured our rights and freedoms, there remains the question of what sort of individual and communal goals we will embrace. Freedom is an important goal, but we may dishonor freedom through personal swinishness as well as through unjust actions toward others.

Thoreau saw his fellow citizens adopting moneymaking and material wealth as their main objectives. He criticized this throughout his life, and ever more vociferously as time went on. But what *positive* political goals might Americans embrace, besides piling up unnecessary wealth? In "Life without Principle," Thoreau proposes human culture and many of the same goals he had already argued for in specifying the good life in *Walden:* fraternity, reverence, creativity, the pursuit of knowledge. He does not translate this into a full political platform, but here and elsewhere Thoreau does offer concrete political proposals (as we saw in our discussion of conservation). Perhaps the key question is whether Thoreau suggests a robust, comprehensive, achievable political ideal: a vision of social flourishing to accompany his keen sense of social degradation. Is a virtue politics possible—or just a virtuous retreat from politics?

Anti-slavery

Thoreau published three substantial anti-slavery works at five-year intervals: "Resistance to Civil Government" (1849), "Slavery in Massachusetts" (1854), and "A Plea for Captain John Brown" (1859).[2] All three denounce slavery and insist that Americans have a moral duty to actively oppose it. Their tone becomes increasingly strident, in line with the political temper of the times.

These pieces contain no detailed discussion of the morality of slavery itself. All humane, thinking persons, Thoreau believes, know slavery is wrong. Some wrongs are so egregious that we are more likely to shudder than argue against them.[3] The proper response may be to heap scorn on their perpetrators and abettors, as when Thoreau speaks of trampling the Fugitive Slave Law in the dust, "and Webster, its maker, with it, like the dirt-bug and its ball."[4]

We need not argue the morality of slavery. The real moral question slavery poses to conscientious Americans is what to do in response to such gross injustice. Thoreau's answer is simple: "I cannot for an instant recognize that political organization as *my* government which is the *slave's* government also."[5] No matter how well the government promotes the interests of the majority, such injustice toward a helpless minority cannot be tolerated. No matter how well the government protects his own interests, Thoreau cannot accept these benefits with a clean conscience. The political connection implicates him in injustice and covers him in shame. Therefore, he asserts, morality demands that he sever the connection—or at least directly and publicly denounce the injustice and challenge that political authority his government itself has undermined.

As in his discussions of personal morality in *Walden,* Thoreau insisted that deeds accompany words. He refused to pay his poll tax for several years, daring the state to imprison him. He wrote and lectured against slavery and invited abolitionists to speak to the Concord Lyceum. He and his family hid runaway slaves and helped them on to Canada, as part of the Underground Railroad. After 1850, such acts of civil disobedience were punishable as felonies under federal law.[6]

While his later writings appeal directly to Christian and patriotic ideals to condemn slavery and prod his fellow citizens into action, Thoreau's arguments in the more philosophical "Resistance" are essentially transcendental or Kantian. Presupposing the humanity of the slave, Thoreau argues the *in*humanity of free citizens who do not recognize the demands of conscience and justice. "Must the citizen ever for a moment, or in the least degree, resign his conscience to the legislator?" he asks rhetorically. "Why has every man a conscience, then?"[7] It is precisely our willingness to accept timeworn injustices that allows them to continue: "the broadest and most prevalent error requires the most disinterested virtue to sustain it."[8] But when we fail to hold ourselves, our neighbors, or our governments to the dictates of morality, we sacrifice our inherent dignity as human beings. "The mass of men serve the State thus, not as men mainly, but as machines, with their bodies," Thoreau believes. "In most cases there is no free exercise whatever of the judgment or of the moral sense; but they put themselves on a level with wood and earth and stones. . . . Such command no more respect than men of straw, or a lump of dirt. They have the same sort of worth only as horses and dogs," to be used by others.[9] Conscience and the freedom to act upon it are what separate us from animals or mere things (like Kant, Thoreau *here* makes no moral distinction between the two). Acting morally ennobles us; failing to act morally soils and dehumanizes us. That is why free citizens should resist slavery.

Again and again, Thoreau asserts the distinctness and superiority of the moral law to all positive law.[10] Again and again, he returns to the point that *principle*—not personal expediency, not economic profit, not legal consistency—demands that we act to right the injustices in our midst. "They who have been bred in the school of politics fail now and always to face the [moral] facts," he complains in "Slavery in Massachusetts": "The judges and lawyers . . . consider, not whether the Fugitive Slave Law is right, but whether it is what they call *constitutional*. Is virtue constitutional, or vice? Is equity constitutional, or iniquity? In important moral and vital questions like this, it is just as impertinent to ask whether a law is constitutional or not, as to ask whether it is profitable or not."[11] We need not assume that Thoreau wants to completely moralize politics (recall the sincere paeans to limited government that open and close "Resistance"). But some political questions rise to the level of issues of justice and demand *moral* answers from governments and citizens alike. The United States Congress and Supreme Court refuse the slave justice. Let the citizen refuse to pay his taxes, then, or storm the jails where fugitive slaves are held. Let the jailor, the tax collector, and the judge resign their commissions, rather than administer injustice; let the state of Massachusetts dissolve its union with Virginia and the Carolinas, rather than become their unjust accomplice.

Thoreau considers and rejects the possibility that he might take a less demanding position toward his government and his fellow citizens. "If I could convince myself that I have any right to be satisfied with men as they are," he writes, "and to treat them accordingly, and not according, in some respects, to my requisitions and expectations of what they and I ought to be, then . . . I should endeavor to be satisfied with things as they are."[12] But he has no such right. Ethics does not turn on what is, but on what ought to be the case. Ethics, in an imperfect world, necessarily includes moments when we refuse to accept the way things are and fight to change them.

Thoreau rounds out his Kantian argument in "Resistance" with a transcendental definition of human freedom. Free will and freedom of conscience constitute true human freedom, which is our greatest good.[13] Conscience and will are superior to brute force, not in the sense of being stronger here in the world, in all cases, but in the sense of being *better* in all cases.[14] While Kant describes this in metaphysical terms in his ethical treatises, Thoreau dramatizes it in "Resistance," mocking the state that imprisoned him: "As they could not reach me, they had resolved to punish my body; just as boys, if they cannot come at some person against whom they have a spite, will abuse his dog. . . . Thus the State never intentionally confronts a man's sense, intellectual or moral, but only his body, his senses. It is not armed with superior wit or honesty, but with superior physical strength."[15] In Thoreau's view, the greatest danger to human freedom is not unjust imprisonment, but our own cowardly acquiescence in injustice, from fear that we might be imprisoned or have our property confiscated. In the face of these threats, Thoreau is defiant: "I was not born to be forced. I will breathe after my own fashion. Let us see who is the strongest. What force has a multitude? They only can force me who obey a higher law than I. They force me to become like themselves."[16] We see here again the Kantian ideas that morality comes to each of us individually, as a "higher law" addressed directly to conscience, and that obeying it is no limitation on human freedom, but rather freedom's prerequisite.

While Kant sought to make metaphysical sense of such constrained, lawful freedom and freely admitted that it could neither be fully explained nor definitely identified here in the world, Thoreau, with his more practical bent, dramatizes action from moral freedom and insists that he will personally uphold this freedom in his own life. Philosophy needs both sorts of efforts, I believe. Thoreau's narrative serves to emphasize the need for personal commitment in ethics. As Gandhi noted appreciatively, Thoreau "taught nothing he was not prepared to practice himself."[17]

Here we come to Thoreau's main claim to fame as a political thinker: his pathbreaking discussion of civil disobedience. That discussion, originally printed in an obscure literary journal where it produced "scarcely a ripple of interest," has had wide political impact.[18] Mohandas Gandhi told a colleague that "Resistance" "contained the essence of his political philosophy, not only as India's struggle related to the British, but as to his own views of the [general] relation of citizens to government." During the crucial months that Gandhi first put nonviolent resistance into practice in South Africa, he recommended study of Thoreau to his associates and translated portions of Thoreau's essay for readers of his newspaper *Indian Opinion*.[19] Martin Luther King Jr., too, cited Thoreau as an inspiration, describing "Resistance" as his "first intellectual contact with the theory of nonviolent resistance." In *Stride toward Freedom*, King wrote that Thoreau helped him clarify the purpose and moral legitimacy of the Montgomery bus boycott.[20] Both Gandhi and King quoted Thoreau while addressing their followers from prison.

In civil disobedience, Thoreau provided what has proven to be a powerful technique for bringing morality into politics. It is a means for the individual conscientious citizen to act, in the face of mass indifference or political stalemate. At the same time, it provides a plausible mechanism to make such individual actions politically effective. Despite the comic aspects of his night in jail (fully acknowledged in "Resistance") Thoreau demonstrates in some detail how such an appeal to conscience might work: an individual acting on principle and willing to endure suffering or injustice himself, because he is fortified by principle; publicizing that action in a way that clearly frames the moral issues involved; thus forcing government agents and his fellow citizens to consider their own complicity in injustice; and reminding all concerned that the status quo is unacceptable, by personally refusing to accept it. "Resistance" suggests how a dramatic gesture may get people's attention and open up space to redefine a political situation. It shows how such gestures may widen our sense of the possible or change our view of action itself. Perhaps others are acting in my name; perhaps inaction is also a moral choice, with important consequences.

In this way, appeal to principle, often dismissed as impractical, may instead be the most practical means to move forward politically. Purity of motives, often derided in the political realm, may strengthen that appeal. In appealing to people's consciences, we ask them to commit, or recommit, to ideals of justice that elevate themselves and society. In the face of the seeming insignificance of the individual, which lends itself so readily to political indifference or despair, Thoreau insists on the necessity and value of individual action. "We are accustomed to say that the mass of men are unprepared," he says, "but improvement is slow, because the few are not materially wiser or better than the many. It is not so important that many should be as good as you, as that there be some absolute goodness somewhere; for that will leaven the whole lump."[21]

While "Resistance" focuses on individual action, Thoreau also contemplates mass civil disobedience and speculates that this might prove a means to defeat injustice without violence: "If the alternative is to keep all just men in prison, or give up war and slavery, the State will not hesitate which to choose. If a thousand men were not to pay their tax-bills this year, that would not be a violent and bloody measure, as it would be to pay them, and enable the State to commit violence and shed innocent blood. This is, in fact, the definition of a peaceable revolution, if any such is possible."[22] Gandhi and King would make nonviolence and mass action central to their political campaigns, developing civil disobedience into an important political tactic and a major force for good in the world.

Thoreau's treatment of civil disobedience can be criticized on several counts. He sometimes seems to confuse civil disobedience as a political tool with civil disobedience as a means to personal purity. He sometimes seems intent on defining a minimal activism that will settle his political accounts once and for all, so that he can attend to more important things. But these lapses are excusable, I think, since they grow directly out of Thoreau's attempt to moralize politics and cannot be completely severed from that attempt.

The pursuit of purity can be pushed too far, but it is part of Thoreau's experience and the experience of others who feel the horror of slavery and know they must respond to it. The desire to keep ourselves and our country morally pure—free of the smell of slavery, "offensive to all healthy nostrils"—is necessarily part of the call to action.[23] Morality necessarily involves action from principle, which brings something radically new and incomparably great into the world, Thoreau believes. "Action from principle,—the perception and the performance of right, —changes things and relations; it is essentially revolutionary, and does not consist wholly with any thing which was. It not only divides states and churches, it divides families; aye, it divides the *individual*, separating the diabolical in him from the divine."[24] Knowing of the civil war to come, we may shudder reading the words "divide states," "divide families." Yet such a will to purity—to separate right from wrong, within our own hearts and lives—lies at the center of morality and is essential to moral and political progress. The trick is to keep our desire to escape this world's impurity from driving us away from politics altogether.

A similar defense may be given for Thoreau's attempts to define a minimal political responsibility. In "Resistance," he gives two answers to the question: when *must* a citizen act to right injustice? First, we must act when an injustice is sufficiently grievous: when, like slavery, it dehumanizes or destroys its victims. Second and at an absolute minimum, we must cease all actions that support such injustice:

> It is not a man's duty, as a matter of course, to devote himself to the eradication of any, even the most enormous wrong; he may still properly have other concerns to engage him; but it is his duty, at least, to wash his hands of it; and, if he gives it no thought longer, not to give it practically his support. If I devote myself to other pursuits and contemplations, I must first see, at least, that I do not pursue them sitting upon another man's shoulders. I must get off him first, that he may pursue his contemplations too.[25]

The two "at leasts" in this key passage suggest that Thoreau would acknowledge further political duties; also, that he might want to specify positive political goals in addition to such negative duties. Yet it makes sense to specify such a minimum, both because some citizens, like Thoreau, recognize legitimate political duties while desiring to keep their political activity to a minimum, and because focusing on minimum moral requirements emphasizes their imperative nature. If justice requires anything, Thoreau says in effect, it requires that we resist slavery.

So Thoreau can meet the preceding criticisms. Where he stumbles badly, however, is in his dismissal of more conventional political activities—voting, petitioning the authorities, organizing new political parties—that may also be essential to challenging injustice:

> All voting is a sort of gaming, like chequers or backgammon, with a slight moral tinge to it, a playing with right and wrong, with moral questions. . . .

Even voting *for the right* is *doing* nothing for it. It is only expressing to men feebly your desire that it should prevail.

I hear of a convention to be held at Baltimore, or elsewhere, for the selection of a candidate for the Presidency . . . but I think, what is it to any independent, intelligent, and respectable man what decision they may come to?[26]

Thoreau's great accomplishment was to put an appeal to conscience at the heart of politics. But once we move beyond the village level, such appeals can only effect real political change by changing laws and policies (as well as hearts and minds). To achieve *this*, as Gandhi and King realized, civil disobedience must be combined with more conventional political activities. Moral action, performed "once and for all," must be combined with the incrementalism and horse-trading of politics. Righteous individuals must combine to form mass movements with their coordinated actions, their leaders and followers. Politics must be moralized—but morality cannot replace politics. Thoreau, arch-individualist, finds this hard to accept.

Lurking always within Thoreau's political writings is the possibility of radical separation. "Resistance" wavers between the goals of effectively challenging injustice and honorably resigning from an unjust world. "What should concern Massachusetts is not the Nebraska Bill, nor the Fugitive Slave Bill, but her own slaveholding and servility," Thoreau thunders in "Slavery in Massachusetts." "Let the State dissolve her union with the slaveholder. . . . Let each inhabitant of the State dissolve his union with her, as long as she delays to do her duty."[27] But disunion would not have solved the problem of slavery *for the slaves*. Nor would the permanent retirement from politics of its most conscientious citizens benefit society.

While Thoreau, Gandhi, and King all emphasized appeals to conscience and principle, only the latter two fully committed to working for justice within a political process. Gandhi and King accepted no separation between themselves and their fellow citizens, even in theory. Among other things, this meant a will to see their political goals through to the end. This commitment involved setting aside personal salvation and working for the good of society, or, perhaps, finding their own salvation in the salvation of their countrymen or race. In the end, of course, it also meant martyrdom for Gandhi, King, and many of their followers. We rightfully honor the men and women who made such sacrifices, while almost all of us decline to follow their examples. And I do not believe that morality *requires* individuals to take on such demanding political commitments.

For these reasons, I am less inclined to blame Thoreau for not becoming a political activist, a role for which he was temperamentally unsuited, than to praise him for providing these great political leaders with a tool to lead more effectively. Civil disobedience has proven a powerful force for justice in the world—as Thoreau insisted it could be.

Citizenship

Two recent, excellent studies of Thoreau's political philosophy locate his main political contributions squarely within his life as a writer. Robert Pepperman Taylor contends that "Thoreau speaks to us as a critic whose primary concerns are the health of the democratic community we profess to value and the integrity of the citizenry upon which any decent democratic community must be built."[28] From this perspective, Taylor shows, virtually all of Thoreau's writings are deeply political, focused on articulating our highest ideals and calling us to live up to them. *A Week on the Concord and Merrimack Rivers* is no mere river jaunt, but a deep exploration of the meaning of American history, including an attempt to come to terms with its violence and injustice. *Cape Cod* is a personal meditation on death, but also on the nature of true charity. *The Maine Woods* chronicles wilderness flora and fauna but also considers how the virtues of the Indian and frontiersman may be preserved in a more settled America.

Jane Bennett emphasizes Thoreau's "distaste for the identity of citizen" and for conventional politics. "I read Thoreau's withholding of taxes as a means toward his more valued end of cultivating individuality," she writes, not "as indicative of a commitment to public service."[29] Bennett locates Thoreau's specifically political contribution as educating his readers in particular "techniques of self-creation" and in challenging them to live consciously and well. The focus is on teaching individuals, one at a time, how to *be* individuals—the only path to true reform. This interpretation finds plenty of support in Thoreau's writings. Even in "Slavery in Massachusetts," a call to action, he wrote: "The fate of the country does not depend on what kind of paper you drop into the ballot-box once a year, but on what kind of man you drop from your chamber into the street every morning."[30]

Thoreau deserves the political credit given him by Taylor and Bennett for his roles as social critic and educator. Still, we should not let these literary contributions obscure his attempt to specify a more immediately engaged citizenship. This might work as an analysis of Thoreau's life, but not of his practical philosophy, which, it would seem, must make a proper place for a citizenship that is open to those who do not have great literary abilities. In his anti-slavery writings as in *Walden*, Thoreau returns repeatedly to the need for action. He explicitly rejects the notion that writing or talking about justice, however eloquently, can take the place of acting to secure it.

Thoreau grapples with specifying a proper, active citizenship but finds grave difficulties in doing so. First, there is his disgust and exasperation with his fellow citizens, repeatedly expressed in his anti-slavery writings. Thoreau believes that the acceptance of slavery shows a sickness deeply embedded in the American polity, and not merely in the South. Think of a country that buys and sells men and women, like cattle, in front of its senate chamber, he remarks in *Walden* (171). Or the "complete servility" of the popular press in reporting the Anthony Burns affair.[31] Or a Massachusetts governor sending one of the commonwealth's own citizens back into slavery, then bragging about it to his political cronies. America's laws and courts, politicians, press, and public all bring disgrace upon her, Thoreau believes.

We tend to look back on the abolitionist movement and later civil rights struggles as noble chapters in our nation's history, helping to fulfill the promise of America. But we can also see the need for them as evidence of Americans' essential ignobility. From within the fray, Thoreau feels himself soiled by having to argue the slavery issue. What sort of people are these among whom I live? he asks. The honest answer is: men who put money and their own self-interest above justice and humanity (or whose inertia allows other men to do so, in their name). We may call our fellow citizens to higher ideals, but in fighting slavery in the political arena, a person must lower himself in order to talk to the dull, unconcerned majority. Furthermore, there is small hope that he will be successful in this; indeed, all the evidence during the late 1840s and 1850s pointed in the other direction. As abolitionism gained ground as a mainstream political movement, the nation's politicians moved toward further accommodation with slavery, abandoning the Missouri Compromise and passing the Fugitive Slave Act.

Hence Thoreau's desire to protest slavery in a way that emphasizes his separation from the polity. Toward the end of "Resistance," he writes: "When I came out of prison . . . I saw yet more distinctly the State in which I lived. I saw to what extent the people among whom I lived could be trusted as good neighbors and friends; that their friendship was for summer weather only; that they did not greatly purpose to do right; that they were a distinct race from me by their prejudices and superstitions."[32] This gets to the heart of the problem. Not only does Thoreau want to separate himself from his neighbors, but to play the only decent role left him in society he believes he has to do so. Nor is this just one man's obstinacy or perfectionism. If we hold ourselves and our fellow citizens to high moral standards—and that we should is axiomatic for Thoreau—we are bound to accentuate this separation.

In addition to the degradation and apparent uselessness of mainstream political involvement, a further reason for abstaining from politics is Thoreau's desire to pursue his own projects of self-improvement, literary creation, and scientific study. In "Resistance," he insists that a man may legitimately have "other concerns" to engage him besides righting the world's wrongs. In "Slavery in Massachusetts," after condemning the politicians for their injustice to the downtrodden slave, he further damns them for taking him away from his proper affairs: "I feel that, to some extent, the State has fatally interfered with my lawful business. It has not only interrupted me in my passage through Court street on errands of trade, but it has interrupted me and every man on his onward and upward path, on which he had trusted soon to leave Court street far behind. What right had it to remind me of Court street?"[33] Commentators often criticize Thoreau for bringing such personal, "selfish" concerns into political discussions, but this begs the very question at issue: What responsibility do we have to involve ourselves in politics? The problem is especially acute when a person feels some political responsibility, but there is no clear way to affect the issue at hand, and that person has important personal projects where she actually can achieve some success. Looking backward, we clearly see that abolishing slavery was infinitely more important than Henry Thoreau saving his own soul or reworking the manuscript of *Walden*. Yet the further inference, that his sporadic anti-slavery efforts had a higher value than his more determined personal projects, is invalid, since it isn't clear that his anti-slavery work had any important effect on the course of events, while his personal and literary triumphs are undeniable. Nor are *we* willing to place a higher value on political action in our own lives. Great injustices and suffering exist in the world today. What have you done to alleviate them?

What *must* we do politically? We saw Thoreau give one plausible answer to this question in "Resistance," where he defined a minimal political responsibility. But Thoreau's recurrent attention to politics and to the meaning of America suggests a wider definition of political responsibility, or at least a wider political concern. In fact, he struggles to balance the personal and the political, and to balance political action with a more detached, intellectual criticism. If Thoreau feels confident in his decision to live a largely private life, an ethical justification of this decision eludes him. The fact that he repeatedly feels the need to justify it (and that those justifications seem so defensive) is suggestive.[34]

This is an important, difficult issue that should not be argued away. In his recent study, Robert Taylor ridicules Thoreau's concern for self-development as "narcissistic," "egoistic," "morally perfectionist," "self-centered," "self-righteous," and "vain."[35] He regrets that self-concern takes him away from his "original project" of social criticism and reform. But for Thoreau, the whole point of a just political order is to encourage self-development and human creativity. Far from a distraction from politics, *these are its ultimate goals*. Another scholar writes convincingly of Thoreau's wish "to redirect the state and its citizens, to shift the goal of politics from the purpose of commerce and the machine to the goal of human development."[36] But if this is so, self-development cannot be a distraction from our true political goals, merely another way—and often the best way—of pursuing them. And when we are forced to fight against greed and rank injustice, rather than get on with life's higher pursuits, some anger toward our fellow citizens seems justified. If we have a responsibility to lift them up, they in turn have a responsibility not to drag us down.

Yet another factor frustrating Thoreau's attempts to specify a proper citizenship is simply the size of the modern nation-state. Thoreau arguably carved out a local citizenship for himself in Concord, based on face-to-face encounters and on educating his fellow citizens. He was a life-long, dues-paying member of the Concord Lyceum: serving several terms as secretary and curator, arranging the annual lecture series, and sometimes putting speakers up at his house. When we add Thoreau's huckleberry parties, his natural history discussions with his neighbors, and his work as official town surveyor, we see a quite civically engaged man—at the local level.

But slavery wasn't going to be defeated at the local level. Nor are most of our important political issues decided there today (America's population stood around 40 million when Thoreau died; it is 294 million and rapidly increasing as this book goes to press). "Resistance" presents civil disobedience as a technique for *individual* action to effect political change on important issues, but the sheer size of the American polity precludes this possibility; in practice, civil disobedience has shown itself an effective tool only in conjunction with large political movements. We feel a justified frustration, contemplating the relative impotence of individual citizens in an indirect democracy. Along with Thoreau, we suspect that our "noblest faculties" and higher ideals are rarely represented in our representative democracy.[37] Even if Thoreau had specified an engaged, local citizenship—and he nowhere does, although he did *live* it, to a degree—these issues of scale would remain.

Thoreau does not provide a comprehensive answer to these problems of modern citizenship, and this is a weakness of his practical philosophy as a whole. But he does articulate aspects of our frustration with modern citizenship that any practical philosophy must address.

Just as *Walden* presents an individual life dedicated to higher goals, we might imagine a whole society so dedicated. This suggests an ideal of political involvement that is aimed at the good of society *and* is uplifting and enjoyable to political participants. Aristotle, who defined human beings as social animals, believed that political involvement was not merely a duty but a basic human good, when performed well in a well-constituted *polis*. This is the positive political ideal that naturally accompanied ancient virtue ethics. It is hard for any real virtue ethicist to give up on this ideal completely.

Sadly, Thoreau never can see his way clear to a life-affirming political role, either for himself or others. Can we see one any more clearly? Those of us working to revive virtue ethics must ask ourselves whether a virtue *politics* is likewise conceivable today. Once again, though, we will have to resist a certain inclination to argue the problem away. For example, Taylor maintains that in diagnosing his sick society and challenging Americans to live up to their ideals, Thoreau was performing the most valuable political service of all. Thoreau suggests something similar, when he writes that only "a very few" citizens "serve the State with their consciences . . . and so necessarily resist it for the most part."[38] Yet even if this is true, the very need for radical social critics and conscientious objectors shows that the polity is out of joint. It suggests a lack of fulfilling roles for conscientious citizens within the existing political framework. The case of John Brown dramatically reinforced these points for Thoreau.

Heroism

Thoreau had met John Brown in 1857, two years before Harpers Ferry.[39] He heard him speak at the Concord Lyceum and invited him to lunch the next day, where they talked for several hours. Thoreau formed a high opinion of Brown's character and contributed a small sum toward his guerilla settlement efforts in Kansas. When the news first broke of Brown's failed attack and capture at Harpers Ferry, there was almost universal condemnation across the country. Staunch abolitionists at best kept silent; even William Lloyd Garrison's *Liberator* denounced Brown's "mad scheme" to foment a slave insurrection in the South.

In this situation, Thoreau did not hesitate to come to Brown's defense. He wrote "A Plea for Captain John Brown" in a white heat, delivering the speech to large audiences in Concord, Boston, and Worcester in an effort to turn the tide of public opinion and raise funds for Brown's family. He wrote two further speeches for ceremonies memorializing Brown. As earlier when advocating civil disobedience, he did not rest content with words. When Francis Jackson Merriam, one of Brown's coconspirators, ill-advisedly returned to the United States, Thoreau helped spirit him back to Canada. All this easily added up to Thoreau's most engaged political hour.

In standing up for his subject in "A Plea," Thoreau emphasizes his patriotism and his idealism. Brown, Thoreau says, is a fitting successor to the minutemen who confronted British regulars at Concord's Old North Bridge. Indeed, he is superior to them in his willingness to face not his country's foes, but his country herself, when she is in the wrong. He is a true Christian, willing to sacrifice himself for humanity. Like the Puritans, he puts love of God and his commandments over money and worldly success—unlike all too many of their Yankee descendants. Thoreau goes further, repeatedly drawing parallels between Brown and Christ, who also died to provide liberty to the oppressed (he titles a later piece "The Martyrdom of John Brown"). Brown is "a transcendentalist above all, a man of ideas and principles. . . . Not yielding to a whim or transient impulse, but carrying out the purpose of a life." Far from illustrating confusion or desperation, as his critics allege, Brown's sacrifice shows the moral law in action. Through his commitment and idealism, he calls Americans back to their fundamental principles:

> He did not value his bodily life in comparison with ideal things. He did not recognize unjust human laws, but resisted them as he was bid. For once we are lifted out of the trivialness and dust of politics into the region of truth and manhood. No man in America has ever stood up so persistently and effectively for the dignity of human nature, knowing himself for a man, and

the equal of any and all governments. In that sense he was the most American of us all.[40]

In defending Brown, Thoreau reiterates points made in his earlier anti-slavery pieces. Rebellion is justified when the government is tyrannical and unjust. The moral law is superior to all positive law. Illegal acts are justified in opposing slavery. These arguments, while important, are not new for Thoreau. What is new is his treatment of heroism: the rare irruption of virtue in the political realm.

Thoreau believes John Brown is a true hero, a fit subject for future painters, historians, and poets. In pleading Brown's case, he hardly mentions politics or policy. Instead, Thoreau describes and defends Brown's character. Several times in "A Plea," he calls Brown "magnanimous": great souled. He shows this greatness in his willingness to sacrifice his own life for the oppressed. Brown is courageous and principled. Like the imagined hero of Thoreau's early piece "The Service," Brown exhibits the soldier's virtues, above all in his single-minded pursuit of his goals. Like the hero of *Walden*, he is a man of Spartan habits, indifferent to wealth or worldly success.[41]

Thrust into the political arena, John Brown embodies Americans' highest religious and political principles, and the people speaking within our churches and legislatures stand revealed in all their smallness and hypocrisy. Here again we face the basic political problem. In the current state of affairs—and maybe in any possible state of affairs—a political hero cannot help but show the inferiority of the multitude. This is true even for a hero such as John Brown, who acts expressly to free the oppressed. Nobility challenges democracy. A democratic hero may not be a contradiction in terms, but as long as the people acquiesce in injustice or otherwise prove themselves degraded, he creates a contradiction in actuality. Moral and political progress depends on making this contradiction explicit.

In "Resistance to Civil Government," Thoreau had expressly called for such heroism. By appealing to people's consciences and forcing them to confront the issue of slavery, a few heroic conscientious objectors could lead more people to act against it. "There are thousands who are *in opinion* opposed to slavery and to war," Thoreau had written, "who yet in effect do nothing to put an end to them."[42] Somehow those thousands had to be forced to act on their opinions.

In John Brown, Thoreau found a hero who forced the slavery issue. One Brown outweighs a million ordinary men, in Thoreau's view. This is not because he succeeds in the ordinary sense: once again, Thoreau reiterates the Kantian position that being right and being successful are two different things. No, Brown was willing to "fail" in his long-shot attempt, in order to appeal to Northern consciences. By forcing the North to stand idly by while he is hung, he makes explicit its past complicity and cowardice. But by dying for their principles, Brown and his men give concrete proof that each of us may sacrifice for higher ideals. Brown's actions, Thoreau thought, had "already quickened the feeble pulse of the North, and infused more and more generous blood into her veins and heart, than any number of years of what is called commercial and political prosperity could." They reinvigorated Thoreau's sense of political possibility, damaged by watching twenty years of politicians' ineffectual avoidance of the slavery issue. Brown's raid showed, at a minimum, that a few principled men could challenge injustice.[43]

It also raised the specter of large-scale violence, which we know was fully realized two years later, with the outbreak of the Civil War. In a recent essay, Lewis Hyde takes Thoreau to task for his virtually unqualified support for John Brown. Hyde sees Brown and Thoreau as two of a kind in their moral certainty and their unflinching application of principle, no matter what the consequences. They arrogate to themselves what he calls "the prophetic voice," which "puts the opposition beyond the pale of speech, or, should oppositional voices arise . . . makes it seem as if they were opposed to nature, the sacred, and the wisdom of the ages."[44] Such a stand is essentially apolitical, Hyde asserts, undermining compromise. The great danger is that it will increase conflict and lead to violence.

Thoreau considers Brown's violence in "A Plea" and approves of it, based on the violence and injustice of slavery: "It was his peculiar doctrine that a man has a perfect right to interfere by force with the slaveholder, in order to rescue the slave. I agree with him. They who are continually shocked by slavery have some right to be shocked by the violent death of the slaveholder, but not others. . . . I shall not be forward to think him mistaken in his method who quickest succeeds to liberate the slave."[45] Slavery denies the most basic human rights, abrogates the social contract, tramples Christian brotherhood into the dirt, directs violence toward the most vulnerable members of society. Slavery only persists by brute force; the slaveholder therefore cannot complain when brute force is directed at him. To say otherwise would be to accept that one man may justly own another.

Thoreau, as we have seen, offered moral persuasion as an alternative to violence in "Resistance to Civil Government." Even back in the 1840s, however, groping for an effective means of *civil* disobedience, he had nevertheless asserted: "When the subject has refused allegiance, and the officer has resigned his office, the revolution is accomplished. But even suppose blood should flow. Is there not a sort of blood shed when the conscience is wounded? Through this wound a man's real manhood and immortality flow out, and he bleeds to an everlasting death. I see this blood flowing now."[46] Violence is an evil: slavery is immoral, in large part, because of its pervasive, dehumanizing violence. But even worse than violence is injustice. Conflict, even war, may be preferable to an unjust status quo.

Such a stance may seem to elevate adherence to principle above any consideration of the consequences of our actions. In "Resistance," Thoreau does contend that there are "cases," both personal and political, "to which the rule of expediency does not apply, in which a people, as well as an individual, must do justice, cost what it may."[47] But this is not to deny the importance of consequences, merely to insist that the justice of our actions must be reckoned among their most important consequences, and that in the case of slavery, a full consideration of the consequences of our actions (and inaction) must consider the consequences for four million slaves and their descendants. We cannot deny these claims, Thoreau believes, without denying morality itself. Again, Thoreau does say: "this people must cease to hold slaves, and to make war on Mexico, though it cost them their existence as a people." But this does not rule out political compromise: it sets minimum moral standards that any compromise should respect. Thoreau does not give a timetable or a preferred means for ending slavery here: he states that slavery must end. Again, he believes this is a clear demand of morality.

Regarding slavery, Thoreau and Brown were indeed moral absolutists. They believed slavery was obviously and grossly unjust, and that slave insurrection and civil war, with all their inherent violence, were justified as means to end slavery. Because chattel slavery's violence was directed toward blacks, most white citizens in antebellum America found it fairly easy to accept, but Brown, Thoreau, and thousands of its better citizens would not accept it. Without their moral certainty and, eventually, without Brown's willingness and the willingness of many of his fellow citizens to fight and die for their principles, slavery would have continued indefinitely.[48] By 1859 there was no hope for compromise on the slavery issue in America. It was time to take sides. To their credit, Brown and Thoreau chose for freedom and humanity.

"When a noble deed is done," Thoreau asks, "who is likely to appreciate it?" and answers, "They who are noble themselves." In this way, Thoreau saw the hero as a touchstone for his society. His neighbors' reactions to Brown showed their characters, he believed: who recognized the possibility of higher motivations or instead spoke of Brown "as an ordinary felon"; who, in judging him, could move beyond the letter of the law to its spirit. In the few weeks between his first and third John Brown speeches, Thoreau saw a marked change in public opinion. At first, there were few good words for Brown, but by the time he was hanged, more people had been won over by his explanations for his actions and the firm way he met his death. In "The Last Days of John Brown," Thoreau could write: "Most Northern men, and a few Southern ones, were wonderfully stirred by Browns' behavior and words. They saw and felt that they were heroic and noble, and that there had been nothing quite equal to them in their kind in this country, or in the recent history of the world."[49]

John Brown provides an interesting test case for considering the role of the hero in a democratic polity. Brown's own actions were premised on the idea that all human beings are created equal. Yet surely Brown exhibited extraordinary courage and self-sacrifice. The very fact that we sometimes need such figures, in order for society to progress, suggests limitations to egalitarianism. But the fact that many people responded positively to Brown's example offers hope. If we aren't really all morally equal—if some, like John Brown, are more brave, eloquent, and magnanimous than the rest—our ability to recognize their greatness and follow them helps justify democracy.

In *Walden*, Thoreau had set himself up as a hero of self-development. In these later pieces, he finally celebrates a political hero. But it is striking that this hero should have been so radically at odds with his own government. While Thoreau as a hero of self-development is free to chart his own course, Brown as political hero must challenge the government, and he pays with his life. Of course, Thoreau nowhere says Brown's way is the only way to engage in politics. But neither does he provide any other positive models, suggesting again his frustration with politics and his difficulty in specifying an honorable, active political role within American society. We can write this difficulty off to the times, which did not teach optimism and provided few examples of political wisdom in action. But if this explains a lacuna in Thoreau's ethical philosophy, it does not fill it.

Meanwhile, as heirs to the dearly bought progress of past political struggles, we must ask how things stand with us today. Who are our political heroes—or do we no longer need heroes? If not, is this because America's citizens or its institutions have improved to the point that we can progress without heroics—or have we simply given up on progress? Above all, are we moving toward what Emerson saw as the special goal of American democracy: "true union as well as greatness"?[50] Or have we settled for a less false union than our forebears and confused greatness with bigness? These remain important political questions.

Anti-mammonism

For Thoreau, it makes no sense to argue against black slavery while living a life of slavish materialism. As we saw earlier, he emphasized the need to grapple with economic questions in order to get right morally. In "Life without Principle," one of his most frequently delivered lectures during the 1850s, he argues that just as false, ignoble, or poorly considered personal economies can lead individuals astray, so a nation devoted to piling up wealth and possessions easily loses sight of the true ends of life.

Thoreau begins the published essay by noting that people typically want lectures that are amusing and that echo rather than challenge their own ideas. Nevertheless, he endeavors to deliver more demanding lectures. "I take it for granted, when I am invited to lecture," he says, "that there is a desire to hear what I *think* on some subject, though I may be the greatest fool in the country,—and not that I should say pleasant things merely, or such as the audience will assent to; and I resolve, accordingly, that I will give them a strong dose of myself. They have sent for me, and engaged to pay for me, and I am determined that they shall have me, though I bore them beyond all precedent."[51] As an educator and citizen, Thoreau sees a duty to challenge his audience. As a writer, he wants to give them the best he has written—whether or not they are quite ready for it.

Here, at the very start of the essay, Thoreau challenges the wisdom of "the market." According to proponents, free markets improve our lives, by delivering more of what we want more efficiently. But in the intellectual realm, accepting market dictates often leads to conventionality and fatuousness, rarely to excellence.[52] Of course, Thoreau as idea-monger must entice people into listening to him. To affect them at all, he must speak to his audience's condition. Thus far he must put himself "on the market." But he cannot give in to the market, since he serves higher ideals largely unrecognized by the majority, hence possessing little market value. Not entertainment, but enlightenment. Not cleverness, but thinking. We must keep our real goals before us and make sure that each foray into the marketplace furthers them. As the essay proceeds, Thoreau systematically develops this point.

As in *Walden*, Thoreau argues that we need high moral standards by which to judge our economic lives and robust values that trump mere moneymaking. Also, that we must avoid getting so focused on efficient means that we lose sight of our proper ends. These points are easy to agree to and equally easy to forget, particularly when the financial rewards for forgetfulness loom large.

A prime example in his time, Thoreau believed, was the California gold rush, which he treats in detail: "That so many are ready to live by luck, and so get the means of commanding the labor of others less lucky, without contributing any value to society! And that is called enterprise! I know of no more startling development of the immorality of trade. . . . It makes God to be a moneyed gentleman who scatters a handful of pennies in order to see mankind scramble for them. . . . What a comment, what a satire on our institutions!"[53] Prospecting differs little from any other sort of gambling. For every one who gets rich, a thousand do not. Most hope to hit the main chance and avoid any work in the future, Thoreau asserts. All are people whose previous work was so unimportant to them that they were willing to give it up on the unlikely chance that they would strike it rich. Even for the lucky few, then, "the gold thus obtained is not the same thing with the wages of honest toil" but denies the value of that toil.

But where lies the real treasure? Thoreau asks. "Men rush to California and Australia as if the true gold were to be found in that direction; but that is to go to the very opposite extreme to where it lies. They go prospecting farther and farther away from the true lead, and are most unfortunate when they think themselves most successful. Is not our *native* soil auriferous?"[54] Cultivate yourself, he suggests, as he had earlier in *Walden*. We should pursue knowledge, build character, do work that we believe in and that makes us and our fellow men and women better and happier. Freedom, integrity, reverence, love, and wisdom are the nuggets that we should be searching out. We will not find them in the mining camps.

It is perhaps understandable that individuals should have fallen into such greedy foolishness. But, Thoreau remarks, the attitude of politicians and thinkers toward the gold rush is no better.[55] They cheer increased wealth and the settlement of the Far West as if these were good in themselves. But more economic activity is just more economic activity. In itself, it is neither good nor bad. In fact, greater per capita economic activity probably means that people are spending more time on the less important things in life; greater wealth probably means they are learning to depend more on luxuries. True, the miners are bringing more gold to the surface, but what of it? "I did not know that mankind were suffering for want of gold," Thoreau writes. "I have seen a little of it. I know that it is very malleable, but not so malleable as wit. A grain of gold will gild a great surface, but not so much as a grain of wisdom."[56]

As wisdom and self-culture are our proper goals as human beings, so they should be the goals of society. Instead, as we ascend to the general, we descend in our aims. "Government and legislation!" Thoreau roars, "these I thought were respectable professions . . . but think of legislating to *regulate* the breeding of slaves, or the exportation of tobacco!" Yet men may well make a profit on these articles, quote the annual yields and the prices current, and consider their lives a success. We must look this in the eye. Slaves and tobacco are no aberrations, but the staple products of whole states. Add luxuries to such inhumane or obviously harmful products, and you will have accounted for most of our country's economic activity. "Such, to a great extent, is our boasted commerce," Thoreau writes, "and there are those who style themselves statesmen and philosophers who are so blind as to think that progress and civilization depend on precisely this kind of interchange and activity,—the activity of flies about a molasses-hogshead."[57] In our day, slavery is long gone from the United States. Yet our government works diligently to open foreign markets to the sale of American tobacco, knowing that this may lead to many thousands of deaths from lung cancer. We are still a long way from disciplining commerce by even our most widely accepted moral principles, which is to say we are a long way from accepting those principles in fact and allowing them to guide our public policy or our lives.

With these comments, Thoreau directly challenges the notion of progress accepted by so many of his fellow citizens, then and now. More money, more technological improvements, and more gross economic activity do not equal progress. Self-culture and character improvement equal progress. *Better* people equal progress—not *wealthier* people or *more* people. "The chief want, in every State that I have been into," Thoreau writes, "was a high and earnest purpose in its inhabitants. This alone draws out 'the great resources' of Nature. . . . When we want culture more than potatoes, and illumination more than sugar-plums, then the great resources of a world are taxed and drawn out, and the result, or staple production, is, not slaves, nor operatives, but men,—those rare fruits called heroes, saints, poets, philosophers, and redeemers."[58]

Thoreau had already delivered a similar political message, more briefly, in *Walden*. "We spend more on almost any article of bodily aliment or ailment than on our mental aliment," he complains there. "Excepting the half-starved Lyceum in the winter, and latterly the puny beginning of a library suggested by the state," there are no means provided for adult education (108). Yet we would devote more resources to our culture, if we kept our true ends in view and really believed in universal human dignity. "In this country, the village should in some respects take the place of the nobleman in Europe," Thoreau argues. "It should be the patron of the fine arts. It is rich enough. It wants only the magnanimity and refinement. It can spend money enough on such things as farmers and traders value, but it is thought Utopian to propose spending money for things which more intelligent men know to be of far more worth" (109). Note how odd it strikes our ears, this talk of "magnanimous" or "refined" villages. It likely sounds precious, pretentious, or elitist. Yet if a community does not recognize intellectual and aesthetic development as valid ends, then it will not support them, and its citizens will be more dimwitted and less appreciative of beauty in art or nature. They will see knowledge and culture at best as "amenities" to be attended to at odd moments, at worst as superfluous distractions from the real business of life.

"In the long run men hit only what they aim at," Thoreau warns us. "Therefore, though they should fail immediately, they had better aim at something high" (27). A society must provide for intellectual and artistic cultivation, if it truly values them. Let us have "whatever conduces to [our] culture," Thoreau challenges his fellow citizens. "Instead of noblemen, let us have noble villages of men. If it is necessary, omit one bridge over the river, go round a little there, and throw one arch at least over the darker gulf of ignorance which surrounds us" (110). Thoreau's whole career, from his writings to his sporadic political activities to his berry-picking parties, can be viewed as an attempt to educate himself, his neighbors, and his readers. On his own view of the purpose of human society, then, he faithfully discharged a citizen's role.

The main problem facing a Thoreauvian politics is that it is easier to see how one individual can act on a noble vision of the good life than how a whole citizenry might. For one thing, it is hard to imagine this nobler society. How would people spend their time in a society where they worked one day out of seven, or six weeks out of the year, as Thoreau recommends? In *Walden,* Thoreau imagines superior societies fleetingly and poetically: economically simple communities set in a distant past ("Nor wars did men molest / When only beechen bowls were in request" [172]) or a timeless eternity (the "larger and more populous house, standing in a golden age," of which he had sometimes dreamed [243]). Neither in *Walden* nor in his later writings does Thoreau specify any of this realistically. Given his stated desire to ground his words in his own experience, it would be difficult to discuss such utopian political ideals in detail, in any case.

Another problem Thoreau faces in translating his vision into political terms is that even if we can imagine a nobler society, it is hard to see how to begin to work toward it in a community of mammon worshippers. Politics, "the art of the possible," is about incremental change and compromise. We may effect a personal revolution without coercion or bloodshed, but not a political one. We may remake our own lives in service to our ideals, and the effort keeps these ideals living and conscious. In the political realm, contrarily, ideals become slogans that, to be effective, must be taken up by the unreflective majority—and Thoreauvian slogans simply aren't as popular as mammonistic ones. It's easier to cater to the appetites of gross feeders than to their fledgling minds.

In America today, Democrats and Republicans differ (more and more slightly) on how to cut the slices, but they both want an ever-bigger economic pie. This despite the fact that material wealth has little to do with happiness; despite the fact that Americans consume more food than we need, leading to a national epidemic of obesity; despite the fact that our effluents threaten to cook the Earth, with potentially catastrophic consequences for our descendants. Worldwide, too, there seems to be a political consensus that economic growth is the holy grail. "And have all the precepts of all the Bibles taught men only this?" Thoreau asks in "Life without Principle," reflecting on the California gold rush. "Is this the ground on which Orientals and Occidentals meet?"[59] As clearly as the answer to the first question is "no," the answer to the second rings out "Yes!" from Tokyo and Beijing as loudly as from Paris or Washington.

Yet another problem for Thoreau is that key parts of his political ideal seem to conflict. For example, his view that luxury harms a democratic polity would seem to call for strong measures to combat it, such as sumptuary laws or caps on personal wealth. But Thoreau nowhere proposes such measures, and his high valuation of individual freedom might make them difficult for him to accept. As an individual, Thoreau could enact freedom and economic simplicity simultaneously at the pond. In politics, these goals conflict.

Partly because of these problems, it is difficult to specify a clear political analog to Thoreau's attempt at self-development in *Walden*—unless it would be Brook Farm and the other idealistic communes of which Thoreau (and Emerson) always remained leery.[60] But maybe this was a mistake. Perhaps such small-scale efforts offer the best chance to actualize Thoreau's vision in the political realm. Even if we do not join intentional communities, most of our positive political possibilities might be local, among our friends and neighbors. We might just have to write off the higher levels of political association as makeshifts to keep the peace, while we work "politically" in what the Greeks would have recognized as real *poleis*—our villages and towns. One problem with *this* solution is that so many political decisions, affecting our ability to live good lives, are made at the state and national levels. Another problem is that we feel implicated in these larger national doings: the Cherokee Trail of Tears and the rush to California in Thoreau's time, the torpedoing of the Kyoto Accord to control global warming and the Iraq war in ours. Responsible—yet impotent to affect them.

Perhaps we are simply at an impasse here, and a large-scale "virtue politics" is impossible. "Life without Principle" suggests as much in its conclusion. After his impassioned arguments for self-development over moneymaking, Thoreau continues airily: "What is called politics is comparatively something so superficial and inhuman, that, practically, I have never fairly recognized that it concerns me at all. . . . I have not got to answer for having read a single President's Message." Thoreau holds out no hope here that politics can be something ennobling to the participant, leading to consciously articulated, positive goals for his society. At best it might sustain such good work by individuals. Maybe that is all we can hope for, and the key to good federal and state government is to limit their scope and develop institutions that will function largely automatically. "Those things which now most engage the attention of men, as politics and the daily routine, are, it is true, vital functions of human society, but should be unconsciously performed, like the corresponding functions of the physical body."[61] Most Americans today treat politics in just this manner, I think, hoping that it will take care of itself—and not just those who are generally apathetic, but many people who are active in all sorts of smaller, more comprehensible projects in their own communities.

But the hope for good yet automatic government is a dangerous illusion. It leaves government in the hands of commercial interests with their selfish, ignoble aims. The common good will not be served by citizens neglecting politics. It is also hard for a genuine virtue ethics to give up on the ideal of active citizenship, when this has been seen as part of our humanity for so long in the Western philosophical tradition. Compare Thoreau's treatment of our more personal "vital functions" in *Walden,* where he says that we must become *more* conscious of these: experience them fully, learn all they have to teach us, and generally make the most of them. We cannot resign our vital political functions in the way he suggests without some loss.

Thoreau himself feels these difficulties. He seems aware of how crabby his own analysis has become and the insufficiency of his purported solution. "Why should we not meet, not always as dispeptics, to tell our bad dreams," he concludes "Life without Principle," "but sometimes as *eu*peptics, to congratulate each other on the ever glorious morning? I do not make an exorbitant demand, surely."[62] The hermit of Walden Pond never gave up the hope for such meetings. Yet he could not see his way clear to how a larger "we" than he normally had use for might meet on this higher plane. Nor did Thoreau come closer to solving this riddle or specifying a "eupeptic" politics in any of his other writings. He leaves us this difficult, unavoidable, necessary task.

Patriotism

In *Walden,* Thoreau penned some of our most memorable words against patriotism, including these from the concluding chapter: "Every man is the lord of a realm beside which the earthly empire of the Czar is but a petty state, a hummock left by the ice. Yet some can be patriotic who have no *self*-respect, and sacrifice the greater to the less. They love the soil which makes their graves, but have no sympathy with the spirit which may still animate their clay. Patriotism is a maggot in their heads" (321). For Thoreau the individual self is greater than any state and should never be sacrificed to it. Self-development and self-exploration should be our goals. *Walden* is the record of such self-exploration, deliberately cultivated far from the distractions of politics and the enervation of daily social contact.

The passage seems to set patriotism—a sentiment of love for one's country—in opposition to these goals. Patriotism, Thoreau tells us, eats away at our brains, like a maggot, slowly but persistently. *Walden* has argued that we must think our way toward a better life. Patriotism destroys this ability to think.

Here is a second passage, from the chapter "The Bean-Field":

> When there was a military turnout of which I was ignorant, I have sometimes
> had a vague sense all the day of some sort of itching and disease in the hori-
> zon, as if some eruption would break out there soon, either scarlatina or
> canker-rash, until at length some more favorable puff of wind, making haste
> over the fields and up the Wayland road, brought me information of the
> "trainers" [Concord's militia in training]. It seemed by the distant hum as if
> somebody's bees had swarmed, and that the neighbors, according to Virgil's
> advice, by a faint *tintinnabulum* upon the most sonorous of their domestic
> utensils, were endeavoring to call them down into the hive again. . . . But
> sometimes it was a really noble and inspiring strain that reached these woods,
> and the trumpet that sings of fame, and I felt as if I could spit a Mexican with
> a good relish,—for why should we always stand for trifles? (160–61)

Again we find thoughtlessness and abdication of self combined with
social conformity, in the image of a swarm of bees. Such a swarm is dangerous, Thoreau suggests, and difficult to control. It must be placated
with honey and semi-domesticated, or be turned loose on outsiders.
Greed and aggression may combine to foster an attack on foreigners, as
in the recently completed Mexican War. Thus a militaristic patriotism
paves the way for the abdication of conscience (a maggot, eating away in
our heads) and the perpetration of injustice. The state hands the soldier
a gun and tells him who to use it against, demanding blind obedience.
The "trifles" we then no longer stand for include morality itself.

Many similarly dismissive references to a militaristic, thoughtless
patriotism can be found in Thoreau's political writings and in his journal.[63] So it might seem perverse to call Thoreau a patriot or to try to
define a Thoreauvian patriotism. Nevertheless that is what we must do.

Treating Thoreau as a patriot underscores the inevitability of the role
of citizen for any morally serious person. Thoreau hates the triviality
and cant of politics; Jane Bennett has well remarked that he "disdains"
conventional politics because it "cultivates skills and habits of mind
inimical to a deliberate life."[64] We have seen that his forays into politics
usually involve protesting government actions, denouncing the moral
indifference of the populace, or making political gestures that emphasize his superiority and separation from the polity. Still, he repeatedly
returns to politics and social commentary, for the simple reason that he
is *not* separate. He is inescapably implicated in the actions of his nation,
responsible (to some unspecifiable but frustratingly nontrivial degree)
for righting current wrongs and safeguarding the promise of America.

Recognizing this patriotic identity is also necessary to understand Thoreau's personal and intellectual achievements. Thoreau went to the woods in order to "live deliberately" and cultivate self-reliance. Yet the path he followed was one that tied him ever closer to the land, as his own true *patria*.[65] He went to pursue self-knowledge—and came to see this as inseparable from knowledge of the society that had done so much to form him. Thus the pursuit of knowledge and right living tied Thoreau ever closer to his surroundings and led to ever-deeper investigations into the history of his country. Inevitably this led to an ardent concern for their future. As Robert Taylor puts it: "there has been no writer with more ambition for America than Henry Thoreau."[66]

Let us look briefly at one leitmotif in *Walden* that bears on the theme of patriotism. The chapter "Where I Lived, and What I Lived For" reaches its crescendo in a famous passage singing the praises of self-development and self-knowledge: "I went to the woods because I wished to live deliberately, to front only the essential facts of life" (90). It begins, however, piano: "At a certain season of our life we are accustomed to consider every spot as the possible site of a house" (81). The paragraph continues with Thoreau imagining himself traveling over the local countryside, "laying out" farms in various spots around Concord township. He might almost be any young man, planning to settle down. Such settling is natural, "at a certain season." Young men and women have the strength and the opportunity to make new lives in settling. This possibility is, or should be, exciting and encouraging (90). It necessitates choices.

Just as important as where to settle, we must decide what type of settlement to make. Before his experiment at Walden Pond, Thoreau writes, he had come close to purchasing "the Hollowell place," a remote farmstead in Concord. Nothing could have been more typical in mid-nineteenth-century America than a local boy taking over a local farm and trying to "make a go of it." We may imagine the close monetary calculations in deciding whether to buy, the attempt to drive the best possible bargain in the purchase. Then moving in, fixing up the buildings, clearing land, planting new kinds of crops, perhaps, or trying new agricultural techniques. The goal might be improved crop yields, generating more income for the farmer and comfort for him and his family. An ambitious, talented, and hardworking young man—such as Henry Thoreau—might hope to make decent profits, add on to his house, buy adjacent property, and one day purchase a house in town.

Yet Thoreau is skeptical of such settlement. He likes the Hollowell farm because it is relatively *un*improved. He writes: "I was in haste to buy it, before the proprietor finished getting out some rocks, cutting down the hollow apple trees, and grubbing up some young birches which had sprung up in the pasture, or, in short, had made any more of his improvements" (83). Rather, Thoreau accepts the farm as it is and loves its wilder aspects. Far from seeking to transform it, he writes: "I knew all the while that it would yield the most abundant crop of the kind I wanted if I could only afford to let it alone." One crop he hopes to reap is a closer relationship to the place itself.

This is not a settlement that seeks dominion or monetary profit. "I love to weigh, to settle, to gravitate toward that which most strongly and rightfully attracts me," writes Thoreau (330). "Settlement" here means belonging to and celebrating a place. One builds on connections: the farm's greatest attraction, Thoreau says, was "the recollection I had of it from my earliest voyages up the river" (83). Settlement means knowing the history of a place. Its past owners, yes, but also its flowers, raccoons, and gnarled apple trees.

Too easily, our settling in life can become the mere making of a living or the heaping up of possessions. We settle ourselves into an unthinking routine (4). At the same time and as a corollary, we set about unsettling the landscape, as in the improvements that Thoreau wishes to forestall by buying the Hollowell place. Such an anxious attempt to transform the world betrays both a mistaken idea of our higher human task, *self*-transformation, and a lack of faith in the goodness of the land itself.

This opening section concludes with Thoreau approvingly quoting Cato the Elder, the famous Roman patriot: "When you think of getting a farm, turn it thus in your mind, not to buy greedily; nor spare your pains to look at it, and do not think it enough to go round it once. The oftener you go there the more it will please you, if it is good" (84). The passage juxtaposes a "greedy buying" with a pleased looking; a hurry to make a profit with a satisfaction in the place itself. To this passage Thoreau adds: "I think I shall not buy greedily, but go round and round it as long as I live, and be buried in it first, that it may please me the more at last." The suggestion is that buying is itself greedy, putting us in a false position toward the land. Our satisfaction will dissipate if we buy greedily: not because we will buy a poor farm, but because we will make it poor, by ignoring what is most valuable there.

Thoreau's wish to be "buried in" the land brings up obvious patriotic connotations: of sacrificing one's life for one's country, of mixing one's flesh with sacred native soil. (Similar references to burial and to the related "burrowing" and "mining" can be found throughout *Walden*, such as at 98, 322.) Thoreau here suggests that going round one's land "as long as one lives" is as patriotic as dying for it. The land needs both defenders and appreciators; a patriot must *live* for his country. What this means is elaborated at greater length in the body of *Walden*, as Thoreau describes his settlement at the pond.

In seeking to redefine settlement, Thoreau touches on a deeply important national theme. The story of America is the story of our settlement: the finding of new lands and the making of new lives upon them. Western expansion was a cause for patriotic celebration in the nineteenth century, and in a famous passage in "Walking," Thoreau identifies with this grand national movement: "Eastward I go only by force; but Westward I go free. . . . I should not lay so much stress on this fact, if I did not believe that something like this is the prevailing tendency of my countrymen."[67] When the westering story is told we tend to emphasize certain heroic aspects of struggle and adventure and the freedom to ditch old lives and old places. Yet this story is, or purports to be, a story of settlement. The trip is heroic, perhaps, but eventually we reach our homestead lands on the Great Plains or in the Willamette Valley. Then must come commitment: the building of communities and the strengthening of ties. Then must come love and appreciation for where we are and who we are with. Failure to realize this means perpetual motion: the sort of rootlessness and heedlessness that are as much failures as a dull, conforming settlement.

As we have seen, Thoreau hated politics. In a journal entry in 1840, he wrote: "If want of patriotism be objected to us, because we hold ourselves aloof from the din of politics, I know of no better answer than that of Anaxagoras to those who in like case reproached him with indifference to his country because he had withdrawn from it, and devoted himself to the search after truth—'On the contrary' he replied pointing to the heavens, 'I esteem it infinitely.'"[68] Thoreau was a young man when he wrote those words. Over time, he moved toward a more earthbound search for truth in the particulars of natural history and the nuanced exploration of American history. The search continued, but unlike Anaxagoras, it took him ever deeper "into place." And as we have seen, a concern for the land and its people meant that he could not remain completely aloof from politics.

Again, Thoreau hated the blind obedience that so many in his time and ours equate with patriotism. "I love mankind[;] I hate the institutions of their forefathers," he wrote in another early journal entry. But the problem is not so much the institutions themselves, as the unthinking way people accept them. In "Resistance," after criticizing those who join the military and "serve the State . . . as machines," he writes that "a very few, as heroes, patriots, martyrs, reformers in the great sense, and *men*, serve the State with their consciences also." Note the positive reference to patriotism here, the key being a thoughtful, critical service. Another key would be a genuine concern for the people themselves, rather than a foolish love for the state, which after all only has value as a tool for safeguarding and improving the well-being of its citizens.[69]

As political developments and his own intellectual growth taught Thoreau, we cannot completely escape from politics. This *is* our country—our history—our people—our land. We can refrain from acting, but others will act in our name. Something new will be made of America, and we will feel proud or ashamed: in any case, we will be implicated. For this reason, we must speak out when actions are done that endanger our country or besmirch its good name. There is no escape from this duty, as Thoreau had imagined in his starry-eyed transcendentalist journal entry. Nor is there an escape from these patriotic connections *into* our moral duties, the kind of solution to political degeneration that Thoreau explores in "Resistance." For even if Thoreau could have effectively forsworn his allegiance to the state, his connection and concern for his country would have remained.

Like Antaeus, Thoreau found strength in his ties to his native earth. He also found strength in American traditions and ideals—sometimes in opposition to them, it is true, but more often in rallying his fellow Americans to extend and live up to them. In "Slavery in Massachusetts," Thoreau writes angrily of the use of his state's militia—descendants of the men who fought for freedom at Lexington and Concord—to return the fugitive Anthony Burns to Virginia and slavery: "I have lived for the last month,—and I think that every man in Massachusetts capable of the sentiment of patriotism must have had a similar experience,—with the sense of having suffered a vast and indefinite loss. I did not know at first what ailed me. At last it occurred to me that what I had lost was a country."[70] As later generations have often been reminded, our institutions of government may become instruments of injustice. But it is not only the threat to our own lives or happiness that moves us to fight injustice. We act because this is our country. We are ashamed of its injustices as we would be of our own and concerned for what sort of country we are leaving our children.

Previous generations of Americans fought to end slavery and imperialist aggression. Thoreau argues that we must also fight to end our ongoing war against nature. In a posthumously published essay, he describes the sugar maples set up on Concord common as a "*perfectly living* institution":

> They are worth all and more than they have cost,—though one of the selectmen, while setting them out, took the cold which occasioned his death,—if only because they have filled the open eyes of children with their rich color unstintedly so many Octobers. . . . No annual training or muster of soldiery, no celebration with its scarfs and banners, could import into the town a hundredth part of the annual splendor of our October. We have only to set the trees, or let them stand, and Nature will find the colored drapery,—flags of all her nations.[71]

Here is an institution Thoreau can wholeheartedly believe in: a benison to all, including future generations. Here, in the person of the anonymous selectman planting trees for his community, is the necessary political complement to the much grander John Brown: an unobtrusive service and incrementalism more suited perhaps to our own time. Here is a patriotism that is fully grounded yet expansive, not drawing lines defensively and saying "us or them," but widening our typical circle of moral concern and inviting in nature.

Like courage, prudence, or, indeed, any virtue, patriotism is liable to a skewed development and to various kinds of misuse. Yet properly developed it is part of a good human life and part of what we owe one another. Put another way, "patriotism" is a necessary word, but one whose meaning we must retrieve. Recall Thoreau's words: "It would seem as if the very language of our parlors would lose all its nerve and degenerate into *parlaver* wholly, our lives pass at such remoteness from its symbols, and its metaphors and tropes are necessarily so far fetched" (244–45). Such has been the fate of "patriotism," a word coined by people who lived much closer to the land than Thoreau's contemporaries or ourselves. It has become a meaningless abstraction for many of us, in part through our mistaking abstractions for our true country. *Walden* suggests that we must retrieve the word by rethinking and reliving it. When we live closer to the land, strive to know it better, and work to protect all its inhabitants, human and nonhuman—that is patriotism. Thoreau's life and writings have much to teach us about how to achieve this.

Foundations

Walden is filled with ethical judgments. What, if anything, justifies them? Casual readers tend to ask the question in personal terms: who is *he* to judge other people's lives, and to judge them so harshly? Philosophers, wary of committing the ad hominem fallacy and mindful that kindly judgments need justification as much as curmudgeonly ones, will de-personalize the question. How, they might ask, does Thoreau ground his ethical judgments? What are his ethical foundations?

Whether they seek them in God, Nature, the structure of reason, or elsewhere, philosophers look to ethical foundations to provide three things. First, these foundations should explain the *force* behind ethical commands and ideals: the legitimate power that we feel they exert over us. Second, they should improve the *accuracy* of our ethical judgments and suggest means to resolve ethical disagreements. Third, ideally, they should provide *certainty* by grounding ethics in universal, unable-to-be-ignored aspects of reality. Most philosophers see these three goals as essentially connected.

In recent years, some have questioned whether this foundational attempt can succeed, and a few philosophers have experimented with ways to "do ethics" without foundations. Some have suggested that ethical analysis can clarify values, even if it cannot justify them; others have emphasized the appeal to local or particular values in justifying particular ethical judgments. *Walden* shows how such a nonfoundational ethics might work. For as we have seen, Thoreau tries to push his readers to make their own values explicit, and he often appeals to ideals that many of them already hold, at least formally. As Christians, for example, they are committed to living reverently and to skepticism about the value of worldly wealth. Many times in *Walden*, Thoreau simply takes these positions as given and judges people's lives accordingly. *Walden*'s success over the years, in provoking thought and challenging readers to live up to their ideals, suggests that such proximate appeals are more valuable than philosophers usually realize.

Given this, we might wonder whether Thoreau does, or should, attempt a deeper, philosophical grounding of his ethical judgments. In fact, *Walden* is centrally concerned with foundational questions (in epistemology, as well as ethics) for all the traditional reasons, including the pursuit of accuracy and certainty in our particular judgments. As discussed below, Thoreau approaches the problem of ethical foundations from a number of different directions. He rests ethical judgments now on nature and now on ideals; now on common sense and now on rare intimations of higher truths that make nonsense of common sense; now on experience and now on a faith that transcends experience. In the end, none of these possible foundations prove completely reliable, and Thoreau forthrightly renounces the hope for certainty in ethics. Nevertheless, alone or in combination these foundations do support particular ethical judgments that provide guidance at particular moments in our lives. Thoreau continues to affirm the possibility of ethical knowledge and the value of acting on its basis.[1]

Contemporary proponents believe virtue ethics' superiority over rival ethical viewpoints rests in part on its greater empiricism: its attentiveness to human nature, its interest in people's actual ethical reasoning.[2] Most contemporary virtue ethicists look to Aristotle as their model for such empiricism. Thoreau advances an *experimental* virtue ethics, which builds on yet challenges Aristotelian empiricism. In Thoreau's view, human nature is more diverse and open-ended than Aristotle realized, so that a consideration of human nature not only grounds basic ethical judgments but also opens up endless ethical possibilities. Because of this, no objective knowledge about human nature in general can take the place of each individual interrogating his or her own experience and testing ideals in life. An open-minded, experimental attitude is key for each of us in pursuing the good life. We improve our ethical knowledge as we work to improve our lives, but some of our most important knowledge will be personal and not clearly applicable to others. Experiments in living, unlike scientific experiments, do not have perfect replicability as a goal. Uncertainty and indeterminacy are ineliminable from ethics, and a convincing ethical empiricism must take this into account.

Still, Thoreau does see some ethical answers as better than others, and he sometimes justifies particular ethical judgments by appeal to more general aspects of reality. By appealing to both nature and ideals, experience and faith, Thoreau propounds a complex or "mixed" foundationalism. I think this will prove stronger than the simpler, single-focus foundational attempts typically favored by philosophers. A mixed foundationalism is truer to how we do, in fact, attempt to ground our virtue ethics judgments. It is superior in making a legitimate place for challenges to those judgments. It employs all the resources at our disposal, rather than pursuing theoretical simplicity past the point of usefulness. Thoreau's foundationalism will prove harder to topple for being true to the complex ways we ground our ethical judgments and to the open-ended nature of virtue ethics.

In the end, Thoreau's complex, mixed foundationalism reserves an important place for free choice: for individuals *building,* rather than merely discovering, ethical foundations for their lives. There is no room, in Thoreau's view, for ethical knowledge apart from personal commitment. In this way, Thoreau returns to an ancient conception of the philosopher as one who lives as well as pursues truth, thereby building the foundations for a higher, more demanding ethics. Self-knowledge and personal commitment are a part of any convincing ethical foundationalism. The casual reader's "who is *he* to judge?" is thus entirely appropriate, as long as he or she continues: "and who then am *I,* and what choices do I face in my own life?"[3]

Thoreau's Naturalism

Philosophers ancient and modern, Eastern and Western, have often located ethical foundations in an unchanging, universal human nature. Aristotle, for instance, argues that our nature as rational, social animals determines our basic needs and higher capabilities. His empirical psychology and political science support his ethics, suggesting how people must structure their lives and societies in order to remain happy and flourishing. For ethical naturalists, human nature grounds ethical truths, which human experience in all ages will tend to confirm.[4]

Thoreau seems to appeal to nature in this traditional way to ground his ethical judgments. The passage describing the penitential brahmins, already quoted, is one clear example of this. It implies that his neighbors' work stunts their natural abilities and literally deforms them. Life naturally moves, is "lively," but the penitents—"hanging suspended, with their heads downward," or holding a pose "until it becomes impossible for them to resume their natural position"—are stuck, unnaturally "fixed" (4). Perhaps like the brahmins, his neighbors have adhered to strange ideas, and this adherence has played them false. A return to a simpler, more natural life and attentiveness to their basic needs will show them the way forward.

The joylessness of Thoreau's neighbors testifies to their failure and impoverishment. Life is good, and human lives should be pleasurable and enjoyable, for the most part. If they aren't, something is wrong with the individuals involved, their situations, or both. Thoreau returns to this theme repeatedly. His life at the pond was pleasant (132), entertaining (160), delicious (129), he says. "Surely joy is the condition of life," he had written earlier.[5]

Other passages in *Walden* continue this naturalism. Thoreau believes new social institutions and technological innovations must have a "foundation . . . in the nature of man," if they are not to take us farther away from true happiness (45). He speaks of the need for simple, "natural means" to restore our happiness, contrasting these both with the complicated machinations of civilized life and the fantastic schemes of many moral reformers (78). In other passages, Thoreau's ethical judgments rest in part on following nature (46) and developing his own true nature (19). He refers often to the essential goodness of wild nature, both to defend it from despoliation and to challenge his readers with the contrast to their own lives (78–79, 165–66). At the end of the chapter "The Ponds," Thoreau calls for human inhabitants who can live in harmony with nature (199–200). As we have seen, Thoreau believes that our flourishing and nature's flourishing are necessarily connected.

All these passages rest, in varied but essential ways, on an ethical naturalism. So does *Walden*'s linking of health and general human flourishing. Like many ancient virtue ethicists, Thoreau sees a strong connection between health and happiness: "All health and success does me good, however far off and withdrawn it may appear; all disease and failure helps to make me sad and does me evil, however much sympathy it may have with me or I with it. If, then, we would indeed restore mankind by truly Indian . . . or natural means, let us first be as simple and well as Nature ourselves, dispel the clouds which hang over our own brows, and take up a little life into our pores" (78). In a sense, a return to life and joy is our chief goal, as well as the general prescription for all our difficulties and failures. In a naturalistic virtue ethics, physical and mental health show that we are on the right track.

Sometimes Thoreau presents his search for unchanging foundations as an appeal to *reality* rather than to nature. In a key passage, he writes:

> Let us settle ourselves, and work and wedge our feet downward through the mud and slush of opinion, and prejudice, and tradition, and delusion, and appearance, that alluvion which covers the globe, through Paris and London, through New York and Boston and Concord, through church and state, through poetry and philosophy and religion, till we come to a hard bottom and rocks in place, which we can call *reality*, and say, This is, and no mistake;

and then begin, having a *point d'appui,* below freshet and frost and fire, a place where you might found a wall or a state, or set a lamp-post safely. (97–98)

Reversing Plato's cave metaphor, Thoreau advises us to work our way downward, through mere opinion concerning appearances. At the bottom, we may "set a lamp-post," its light symbolizing knowledge. To succeed, we must pass by our social and intellectual constructions as so many impediments and delusions, so as to reach "reality": what truly *is,* not today or tomorrow, here or there, but now and forever, whenever and wherever a man or woman may struggle through to see it. Placed at the end of *Walden's* second introductory chapter, this peroration implies that knowledge of the way things are would justify Thoreau's life and help to guide *us* as we make our own decisions. Instead, we have been told a few lines earlier, "men establish and confirm their daily life of routine and habit every where, which still is built on illusory foundations" (96). Whether speaking of nature or reality, the implication is that ethical justification and guidance depend on foundational knowledge.

As Julia Annas notes in her study of the ancient virtue ethics tradition, the appeal to nature has historically played several key roles in ethical philosophy. Perhaps the three most important have been nature as "the given," nature as a foil for convention, and nature as underwriting ethical objectivity and certainty. Thoreau makes all three sorts of appeals in *Walden.* All have some merit, but they mislead us when pushed too far as justifications for our ethical judgments.[6]

Annas writes that "*nature*" sometimes represents "*the given* facts about ourselves which ethical theory has to respect" (italics added).[7] The facts of human nature—what we truly find enjoyable, our real capabilities, our genuine interests and actual activities—suggest particular goals and pursuits. These facts limit what visionaries and social engineers may define as human happiness or excellence. Visions of unattainable excellence are largely pointless, while consideration of our actual alternatives preserves the practical usefulness of ethical discussion.

As we have seen, Thoreau appeals to nature in this sense of "the given." People have bodies and minds that must be exercised if they are to remain happy. We have capabilities to know and enjoy nature that in many cases are barely utilized. Many common activities provide opportunities for enjoyment and enlightenment. In all these cases, the ubiquity of particular capabilities or activities helps justify Thoreau's judgments that "we"—implicitly, all his readers—should pay attention and try to make the most of them. Beyond this, Thoreau asks each reader to attend personally to the most basic aspects of his or her life. "What do you really find enjoyable?" Thoreau asks. "Find out and pursue that."

However, this appeal to "the given" has limits. First, the given is to some degree particular. You and I will have somewhat different proclivities and abilities, suggesting different paths to happiness. Thoreau sounds this theme early in *Walden,* saying "nature and human life are as various as our several constitutions. Who shall say what prospect life offers to another?" (10). Ethical naturalists have tended to see these differences as relatively unimportant. But once we move beyond the simple "thou shalt nots" that allow us to live in relative harmony with one another to the life decisions that play a large role in making us who we are, individual differences can loom large. In making a compatible marriage or choosing a career in which I have real abilities, self-knowledge seems more important than a general understanding of human nature. To know how to live we must find some stable foundation and commit to it, Thoreau believes: "the perennial source of our life, whence in all our experience we have found that to issue." However, "this will vary with different natures . . . the place where a wise man will dig his cellar" (133).

Most ethical naturalists believe that a general account of human nature can justify *universal* ethical judgments, binding on all human beings. Thoreau doubts this. In the midst of criticizing overconsumption and the pursuit of luxury in the strongest possible terms, he pauses to qualify his statements: "I do not mean to prescribe rules to strong and valiant natures, who will mind their own affairs whether in heaven or hell, and perchance build more magnificently and spend more lavishly than the richest, without ever impoverishing themselves, not knowing how they live. . . . I do not speak to those who are well employed, in whatever circumstances, and they know whether they are well employed or not" (16). This is less rhetorical modesty than philosophical scruples. From long observation, Thoreau believes that the fruits of luxury are mostly rotten, but he cannot say that they *always* are. He lacks the universal human knowledge and the personal experience with wealth and luxurious living that would give his words added weight. It is up to each individual reading his account to decide the proper role of economic consumption in his or her life. Regardless of what Thoreau thinks the best answers would be for most readers, he insists that ethical knowledge only comes when individuals interrogate their own lives.

The example of Alek Therien, discussed earlier, emphasizes the importance of particularity in virtue ethics. A good part of *Walden*'s ethical message can be summed up in the imperative to strive for moral, intellectual, and spiritual improvement. Yet this imperative gains no purchase on Therien, who (as Thoreau presents him) cannot strive or understand the need to strive. The possibility for such striving is "given" to most people, Thoreau believes, but apparently not to everyone. However, other people's insufficiencies or our own doubts about the universality of an imperative to strive do not let *us* off the hook. It is up to each of us to learn our own nature, clarify our responsibilities and possibilities, and act on that basis.

A second limit to the appeal to "the given" comes about because human nature itself may change. Our activities, our interests, and even our basic capabilities may evolve over time. Given many centuries in which to cumulate, these changes could become immense. Aristotle's current followers ignore this possibility, assuming that any changes in human nature are too minor or too gradual to make any difference to ethics.[8] But this seems a mistake, given our knowledge of a deep human prehistory stretching back tens or hundreds of thousands of years, and the rapidly accelerating pace of technological and social change in our own time. The appeal to the given works largely by clarifying human possibilities, but we have little reason to assume that the possibilities open to human beings ten thousand years ago and ten thousand years hence were or will be very similar to our own.

Thoreau is more alive than most virtue ethicists to the possibility of radical changes in human nature. I think this is partly because his ecological sensibility makes him less inclined to separate radical changes in the environment from radical changes in people themselves. "Who knows what the human body would expand and flow out to under a more genial heaven?" he writes in *Walden* (307). He describes the movement from an outdoor to an indoor life as momentous in human history, changing our experience of the world and ultimately our selves (28). The coming of the railroad, he thinks, makes people more alert: for better or worse, they begin to think and live "by railroad time" (117–18). Sleeping under the stars and walking across the landscape are very different experiences from sleeping under a roof and riding the train. These social and technological changes make some paths more difficult to follow and others easier. Possibilities and actualities change. *We* change.

What then remains of value in appealing to nature as "the given"? Once we acknowledge the evolving particularity of human nature and discard any conservative bias toward the current, the normal, or the prevalent, we are still left with personal and political decisions concerning how to live.

Arguably, such decisions should be made on their merits, based on a realistic assessment of our possibilities. Insofar as an appeal to nature represents an appeal to continue the status quo or to prefer the normal *in lieu of giving reasons for doing so,* it should be rejected. There may be good arguments for ethical or political conservatism, based on the goodness of the status quo or on human beings' infinite capacity to make mistakes. But these arguments must stand on their own merits—invoking "naturalness" adds nothing to them.

A second important use of the appeal to *nature* is *as a means to challenge convention.* Nature "is an important element in the revisionary aspect of ancient ethical theories," Julia Annas writes; "what is natural is opposed to what is merely conventional."[9] Chief among the "shams and delusions" that Thoreau seeks to work through are the conventional beliefs of his neighbors and past authorities about the nature of the good life (97–98). Living apart from society opens up a space from which to criticize tradition and public opinion. Living closer to nature helps Thoreau distinguish his needs from his wants and to decide which of his wants are worth satisfying.

Strictly speaking, however, such criticism may be done without appealing to nature; living deliberately and closely interrogating our own experience are the keys. Thoreau juxtaposes his life at Walden Pond with more conventional lives, and the juxtaposition itself allows for ethical comparison. Virtue ethics requires such comparisons and such thoughtfulness. But although we may oppose simpler, older, or less complicated ways of living to what is conventional, we may also consider the unconventional, the "not yet tried," or even other conventions. The main point is this: when we go on to ask which ways of living are actually best, "naturalness" does no justificatory work.

This is shown, for example, in Thoreau's discussion of houses and house building in *Walden* (27–50). He describes the houses built by a wide variety of Concord's past and present inhabitants: Indian wigwams and the sod houses of the first white settlers, the extravagant mansions of the wealthy, and his own small house. He imagines living in a tool chest by the side of the railroad and the "larger and more populous house" that is part commune, part medieval manor hall (243–44). These comparisons open up possibilities. The discussion suggests that an individual can build a house that serves her conscious purposes and does not involve her in superfluous ones. Thoreau argues against luxury and for simple, inexpensive construction, but he gives reasons for this. Indian wigwams are not judged superior to Concord's mansions because they were more primitive or natural. They were superior, rather, in not requiring great expense of trouble or time. Simpler houses are also superior in a democracy, because they do not advertise differences in wealth and thus discourage envy, greed, and conspicuous consumption.

"Consider first how slight a shelter is absolutely necessary," Thoreau begins this discussion, but it *is* a beginning (28). We cannot define "the natural" as the minimum we can get by with, because nothing is more natural for human beings than to consume more than this minimum. Nor can we assume that such minimalism *necessarily* leads to the best possible lives. The Fields family, living in their squalid shack, suggests otherwise. In building and furnishing his house, Thoreau goes beyond what is absolutely necessary to provide what is comfortable and allows for his proper pursuits. He practices simple living because he values his freedom and the intellectual and creative activity it makes possible. These are persuasive reasons for living simply, regardless of the naturalness of such a path or conventional opinions for or against it.

An *environmental* virtue ethics, such as Thoreau's, must be especially aware of these limits to the appeal to nature. As Holmes Rolston succinctly puts it: "the danger here is that any secretly desired conduct can somehow be construed as natural and found virtuous."[10] Or that any conduct with which environmentalists disagree may be defined as unnatural and condemned on that basis. Environmentalists often advocate leaving wild nature "as is" and express indifference or scorn for the blandishments of civilized consumerism. The temptation is to define leaving nature alone as natural and the pursuit of expensive consumer goods as unnatural, allowing that to stand as their condemnation.

Such arguments are open to the obvious rejoinder that it is natural for humans to tamper with nature and pursue artificial pleasures. Our *current* human nature is arguably a highly conventional and artificial construct. In short, it is now natural for us to lead quite unnatural lives! Furthermore, invoking "naturalness" as a reason for pursuing a certain course is open to the retort: "Okay, I would rather do what is *un*natural. So what?" The correct response is "*This* is what," specifying consequences. These consequences do the actual work of convincing people, if anything does. Invoking "the natural" provides no further justification.

A third important aspect of the appeal to nature involves *nature underwriting ethical objectivity and certainty.* To "settle ourselves, and work . . . till we come to a hard bottom and rocks in place, which we can call *reality* . . . and then begin"—this passage expresses the hope that we can build lives based upon our own well-considered beliefs, rather than upon convention. These beliefs will certainly reflect our intellectual limitations; they might well be false, referring not to reality itself, but merely to what we "can call" reality. But these beliefs will be ours. Any virtue ethics must retain this hope for conscious action and integrity. The passage also expresses the hope that we may know and even touch a reality that is beyond all "poetry and philosophy and religion" but is that of which they speak: what we can *truly* call reality. Like acting consciously, the pursuit of knowledge and direct contact with nature are important elements in Thoreau's conception of the good life. Here, too, I believe virtue ethics should retain these goals.

However, the passage also may be taken to express the more problematic theoretical hope that our virtue ethics judgments may be grounded upon a correct specification of human nature and that Nature of which we are a part. Then, the passage suggests, we will *know* that we are choosing correctly and may begin our efforts with complete assurance. But these are vain hopes, at least for our mature life decisions. Thoreau elsewhere warns us that we must act in the absence of such ethical certainty (71). No matter how solid the foundations, they cannot guarantee the beauty or durability of the house or ensure that we have built the best possible dwelling.

We may be sure, for example, that we should not keep children inside twenty-four hours a day without opportunities to run and explore out-of-doors. Their nature suits them for such play and exploration: their happiness and development demand it. But whether you or I should give up a job working in the woods as a forester to supervise other foresters from an office may not be so clear. For better or worse, our nature and our societies provide varied opportunities, and we must often choose without clear knowledge of which one is best. But assume that consideration of your own personality and situation makes this decision an easy one: obviously, you will be happier working in the woods, and the extra money isn't likely to be important to you or your family. Still, you cannot say that your answer would suit everyone. Otherwise put: your subjective certainty does not translate into objective certainty. Indeed, the fact that personal, subjective knowledge does sometimes clarify such important decisions calls the value and possibility of ethical objectivity into question. *Walden* makes much of this, insisting that *personal* knowledge is the key to right living.

Certainly, virtue ethics judgments may be dismissed if they make demonstrably false claims concerning human (or nonhuman) nature. But human nature and human societies are complex, opening up numerous possibilities. Appeals to human nature to determine the relative superiority of particular lives or paths are rarely convincing. Finally, no amount of success in specifying human nature or predicting human behavior will completely remove uncertainties concerning how to live well, since we can try new paths and radically change our lives. This becomes clearer when we consider the idealistic half of Thoreau's ethics, the necessary complement to his naturalism.

Thoreau's Idealism

We have looked at numerous passages that emphasize Thoreau's ethical naturalism. Elsewhere in *Walden,* Thoreau highlights the importance of ideals in ethics.[11] While our conceptions of human nature are necessarily backward looking, built upon what people have been and done up to this point in history, ideals look to the future. They may call the goodness of entrenched realities into question and open up possibilities never before conceived. For these reasons and others, idealism is a necessary part of virtue ethics.

Early in *Walden,* Thoreau emphasizes the importance of being able to imagine new possibilities in order to improve our lives: "Self-emancipation even in the West Indian provinces of the fancy and imagination" cannot be brought about by any outside reformer (7–8). Actual, physical freedom could not be taken for granted in antebellum America. But a complete freedom also encompasses free thought and imagination, the keys to free choice. It is interesting how often Thoreau thus pairs "fancy and imagination" (85, 215, 242). The imagination is clearly both a desiring and a creative power for him, and part of what it may create are new, better ways of life. Thoreau seeks to live a life at the pond that is not only healthy and enjoyable but also "agreeable to the imagination" and to his ideals (47). The woodchopper Therien, on the other hand, a "natural man" with no inclination to better himself, does not have a new idea from one season to the next (149).

Thoreau's appeals to "reality" can support either naturalism or idealism. Early on, his desire for ethical knowledge seems to lead toward naturalistic foundations: the "Realometer" measures how far appearance and convention have obscured a healthy, natural way of life (97–98). But later, he states that health and success may well be sacrificed to "a life in conformity to higher principles," suggested not by nature but by our "genius." "The greatest gains and values are farthest from being appreciated," he writes now. "We easily come to doubt if they exist. We soon forget them. They are the highest reality" (216). *Walden*'s "Conclusion" reiterates the call to idealism and again questions the goodness of what is the case, now calling this an inferior reality: "If the condition of things which we were made for is not yet, what were any reality which we can substitute? We will not be shipwrecked on a vain reality" (326). The book's final paragraph contains one final call to "realize" our ideals here in the world (333).

Of course, human ideals are not always superior to the realities that their creators wish to displace. Thoreau mentions the impractical schemes of dreamers such as the Brook Farmers (119), the diseased imaginings of starving people (136), and other cautionary examples. Above all, he ridicules those who would rather talk about their ideals than try them out in life: "men of ideas instead of legs, a sort of intellectual centipede that made you crawl all over" (152). Like hidebound realists who refuse to try anything new, such lazy idealists also keep us earthbound by obscuring the need to act. Yet despite these qualifications, idealism is necessary to ethics. Thoreau sometimes suggests that we may directly intuit or see the truth of ethical ideals and principles (96–97). At other times, he emphasizes that ideals only prove their superiority when we try them out and make them a part of our direct experience.

Thoreau's idealism is fully displayed in his arguments for vegetarianism in the chapter "Higher Laws." Thoreau makes it clear there that he believes hunting and fishing have a strong foundation in human nature. Meat and fish taste good to us, and though it isn't in fact true that we need to eat meat for our health—this is one of those popular beliefs proved false, at least for him, by his own experience—it also isn't true that moderate meat eating harms our health. Like many of his neighbors, Thoreau has a natural instinct to fish; he enjoys it and is good at it. Perhaps most important, hunting and fishing help develop our natural capabilities for enjoying and learning about nature (210, 212). Given the important role that connecting to nature plays in Thoreau's conception of the good life, these are important points in favor of these activities.

Nevertheless, he argues against them, believing that the experiences of hunting or butchering domestic animals will in time teach attentive individuals that there are better, less violent ways to live. "Though the results were bodily weakness," Thoreau asserts, "yet perhaps no one can say that the consequences were to be regretted, for these were a life in conformity to higher principles" (216). While these higher principles are not explicitly stated, his remarks suggest support both for the utilitarian "cause no unnecessary suffering" and the animal rightist's "do not kill intrinsically valuable beings unnecessarily." As we have seen, Thoreau tries to follow these principles in his life at the pond. Thoreau does not believe such principles can be grounded in human nature; they must *improve* human nature. He does not believe they are self-evident or necessary truths of reason. Indeed, he is skeptical about how far reason can take us here, suggesting that "it may be vain to ask why the imagination will not be reconciled to flesh and fat," but immediately adding, "I am satisfied that it is not" (215). Hearing the cry of the hare or the bleating of lambs as they are slaughtered is the strongest argument for utilitarian charity. Seeing the variety and complexity of our "Brute Neighbors" is the strongest argument for not ending their lives unnecessarily. Arguably, direct experience is stronger than abstract argument here.

Such passages suggest that experience itself may serve as Thoreau's ethical foundation. In "Higher Laws" he says that he speaks from "an unusually complete experience," as if this warrants his ethical position (214). Elsewhere he emphasizes the importance of learning from experience (55, 61) and insists that only personal experience will teach us the most important ethical truths (133). Yet we cannot *rest* in experience, or in our intuitions from experience, any more than we can rest in nature or our natural appetites and inclinations. Our experience may be "partial" (9, 324). Experience may not make us wiser but only more resigned to the status quo, if it is the experience of failure (96). Most important, experience may be tested or "belied" by faith (9), just as nature may be belied by our ideals. We may have intimations of a better world than we have yet experienced—and who can say that this would not, truly, be a better world and one that our descendants may one day experience, even if we cannot (268–69)? While our conception of nature is backward looking, experience is always centered in the present, happening right now. That is why both nature and experience can always be challenged by imagination, faith, or forward-looking ideals. In a sense, experience *is* Thoreau's ethical foundation, but its answers to our ethical questions are provisional at best.

The discussion in "Higher Laws" recognizes that our natural appetites can lead us astray, or at least "downward." Following out the logic of his argument leads Thoreau to deny appetite and decry human nature. "We are conscious of an animal in us," he writes, "which awakens in proportion as our higher nature slumbers. It is reptile and sensual, and perhaps cannot be wholly expelled; like the worms which, even in life and health, occupy our bodies. . . . I fear that it may enjoy a certain health of its own; that we may be well, yet not pure" (219). Having suggested earlier that we should pursue our ideals beyond bodily health, if necessary, Thoreau here reminds us that we may have a certain animal healthiness—and by implication, achieve a certain type of happiness focused on physical pleasure—that yet conflicts with our higher ideals and goals. Here he argues for privileging ideals over our animal nature, concluding that "nature is hard to be overcome, but she must be overcome" (221). Considering their source, these words cannot fail to shock, as does the quote from John Donne that precedes them:

> How happy's he who hath due place assigned
> To his beasts and disaforested his mind! (220).

Ideals and principles may trump realities, showing us a goodness to which we should sacrifice the natural goods of bodily health or pleasure.

This discussion shows the necessary place for anti-naturalism in virtue ethics. We have all felt the tug between our physical appetites and higher goals, and ethics necessarily involves disciplining our natural inclinations in the service of our articulated ideals. Here are aspects of life that support ethical idealism. Just so, the partial conjunction between health, strength, and vitality, on the one hand, and human happiness and excellence, on the other, makes an ethical naturalism plausible.

However, pushed far enough—pushed as far as philosophers typically push them, in order to find the guidance and certainty they desire—neither of these meta-ethical positions are convincing. A naturalism such as Aristotle's that seeks to ground our ethical judgments in human nature eventually confronts indeterminate aspects of human nature that allow for various sorts of development. It confronts ways in which following ideals may improve (rather than perfect) human nature. An ethical idealism such as Kant's, on the other hand, cannot explain why an individual should follow moral rules "legislated" by his higher or ideal nature. Kant's own justification seems to rest, finally, on an implicit equation of our ideal with our real selves, which individuals are always free to deny.[12] In different ways, both Aristotle and Kant are brought up short by our actual, yet incompletely determined, human nature.

In the end, the difficulty of specifying a meta-ethical position from which to derive clear, unambiguous ethical judgments rests on the impossibility of privileging either our ideals or our human nature. Thoreau, to his credit, keeps worrying about this issue in *Walden*. Even the idealistic "Higher Laws" begins with the assertion: "I found in myself, and still find, an instinct toward a higher, or, as it is named, spiritual life, as do most men, and another toward a primitive rank and savage one, and I reverence them both. I love the wild not less than the good" (210). This suggests that higher and lower aspects are equally real and equally legitimate parts of us that need to be accommodated in our ethical ideal. Those readers inclined to take "Higher Laws" as moving from a false or lower naturalism to a true or higher idealism should remember that the following chapter, "Brute Neighbors," returns us again to nature and wildness; also, that despite his reliance upon the traditional ethical dichotomy of higher and lower, Thoreau also questions that dichotomy: "Heaven is under our feet as well as over our heads" (283).

On the practical level, *Walden* attempts to specify an ideal that combines the best of nature and culture: wild freedom and "life according to principle." On the theoretical level it seeks a meta-ethics grounded in nature and the ideal: what is and what might and perhaps ought to be. At both levels conflicts, uncertainties, and contradictions are ineliminable. Thoreau's justification for his position can only be that his more encompassing ideal and broader meta-ethics are more attractive and plausible than the narrower alternatives typically put forward by philosophers.

Just as it draws on an empirical conception of human nature, virtue ethics builds on our ethical "common sense." First, it accepts the practical postulates that we can know right from wrong and that we can freely act on the basis of that knowledge. Whether or not we can prove these postulates true, we need them. They allow us to strive as individuals and debate ethical positions among ourselves. Second, virtue ethics builds on common sense by seriously considering popular conceptions of the good life. These demand our attention, since they might be right and since any other conceptions we put forward will have to compete against them. Yet common sense rests, in the end, on common experience. If we take seriously the injunction to live the best lives possible, this should lead us beyond common experience and beyond what our society takes as commonsense ethical truth. Ethical theory should clarify and deepen common sense, while our actual lives should transcend it.[13]

Walden illustrates the proper role of common sense in virtue ethics. Recall that Thoreau moved to Walden Pond "to transact some private business," relying on his "enterprise" and "common sense" to get started (19–20). Throughout the book's first chapter, Thoreau refers time and again to the basic means/ends calculations that are part of our ethical common sense and to obvious, widely acknowledged goods such as pleasure and health. These moves will always remain useful in virtue ethics, because these basic goods *are* good, and we all continually make simple mistakes in trying to achieve them. The appeal to common sense also remains useful because regardless of whatever higher goals an individual may advocate, most of the people he talks to will take a more commonsense view of human happiness. To talk to people, we usually must talk commonsensically.

On the other hand, living a good life should itself affect our ethical views. The individual who seriously strives to live well will follow the effects of her actions further than others, plumb their meaning more deeply, and think more clearly about ethical issues. She will try new ways of living and obtain a richer and wider experience. If this is not all a delusion, it should move her beyond common sense. (If it is a delusion, then ethical philosophy is a waste of time.) Such a person's contributions to ethical discussions must express her uncommon experience and understanding. Examples from *Walden* include Thoreau's paean to dawn and unlimited human possibilities (88–89), his description of merging with Walden Pond (193), and many more. So he writes, in *Walden's* "Conclusion": "I fear chiefly lest my expression may not be *extra-vagant* enough, may not wander far enough beyond the narrow limits of my daily experience, so as to be adequate to the truth of which I have been convinced. . . . Why level downward to our dullest perception always, and praise that as common sense? The commonest sense is the sense of men asleep, which they express by snoring" (324–25).

It might seem as if all our experiences, insights, or ethical assertions should be able to be expressed in simple language that could be widely understood. Certainly ellipsis and periphrasis do not guarantee profundity or truth. Yet our rare experiences do seem to call forth poetry. When we remind ourselves and our neighbors of them, we need the help of more suggestive and soaring, and less commonsense, language. "The words which express our faith and piety are not definite; yet they are significant and fragrant like frankincense to superior natures" (325). Particularly grand or unusual language may in itself suggest the possibility of experiences beyond the commonplace (regardless of whether it is necessary to convey cognitive content).

In any event, the point is not to privilege poetically expressed ethical assertions, but to deny any compelling weight to ethical consensus or to our own common ethical intuitions. The point is to entice us further down the road to excellence, which, Thoreau believes, is always the road less taken. "We are enabled to criticise others only when we are different from & in a given particular superior to them ourselves," he writes in his journal. "I am sane only when I have risen above my common sense—

When I do not take the foolish view of things which is commonly taken . . . Wisdom is not common."[14]

This suggests an important limitation to the whole foundational project. "Grounding" brings us down to where most people are. But that is not where real virtue ethicists want us to be! So there is a sense in which "grounding," "resting," and "foundations" are bad words in virtue ethics in a way they are not in an egalitarian ethics focused solely on our rights and responsibilities toward others. Indeed, the foundational project is likely to play out differently in these two kinds of ethics. Egalitarians can never overemphasize commonalities and shared vulnerabilities. These make their case. But proponents of excellence must emphasize differences in our achievements and the importance of these differences. Otherwise, there is no reason to strive. Egalitarians keep us at the foundational level, in a sense, while true virtue ethicists take us from the basement to the roof and ask us to add a story or two ourselves.

Thoreau identifies the great ethical danger in common sense as asking too little of ourselves. "By closing the eyes and slumbering," he writes, "and consenting to be deceived by shows, men establish and confirm their daily life of routine and habit every where, which still is built on purely illusory foundations" (96). Living thus lazily, we will not lack for company or assurances that this is all that there is to life. Spend time with philosophers, on the other hand, and they likely will charm you with fair visions and make you discontented with your life, as you sit "building castles in the air for which earth offers no worthy foundation" (269–70).

Taken as a whole, *Walden* supports a dialectical meta-ethics. We attend to common sense and human nature for information on how to improve our lives. That is what Thoreau asks his neighbors to do in the first few pages of the book. He wants them to ask themselves if they are emotionally satisfied and physically flourishing: whether they are *actually* happy. This will suggest possible improvements. Yet even as we interrogate our experience, we must "have some faith left which belies that experience" (9). We must keep ourselves alive to ideals, because there may be ways to improve our lives that the world will tend to disparage and deny. We should pursue higher paths, if we have the strength to do so. Still, human nature is not infinitely plastic, and we must try our ideals in life, which will prove some of them false, unrealizable, or otherwise unworthy. So the dialectic continues—one that *Walden* captures in the words "nature" and "ideal," "reality" and "imagination," "experience" and "faith," "common sense" and "extravagance." While this dialectic will not lead to absolute ethical certainty or help us live perfect lives, we may hope that it will lead to ethical knowledge and help us live better lives.

The problem, obviously, is that once we no longer privilege either human nature or our ideals, then ethical indeterminacy and uncertainty, which seemed merely matters of temporary ignorance, threaten to become permanent aspects of the human condition. Yet this seems to be our situation, because new ideals are always possible and cannot be ruled out a priori, because human nature itself is slowly changing, and because no privileging of the one over the other can be accepted. Then what is the value of pursuing greater clarity or consistency in our lives? Perhaps the strongest justification for such efforts is simply a pragmatic belief that we will live better lives if we make them. *Walden* provides stirring calls to "know thyself" and live with integrity and, beyond these, Thoreau's example of a life lived in obedience to these calls. That example is important. Our lives themselves must help provide the ethical foundations that modern philosophers had hoped to build solely from theories.

Thoreau's Experimentalism

Thoreau proposes an experimental virtue ethics. Throughout *Walden*, he speaks of his stay at the pond as an experiment (55, 84, 323) or as offering opportunities for particular experiments (65, 246). His deliberateness in action, his careful reporting, and even his eventual leave-taking all emphasize the experimental nature of his sojourn. He speaks of life itself as a great experiment (9) and insists that individuals who have actually experienced a way of life are best positioned to judge its success (16).

For Thoreau, no general account of the good life can ever supersede individual judgment; no appeal to the real *or* the ideal can answer our questions once and for all. While this complicates our ethical judgments, it also opens up exciting ethical possibilities. "How could youths better learn to live than by at once trying the experiment of living?" Thoreau asks. They should not merely play or study life "but earnestly *live* it from beginning to end" (51). In *Walden*'s conclusion he generalizes this point, finding our individual opportunities and the broader prospects of humanity equally exhilarating: "What youthful philosophers and experimentalists we are! There is not one of my readers who has yet lived a whole human life. These may be but the spring months in the life of the race" (331).

In a sense, experience itself is foundational for Thoreau. But this will not be a traditional sort of foundation, since experience—as opposed to our generalizations about it—is always personal, new, and potentially unsettling. The infinite revisability and uncertainty of such a virtue ethics must be emphasized. For all his idealism and unconventionally, Thoreau insists that only by trying our ideals in life can we find out whether they are good ideals; only by trying unconventional paths can we know whether they are better than more conventional ones. Sometimes they will not be better: *Walden* mentions some of its author's own failed experiments (59), as well as the "fantastic enterprises and sentimental experiments" of the reformers (119).

Arguably a complete ethics must include both an Aristotelian empiricism and a Thoreauvian experimentalism. Aristotle, the paradigmatic systematic philosopher, never forgets that knowledge involves the careful description of particulars as well as the clear specification of general principles. Within ethics, an Aristotelian empiricism gives an account of the goals actually pursued and values actually held by individuals from a wide variety of societies. Popular opinions concerning the good life may be criticized either in terms of human nature or in terms of our ideals. But such an empiricism also shows a willingness to say: "All right. Given that this *is* our concept of the good life, what follows?" It takes certain ends as given, not from the beginning, but at particular moments in the debate. This recalls philosophy from empty theory building to Aristotle's notion of practical reason as thought in the service of right action. It also provides solid empirical foundations for ethics.

A Thoreauvian experimentalism goes further. It explicitly rejects the idea of an unchanging human nature and denies that appeals to human nature fully ground ethical judgments.[15] Instead, it sees life as a series of experiments that we evaluate as we go along. This is how Thoreau presents his stay at the pond. Just as the natural scientist sets rigorous parameters for his experiments in order to ask nature particular questions, so Thoreau hoped to answer questions concerning the good life by placing himself in the proper contexts to test them. Some of these questions were quite specific. Can a person live on a cheap, simple vegetarian diet without losing health and vigor? Can he live alone and not be lonely? Other questions were more complex and their answers correspondingly complicated or ambiguous. What does "living close to nature" mean? (Is it a matter of physical proximity, mental or spiritual openness, or what?) Are my hopes for "farming poetically" romantic moonshine, or can I truly live them?

Ethics involves testing ideals in life—not merely in the negative sense of seeing how far human nature can be bent, but in the positive sense that the answer to the question "Is this path good?" must be given to individuals in their own experience. Seeking such answers demands initiative and effort and is itself an important part of the good life. A person deciding between live alternatives cannot fall back on a theory of human nature, or on rules derived from general principles, or on moral guides. If he does, Thoreau believes, he forsakes his exploratory birthright—and is also more likely to take the wrong path.

While one main job of ethical philosophy is to generalize about the nature of the good life, another is to open the reader to the fact of possibility and to the variety of possibilities available in life. We may imagine an "experimentalist" writer on virtue ethics solely focused on the latter job. She is not concerned with which possibilities her readers choose—only *that* they choose. Such an experimentalist might describe her own experiments omitting all "shoulds" and "oughts," leaving it completely up to her readers to decide how or whether her experiments applied to their own lives.

Thoreau, however, is not this sort of experimentalist. He definitely believes some ways of living are better than others and that most people sell themselves short: "The greater part of what my neighbors call good I believe in my soul to be bad" (10). There is some tension here between Thoreau's position that ultimate ethical judgments are reserved to each individual and his assertions that certain ways of life are limiting, slight human nature, or are ignoble and wrong. But the tension is partly one of style rather than substance. Because he states his positions so forcefully, it is sometimes difficult for a reader to imagine that Thoreau does not believe himself in possession of timeless and certain ethical truth. Yet as standard practice within the natural sciences demonstrates, the clear and forceful presentation of opinions is compatible with doubt as to their certainty and with eagerness to have them tested in new, independent experiments.

Thoreau as experimentalist says to his readers: this was my experiment. Here is how a person can fill up his time and what he can create—a certain type of life, a literary work called *Walden*—if he puts aside a more conventional life. Here is what I have to say concerning my experiments and activities and how they compare to my neighbors'. If you feel like taking such a path, it is possible. If your bent is in this direction, you have options.

At the same time, Thoreau unmistakably underlines the limits to his experiment. Despite any ethical knowledge that it might have made possible, it is still just one man's account of two years of his life. Any lessons learned will have to be applied in new ways in the future, and both the lessons and the life itself may grow stale with time. He writes in *Walden*'s concluding chapter: "I left the woods for as good a reason as I went there. Perhaps it seemed to me that I had several more lives to live, and could not spare any more time for that one. It is remarkable how easily and insensibly we fall into a particular route, and make a beaten track for ourselves. I had not lived there a week before my feet wore a path from my door to the pond-side.... How deep the ruts of tradition and conformity!" (323).

We must keep ourselves awake and try new experiments: "in view of the future or possible, we should live quite laxly and undefined in front" (324). Thus only may we do justice to our principles. In the years following *Walden*'s publication, for example, Thoreau's principle of serving his community through contradiction led him to defend John Brown. His personal goal to know wild nature took him in an increasingly scientific direction, one far removed from the poetic romanticism of his youth. These further experiments grew naturally out of his own previous efforts and larger social developments to which he was forced to respond. Like previous experiments, however, they were carried out locally, in the streets and meeting halls, the fields and forests in and around Concord township. Such focus provided the best opportunities for Thoreau to understand and implement *his* ethical truth.

Somewhat paradoxically, a true empiricism undermines an objective, naturalistic foundation for virtue ethics. For the evidence argues against an unchanging human nature, against the superiority of the normal and the conventional, and for the importance of ideals in human life. We are the animals who transform and transcend our nature—sometimes with positive results. So a true empiricism must make a proper place for ideals and ethical "possibilism."

A true empiricism will also recognize the qualified usefulness of ethical theory and general accounts of the good life. The fact of a basic structure to human experience both lends a certain objectivity to some ethical judgments and allows for cross-cultural comparisons. This basic structure assures that Aristotle and Thoreau have something to say to all of us. But it does not fully *justify* what they have to say. Such a justification can only come to each of us within our own experience. So a true empiricism must make a place for subjectivism and particularity in judging our alternatives—not as a temporary failure or necessary limitation, but as a positive and ineliminable feature of ethics.

Theoretical specification of human nature or the general structure of experience is one direction ethical philosophy can take. Another direction is more individualistic, involving a careful description of one's own experience. This second, more personal and descriptive path, well illustrated in *Walden,* may be more effective in reawakening readers to their own ethical experience. Yet a third direction the philosopher may take involves *living* a rigorous and principled life in pursuit of wisdom or other ideals. Because excessive theorizing impedes these second and third paths, theorizing must be treated warily. Thoreau's advice to his readers to "step to the music which [they] hear, however measured or far away" (326), and his recognition of exceptions to his general pronouncements suggest that he might reject the attempt to construct a theory out of his remarks. So, of course, does the fact that he constructs no such theory himself.

How can an Aristotelian empiricism—with its attention to our existing beliefs and goals, its concern with human nature, and its tendency to theorize—coexist with a Thoreauvian experimentalism, which emphasizes ideals, individual choice, and the actual attempt to live a good life? I see no easy answers to this question. But it seems to me that a correct, comprehensive empirical ethics will:

insist that there are better and worse choices and lives without insisting on a single, all-embracing account of the good life, on certain and complete ethical knowledge, or on a moralistic imposition of rules on others.

juxtapose objective, general accounts of the good life with subjective, personal accounts of good lives.

recognize both the existence and the *creation* of ethical value, as individuals instantiate particular values through their actions and create new ways of life.

strike a proper balance between ethical justification and ethical clarification and between discussing ethics and living them.

Philosophical Foundations

Among the ancients, a person's philosophy was his credo for how to live, while the title "philosopher" was reserved for those who committed themselves to "plain living and high thinking."[16] Although it no longer has these meanings within academia, standing rather for a certain scholarly training and particular theoretical interests, philosophy retains these older connotations among the general public. Here, as in other respects, Thoreau articulates the ancient views in a modern form, insisting that the philosopher live his philosophy:

There are nowadays professors of philosophy, but not philosophers. Yet it is admirable to profess because it was once admirable to live. To be a philosopher is not merely to have subtle thoughts, nor even to found a school, but so to love wisdom as to live according to its dictates, a life of simplicity, independence, magnanimity, and trust. It is to solve some of the problems of life, not only theoretically, but practically. (14–15)

Similar references to philosophy as a vocation or way of life recur throughout *Walden* (56, 173–74). Living according to reason's dictates, as well as one can know and apply them, is the clearest evidence that a person does, in fact, love wisdom. Merely to discuss life's problems and possibilities as interesting topics for conversation is good evidence that one loves not wisdom but rather contention, cleverness, or logic chopping. For as Aristotle reminded his students, "the aim of studies about action, as we say, is surely not to study and know about a given thing, but rather to act on our knowledge."[17]

This demand for personal commitment is fundamental to Thoreau's ethics. He returns to the need to integrate thought and action in "Life without Principle," asserting that "the title *wise* is, for the most part, falsely applied. How can one be a wise man, if he does not know any better how to live than other men?—if he is only more cunning and intellectually subtle? . . . It is pertinent to ask if Plato got his *living* in a better way or more successfully than his contemporaries,—or did he succumb to the difficulties of life like other men? Did he seem to prevail over some of them merely by indifference, or by assuming grand airs? or find it easier to live, because his aunt remembered him in her will?"[18] Plato himself would probably have agreed that such questions are pertinent. His dialogues match words to deeds in presenting Socrates as the prototypical philosopher; his school, the Academy, emphasized right living, along with philosophical study. Yet most contemporary moral philosophers find such questions highly impertinent, believing that ethical doctrines can and should be discussed with no reference to those who propound them. To do otherwise is to fall into the ad hominem fallacy and forfeit objectivity, our best chance to find ethical truth.[19]

Thoreau rejects this view for three reasons. The first, obvious reason is that the modern view tends to undermine integrity and encourage hypocrisy, as we talk about our most important problems absent a commitment to do anything about them. One of the best things about teaching introductory philosophy classes is that my students will remind me of this, given the opportunity. Thoreau's second reason, as we have seen, is his belief that personal experience is the key to ethical knowledge. Third, Thoreau demands that we live our ethical answers because foundations are not just found, but also made. Leaving the pond, he wrote:

> I learned this, at least, by my experiment; that if one advances confidently in the direction of his dreams, and endeavors to live the life which he has imagined, he will meet with a success unexpected in common hours. . . . In proportion as he simplifies his life, the laws of the universe will appear less complex, and solitude will not be solitude, nor poverty poverty, nor weakness weakness. If you have built castles in the air, your work need not be lost; that is where they should be. Now put the foundations under them. (323–24)

This reverses traditional foundational thinking: we must create foundations, rather than finding them ready-made. With effort we can live our ideals, testing them in life and life by them. Thoreau does not quite say that we thus change nature—the laws of the universe are not changed; they *appear* different. Yet wasn't that one of the great lessons of the "nervous, bustling, nineteenth century" and its twin intruders, the railroad and the telegraph? And hasn't the twentieth century confirmed the lesson? There is no unchanging nature; individually and collectively, we partially create the framework of our lives (another meaning for "nature"). Better to do this consciously, in the service of noble ideals, like the artist of Kouroo, than to live life unconsciously and habitually in the old ruts, or the new ruts laid down by "market forces."

Like twentieth-century ethicists, Thoreau often discusses the need for ethical foundations. But rather than look for ethical foundations in true doctrine or an unchanging nature, Thoreau insists that we build them in our own lives (46, 330). Living according to our principles and judging those principles by our own experience gives our words weight. If this does not fully justify our ethical judgments to others, it is arguably a precondition for our attempts to justify them to ourselves. Furthermore, a basic right-living is the foundation that will support our higher efforts: "Before we can adorn our houses with beautiful objects the walls must be stripped, and our lives must be stripped, and beautiful housekeeping and beautiful living be laid for a foundation" (38). Knowledge can further these efforts, but it cannot take their place.

A purely intellectual foundationalism in ethics will inevitably fail. It looks for certainty where we cannot have it, since no philosophy or creed will fully justify our actions or guarantee the success of our experiments. It puts knowledge in the place of action, when our ethical foundations must be actively laid. (*Walden* is, among other things, the story of a man building a house.) And it fails to attend to the foundational metaphor itself, for after all foundations are not ends but beginnings: the solid ground on which higher things can be raised. Failure to appreciate this last point has been the cardinal failure of twentieth-century ethical philosophy.[20]

While Thoreau's foundationalism opens up ethical uncertainty, it also opens up room for individual choice and exploration. Clearly there can be no end to these efforts (besides the obvious one). If we have great hopes for this life, we must lay the foundations ourselves and attend to them continually. Every success or failure is, or may be, the foundation for new efforts. Sometimes it is time to settle and sink our foundations deeper; sometimes it is time to pull up stakes and leave the pond. If we have been attentive, we will find guidance for our next endeavors and good stories to tell. We will also be better people.

Death

If "to be a philosopher . . . is to solve some of the problems of life, not merely theoretically, but practically," death might be our greatest philosophical challenge. The ancients sometimes described philosophy as a training for death. How to accept rather than fear it; how to use it as an incentive to live well; how to die gracefully and with dignity. By the end of his life, Thoreau had learned these lessons. In the final analysis, his death is the most eloquent testament to the success of his life and a final, valuable window into his ethics.[1]

Over the years, Thoreau meditated much on death. In his early twenties, he asked his journal: "How may a man most cleanly and gracefully depart out of nature? At present his birth and death are offensive and unclean things. Disease kills him, and his carcass smells to heaven. . . . His carcass invites sun and moisture, and makes haste to burst forth into new and disgusting forms of life with which it already teemed."[2] Here we see Thoreau's familiar discomfort with bodily things, married to a (perfectly understandable) desire to transcend such gross corporeal decay. As the passage continues, Thoreau gropes for an answer to this unpleasant reality. Live temperately, he suggests: "put away beef and pork—small beer and ale." May we not die like trees, he wonders, which "wither and dry up," and stand "clean" and "without shame or offence amidst [their] green brethren"; or like the mollusk, which "casts his shell with . . . little offence"? Finally, Thoreau settles on cremation as "more tidy" than burial in the earth, a true purification, allowing "our spirits [to] ascend pure and fragrant from our tainted carcasses."

But life is the only answer to death. By the time Thoreau wrote *Walden,* he had come to realize this. There Thoreau's exuberant spirits and love of life sweep all before them. He can write of a dead horse near the path to his house, "which compelled me sometimes to go out of my way, especially in the night when the air was heavy, but the assurance it gave me of the strong appetite and inviolable health of Nature was my compensation for this" (318). We may pull out a handkerchief and cover our noses; still, we should be cheered to see the vultures digging into the carcass. Life—*all* life—is good, vultures as well as bluebirds, worms as well as butterflies, funky, phallus-shaped toadstools as well as primroses and huckleberry bushes.[3] And while individual lives come and go, life goes on: "I love to see that Nature is so rife with life that myriads can be afforded to be sacrificed and suffered to prey on one another; that tender organizations can be so serenely squashed out of existence like pulp. . . . With the liability to accident, we must see how little account is to be made of it. The impression made on a wise man is that of universal innocence. Poison is not poisonous after all, nor are any wounds fatal" (318). This is nature's lesson. Having worked long and hard to place himself within nature, Thoreau was not inclined to exempt humanity from the general scheme.

Walden's penultimate chapter, "Spring," denies the need for personal immortality, the Christian answer to the problem of death. As the days lengthen, as the geese return, as the first spears of new grass shoot up in the meadows, we realize simply: "Walden was dead and is alive again" (311). Nature's immortality is enough: "In a pleasant spring morning all men's sins are forgiven. . . . While such a sun holds out to burn, the vilest sinner may return" (314). We need not hanker after God or nuzzle up to him. Spring itself gives the lie, or answer, to death. Appreciate that, Thoreau says. You will never get closer to eternal life.

In his mid-twenties, the agonizing death of his brother John, from lockjaw, temporarily incapacitated Thoreau. He came down with a case of "sympathetic" lockjaw, exhibiting many symptoms of the disease. He lingered in bed for a month and plunged into a depression that lasted much longer. In a journal entry composed two months after his brother's death, Thoreau wrote: "I live in the perpetual verdure of the globe—I die in the annual decay of nature."[4] This terse sentence is not elaborated; it is impossible to say whether he wrote it as an antidote or an expression of his despair. But ten years later, Thoreau believed these words deeply, having lived and celebrated ten more seasons of life and death in nature. "Ah!" he wrote in *Walden:*

> I have penetrated to those meadows on the morning of many a first spring day . . . when the wild river valley and the woods were bathed in so pure and bright a light as would have waked the dead, if they had been slumbering in their graves, as some suppose. There needs no stronger proof of immortality. All things must live in such a light. O Death, where was thy sting? O Grave, where was thy victory, then? (317)

This is the great hope, not for us as individuals or for our souls, but for life itself: for the forests, ponds, and meadows, which may continue to teem with life, including ripe berries for the children who will come after us. The man who has let go his own importance and learned this lesson may carry spring in his heart in all seasons.

"I went to the woods because I wished to live deliberately," Thoreau had written, to face life and "learn what it had to teach, and not, when I came to die, discover that I had not lived" (90). Nothing poisons life, and especially life's end, more than regret for past sins and missed opportunities. Nothing better resigns us to death than a life well spent, rich in memories and accomplishments. Thoreau lived his life fully and well. When it came time to die—too soon, at age forty-four—he was ready.

Thoreau's journal entry for November 25, 1860, is filled with the phenomena of late fall in New England: crows beginning to flock, a few last maple keys hanging on the trees, cold night winds shaking the house and exposing "a general deficiency of bedclothes." Most of the entry discusses forest succession, a central interest of Thoreau's during his last years. "How commonly you see pitch pines, white pines, and birches filling up a pasture," he writes, "and, when they are a dozen or fifteen years old, shrub and other oaks beginning to show themselves, inclosing apple trees and walls and fences gradually and so changing the whole aspect of the region. . . . I confess that I love to be convinced of this inextinguishable vitality in Nature. I would rather that my body should be buried in a soil thus wide-awake than in a mere inert and dead earth."[5] A week later, while out counting tree rings on a raw day, Thoreau caught a cold, which developed into acute bronchitis. Confined to the house for most of the winter, he rallied enough to take short walks and wagon rides around Concord. But a trip to Minnesota in summer, to recover his health, proved a failure, and he came back sicker than he had left. Tuberculosis held him in its grip.

Returning home from his trip out West, Thoreau faced the fact that he might have seen his last spring. He worked on his manuscripts, walked ever-smaller circuits around Concord, chatted with friends and neighbors, and generally enjoyed life for as long as he could. In August, he visited a friend at his home on Massachusetts's south shore, taking short walks and botanizing for several days. "But his invalidism restricted his activities," his biographer reports. "He refused to go swimming and at night requested a secluded bedroom so that his coughing would not disturb the others." In September, he made his final visit to Walden Pond, and in November, he made a last, short entry in his journal, which he had kept faithfully for nearly twenty-five years. Later that month, a visitor at Emerson's noted that Thoreau, who had come to borrow a book, looked "much wasted" and that "his doom [was] clear." Still, he "talked in the old strain of wise gravity without either sentiment or sadness" and kept "the same habitual erect posture, which made it seem impossible that he could ever lounge or slouch."[6]

As long as possible, Thoreau continued to arrange his notes and compile lists of the natural phenomena of Concord, with an eye toward realizing one or more of his large, unfinished natural history works. Finally, in February 1862, he laid these aside and busied himself with putting some of his lectures in essay form. "Autumnal Tints," "Life without Principle," "Wild Apples," and "Walking" were dispatched for publication, in short order. The money would help provide for his remaining family.

The reports of friends, relatives, and others who visited him in these last months agree that he continued stoic and cheerful to the end. His sister Sophia, his primary nurse, wrote in a letter: "His spirits do not fail him, he continues in his usual serene mood, which is very pleasant for his friends as well as himself." Sam Staples, Thoreau's jailer so many years before, came to visit. "Never spent an hour with more satisfaction," he later told Emerson. "Never saw a man dying with so much pleasure and peace." Replying to a fan letter from an aspiring poet, Thoreau, no longer able to write, dictated a response: "I have intended to answer before I died, however briefly. I am encouraged to know, that, so far as you are concerned, I have not written my books in vain. . . . You ask particularly after my health. I *suppose* that I have not many months to live; but, of course, I know nothing about it. I may add that I am enjoying existence as much as ever, and regret nothing."[7]

His final illness was perhaps the most social period of Thoreau's life, with friends and neighbors visiting often. The Hawthornes brought a music box to cheer the invalid; Mrs. Alcott sent over spearmint from her garden to make a tonic tea; and the neighborhood boys brought game for Thoreau to eat. (Although the record is not conclusive, it suggests that Thoreau cast his final vote for "the wild" rather than "the good" in this matter.) "The devotion of his friends was most rare and touching," his sister wrote; "his room was made fragrant by the gift of flowers from young and old; fruit of every kind which the season afforded." A neighboring child remembered, many years later, that "in his last illness it did not occur to us that he would care to see us." But Thoreau watched the children passing in front of his window and asked his sister to invite them in. "After that we went often, and he always made us so welcome that we liked to go. I remember our last meetings with as much pleasure as the old play-days."[8]

Thoreau's friend Daniel Ricketson, a confirmed hypochondriac, unable to resign himself to his impending loss, wrote numerous letters during these last few months. He suggested new doctors, assured Thoreau that he would get better, begged Thoreau himself for such assurances. "Truly you have not lived in vain," Ricketson wrote a few weeks before Thoreau's death, "your works, and above all, your brave and truthful life, will become a precious treasure to those whose happiness it has been to have known you, and who will continue to uphold though with feebler hands the fresh and instructive philosophy you have taught them." But he could not bear the thought of seeing Thoreau in his weakened condition or the emotional shock of a personal leave-taking. Hearing this, Thoreau whispered to his sister: "Now Ricketson ought to come and see me; it would do him good."[9]

"Be it life or death, we crave only reality," Thoreau had claimed in *Walden*. "If we are really dying, let us hear the rattle in our throats and feel the cold in our extremities; if we are alive, let us go about our business" (98). Brave words! For a long time now, Thoreau had been unable to keep warm. Refusing opiates for his pain and sleeplessness, he told his friend Ellery Channing that "he preferred to endure with a clear mind the worst penalties of suffering, rather than be plunged in a turbid dream of narcotics." Nor would he fall back on the comforts of ortho-dox religion. When a pious aunt asked him if he had made his peace with God, he answered: "I did not know we had ever quarrelled, Aunt."[10]

A few days before Thoreau's death, Parker Pillsbury, abolitionist and old family friend, came to pay his respects. Thoreau looked "deathly weak and pale," Pillsbury later remembered, and they talked only briefly. "You seem so near the brink of the dark river," the former minister commented as he got ready to leave, "that I almost wonder how the opposite shore may appear to you." To which Thoreau answered: "One world at a time."[11]

On May 6, 1862, Henry Thoreau died. The funeral service was held in the First Parish Church, the same church from which Thoreau had resigned so many years previously. Emerson read the eulogy, sketching Thoreau's life and character in bold strokes:

> He declined to give up his large ambition of knowledge and action for any narrow craft or profession, aiming at a much more comprehensive calling, the art of living well.

> He chose to be rich by making his wants few, and supplying them himself.

A very industrious man, and setting, like all highly organized men, a high value on his time, he seemed the only man of leisure in the town, always ready for any excursion that promised well.

Thoreau was sincerity itself, and might fortify the convictions of prophets in the ethical laws by his holy living. It was an affirmative experience which refused to be set aside.

So much knowledge of Nature's secret and genius few others possessed, none in a more large and religious synthesis.

Emerson could not resist making Thoreau out to be a bit more of an orthodox transcendentalist than he was, saying that "there was an excellent wisdom in him, proper to a rare class of men, which showed him the material world as a means and a symbol." And as with all his portraits of "representative men," Emerson felt compelled to add some criticism, as a tribute to the ideal that his friend suggested. "His virtues, of course, sometimes ran to extremes," he remarked, mentioning Thoreau's "dangerous frankness" and his "inexorable demand on all for exact truth." "I think the severity of his ideal interfered to deprive him of a healthy sufficiency of human society."[12]

Still, Emerson's love and respect for his friend are evident throughout his address, which portrays Thoreau as having largely met "the challenge" he had presented to the American scholar so many years previously: to "exercise the highest functions of human nature" and to be "the world's eye, the world's heart."[13] "The scale on which his studies proceeded was so large as to require longevity," Emerson concluded, "and we were the less prepared for his sudden disappearance. . . . It seems . . . a kind of indignity to so noble a soul, that it should depart out of Nature before yet he has been really shown to his peers for what he is. But he, at least, is content. His soul was made for the noblest society; he had in a short life exhausted the capabilities of this world; wherever there is knowledge, wherever there is virtue, wherever there is beauty, he will find a home."[14] A moving tribute, although Thoreau would surely have smiled at the notion of exhausting nature's capabilities in a single lifetime. After readings from Thoreau's works and a final prayer, the service was over.

Concord village had about four hundred schoolchildren in 1862: three hundred took part in the procession from the church to the new burial ground, where Thoreau's body was laid to rest in the family plot. It was a lovely spring day. Louisa May Alcott, who was present, later wrote to a friend: "It seemed as if Nature wore her most benignant aspect to welcome her dutiful & loving son to his long sleep in her arms. As we entered the church yard birds were singing, early violets blooming in the grass & the pines singing their softest lullaby, & there between his father & his brother we left him, feeling that though his life seemed too short, it would blossom & bear fruit for us long after he was gone."[15] So it has and so it may. Henry Thoreau's life and philosophy will continue to instruct and inspire, as long as there are people who find joy in nature and challenge in the pursuit of virtue.

A Note to the Reader

If you agree with Henry Thoreau's environmental philosophy, you might consider joining one of the many fine organizations dedicated to promoting it. As Thoreau said, "to act collectively is according to the spirit of our institutions."

The Walden Woods Project is a charitable organization working to protect land of ecological and historical significance in the area surrounding Walden Pond. It also supports the Thoreau Institute and its educational initiatives related to the study of the environment and the humanities. To date, the Walden Woods Project has raised over $23 million to protect nearly one hundred acres in historic Walden Woods and to establish the Thoreau Institute. For more information, contact the Walden Woods Project, 44 Baker Farm Road, Lincoln, MA 01773-3004. Phone: 781-259-4700. Email: wwproject@walden.org. Web site: www.walden.org.

The Maine woods made such a deep impression on Henry Thoreau that he called for the creation of a "national preserve" to protect them. Today the grassroots group RESTORE: The North Woods is spearheading efforts to create a new Maine Woods National Park encompassing 3.2 million acres, an area larger than Yellowstone and Yosemite combined. The Park will restore native wildlife and ecosystems, provide wilderness recreation, diversify the local economy, and shift land-use control from corporations back to the public. To learn more about this visionary effort, contact RESTORE: The North Woods, PO Box 1099, Concord, MA 01742. Phone: 978-287-0320. Email: restore@restore.org. Web site: www.restore.org.

The Wilderness Society is devoted to protecting American wilderness through a combination of science, advocacy, and education. Among many valuable activities, it maintains one of the most effective lobbying offices in Washington and organizes local "forest watch" groups to monitor public lands across the country. Wilderness Society efforts have led to the permanent protection of wilderness areas totaling tens of millions of acres, from Alaska to Florida, and to improved stewardship on public lands not formally designated as wilderness. To learn more, contact the Wilderness Society, 1615 M Street, NW, Washington, DC 20036. Phone: 1-800-843-9453. Email: member@tws.org. Web site: www.wilderness.org.

The Sierra Club, founded by Thoreau fan John Muir, is America's oldest, largest, and most influential grassroots environmental organization. From the halls of the Capitol to city council meetings, the Sierra Club works to defend our communities and our public lands. Join their seven hundred thousand members as they explore, enjoy, and protect the wild places of the earth. Sierra Club, 85 Second Street, 2nd Floor, San Francisco, CA 94105. Phone: 415–977-5500. Email: information@sierraclub.org. Web site: www.sierraclub.org.

Notes

The Challenge

1. Emerson, "The American Scholar," in *Oxford Authors*, 37. For accounts of Emerson's speech, Thoreau's response, and their growing friendship, see Harding, *Days of Thoreau*, 50–51, 59–66; Richardson, *Henry Thoreau*, 18–23, 96–100; Richardson, *Emerson*, 262–65, 280–85. Throughout this book, I rely on the excellent scholarship of Walter Harding and Robert Richardson Jr. for much of my understanding of Thoreau's life and work.
2. Emerson, *Oxford Authors*, 37.
3. Ibid., 50–51.
4. Ibid., 38.
5. Ibid.
6. Ibid., 38, 41.
7. Ibid., 50.
8. Ibid., 40.
9. Ibid.
10. Ibid., 49.
11. Ibid., 49–50.
12. Ibid., 43.
13. Ibid.
14. Ibid., 43, 45.
15. The best introductions to virtue ethics remain Alasdair MacIntyre's scholarly *After Virtue* and Richard Taylor's polemical *Virtue Ethics*. For Emerson as virtue ethicist, see Van Cromphout, *Emerson's Ethics*, 57–59; Robinson, *Emerson and Conduct*.
16. Emerson, *Oxford Authors*, 46.
17. Ibid., 51–52.
18. Ibid., 47.
19. Ibid., 51. Several commentators have recently argued that Kant does, in fact, support self-cultivation and the comprehensive pursuit of excellence, mostly on the basis of some cursory remarks in part two of *The Metaphysics of Morals*. Particularly ingenious constructions utilizing these few slender reeds are Baron, "Kantian Ethics"; O'Neill, "Kant's Virtues," in Crisp, *How Should One Live?* 77–97.
20. Emerson, *Oxford Authors*, 52.
21. Ibid., 3.
22. Ibid., 50.
23. Richardson, *Emerson*, 263.
24. Emerson, *Oxford Authors*, 39.

25. Thoreau, "The Service," in *Reform Papers*, 5–6, 8, 9–10.
26. Thoreau, "Sir Walter Raleigh," in *Early Essays*, 197, 181, 178.
27. Ibid., 199–200.
28. Ibid., 192; see also 179.
29. Ibid., 216.
30. Thoreau, "Natural History of Massachusetts," in *Natural History*, 5, 25.
31. Ibid., 5.
32. Ibid., 29.
33. Emerson, *Oxford Authors*, 14.
34. Van Cromphout, *Emerson's Ethics*; Neufeldt, *Economist*.
35. Botkin, *No Man's Garden*; Shi, *Simple Life*. Articles by Joseph Wood Krutch, Lewis Mumford, and many others in the latter volume refer to Thoreau.

Life

1. Thoreau began writing *Walden* in 1846, while still at the pond. The manuscript underwent six major revisions before publication in 1854 (Shanley, *Making of* Walden).
2. Samuel Taylor Coleridge, "Dejection: An Ode," in Wolfson and Manning, *Anthology*, 520–21. Coleridge was a leading transcendentalist thinker who helped bring Kant's philosophy to the English-speaking world. In opposing him here, Thoreau perhaps also signals his desire to reorient transcendentalist philosophy or fashion it into something more useful for his own purposes. For example, Coleridge's narrator insists that human beings are superior to the rest of nature and that only human subjectivity gives nature meaning and value: "O Lady! we receive but what we give / And in our life alone does Nature live." Thoreau rejects these positions decisively. Perhaps by referencing Coleridge here, he means to connect despair and alienation, on the one hand, and this human exceptionalism, on the other. For a good discussion of Coleridge's and Thoreau's epistemological differences, see Walls, *Seeing New Worlds*, chapter 2.
3. Thoreau, *Journal 4*, 416 (April 2, 1852). Where possible, I reference Thoreau's journal in the new Princeton edition, using the 1906 edition for later volumes. Following common practice, I cite volumes in the new edition by arabic numeral, volumes in the old edition by roman numeral.
4. Ibid., 340 (February 10, 1852).
5. See for example Martha Nussbaum, "Non-Relative Virtues," 243. Thoreau also uses the terms "living well" and pursuing his "chief end" to describe his overall goal: these are also words and phrases used by recent scholars to translate and resurrect the proper ancient Greek understanding of *eudaimonia*. "Living well": *Walden*, 51, and J. L. Akrill, "Aristotle on *Eudaimonia*," in Rorty, *Aristotle's Ethics*, 17. "Chief end": *Walden*, 8, 90–91, and Annas, *Morality of Happiness*, 46.
6. See Richardson, *Henry Thoreau*, 54–57; and Van Cromphout, *Emerson's Ethics*, 78–84.

7. On the capabilities approach, see Amartya Sen, *Commodities and Capabilities,* and Nussbaum, "Non-Relative Virtues."

8. As noted by William Rossi, editor of Thoreau, Walden *and Resistance,* 5. Thoreau also refers to the catechism earlier in *Walden* (Princeton edition, 9).

9. Cogent arguments against such a narrow view of ethics are presented in Kelly Rogers, "Beyond Self and Other" and David Schmidtz, "Self-Interest: What's in It for Me?" both in Paul, Miller, and Paul, *Self-Interest,* 1–20, 107–21.

10. Thoreau also works to instill this sense of self-importance in himself. "May I so live and refine my life as fitting myself for a society ever higher than I actually enjoy," he writes in his journal. "May I be to myself as one is to me whom I love—a dear & cherished object. . . . May I dream that I loved & practiced virtue" (*Journal 3,* 311–12 [July 16, 1851]). This passage suggests the necessary connection between a strong self-interest and any genuine ethics of aspiration.

11. *Health* (also "hardiness"): Thoreau several times speaks of his willingness to sacrifice health for higher goods (*Walden,* 27, 60, 61).

    Pleasure is occasionally mentioned favorably in a fairly direct way, as on 240. More often it is assumed to be good, and more specific pleasures are noted.

    Rich experience: 42, 46, 51, 53, 61, 90.

    Self-culture: 40, 77, 109–10, 328.

    Freedom (also "independence") is one of Thoreau's most frequently mentioned goods (7, 8, 12, 15, 33, 37, 45, 56, 60, 63, 70, 84, etc.).

    Friendship receives its fullest discussion in *Week,* 259–89. In *Walden,* the chapter entitled "Solitude" asserts a certain independence from the need for human friendship, while in "Winter Visitors" Thoreau obliquely discusses his friendships with fellow transcendentalists Channing, Alcott, and Emerson (*Walden,* 129–39, 267–70).

    Knowledge: 18, 20, 90, 95–97, 100, 321–22, 327, 330–31.

    Reverence: 69, 88, 111, 138, 165–66, 201, 217, 221.

    Achievement in his chosen calling—writing—is referred to obliquely yet stirringly at 16–21, 162.

12. Two good examples are Susan Wolf, "Happiness and Meaning: Two Aspects of the Good Life," in Paul, Miller, and Paul, *Self-Interest,* 207–25; and Tuan, *Good Life.*

13. Marcus Aurelius, *Meditations,* 33, 43. Aristotle doesn't say much directly about health in the *Nicomachean Ethics.* I take his brief notice that health is commonly believed to be important to happiness (book 1, chapter 4) and his positions that happiness is "the most complete" human end and that it involves the "proper functioning" of human beings (book 1, chapter 7) to imply that health is essential to happiness (Aristotle, *Ethics,* 3, 7–9).

14. Sen, *Standard of Living,* 27–28.

15. Thoreau does not separate consideration of the ultimate value of ends from consideration of the best means to achieve them. Like ancient virtue

ethicists, he moves seamlessly from the most profound and general questions to the most specific and trivial. He praises just this in his comments on the ancient Indian scripture, "The Laws of Menu" (221). Like the ancient moralists, Thoreau countenances no distinction between pure and applied ethics.

16. Thoreau, "A Plea for Captain John Brown," in *Reform Papers*, 138.
17. Aristotle, *Ethics*, 8 (book 1, chapter 5).
18. At a minimum, Therien's example casts doubt on the possibility of universal judgments in virtue ethics. More, perhaps Therien represents a different and a better path than Thoreau's for virtue ethics, or at least a better path for many people. We should remember that ancient virtue ethics had views counter to the mainstream Confucian and Aristotelian injunctions to strive for personal excellence. Ancient Taoists apparently believed that people overemphasized differences in individual human virtue. According to them, everyone shared a basic goodness, which striving could only confuse and conceal. Similarly, the ancient Greek Cynics advocated lives of simplicity, naturalness, and lack of striving. Like the Taoists, they mocked social conventions and philosophical theorizing. Therien does not strive or question, yet he exhibits the sort of natural goodness and acceptance of his lot in life that the Taoists and Cynics would have equated with virtue. Such ideas have been largely ignored in the contemporary virtue ethics revival; not because they are rationally untenable, I believe, but because they are uncongenial to the scholarly mandarins writing the books. Yet these are perennial alternatives within virtue ethics, ineradicably grounded in human experience. Thoreau to his credit seriously considers them, entertaining both the ideas that Therein is subhuman and superhuman.
19. Thoreau, *Correspondence*, 412 (March 5, 1856).
20. William Wilberforce was a leader of the British anti-slavery movement during the first third of the nineteenth century. Like the ancient virtue ethicists, Thoreau sometimes challenges his readers by asserting their voluntary or de facto slavery. Compare Thoreau, *Reform Papers*, 91 and 174, with Epictetus, "Encheiridion," in Guignon, *Good Life*, 58 (no. 14).
21. Thoreau, *Journal 1*, 137–38 (June 21, 1840).

Virtue

1. See MacIntyre, *After Virtue*; Richard Taylor, *Virtue Ethics*; Hursthouse, *Virtue Ethics*.
2. Ancient and modern conceptions of virtue have exhibited much diversity, of course. Still, a general trend to a narrow, more moralistic conception of virtue in the modern era is readily apparent, in philosophy and in common English usage. See MacIntyre, *After Virtue*, for a plausible account of this narrowing in Western philosophy. For the narrowing of "virtue" in common English usage see the *Oxford English Dictionary*. For an argument against a strong modern-ancient dichotomy, see Sherman, *Necessity of Virtue*.

3. Kant, *Practical Philosophy*, 62.
4. Aristotle, *Ethics*, book 2, chapter 6.
5. Thoreau, *Journal 1*, 92 (December 1839), emphasis added.
6. Thoreau, *Week*, 132.
7. Thoreau, *Journal 5*, 79 (June 5, 1852).
8. Thoreau, *Reform Papers*, 5.
9. Ibid., 15.
10. Aristotle, *Ethics*, book 7, chapter 1.
11. Note that neither of these challenges to action can gain purchase without the recognition that some lives are superior to others. If different endowments don't really matter, why bother to improve opportunities for the less fortunate? If different accomplishments are unimportant, why strive to accomplish more in your own life?
12. For any genuine virtue ethics, there is no avoiding this need to justify a strong measure of self-interest and to limit the moral claims of others upon us. In an otherwise perceptive discussion of Emerson's virtue ethics, Stanley Cavell tries to argue away a similar criticism of conventional philanthropy and unjustified moral demands in Emerson's "Self-Reliance" (Cavell, *Emersonian Perfectionism*, 134–37).
13. This discounting of intellectual virtue and accomplishment can be seen in our use of the phrases "good man," "good woman," "good person." It sounds funny to us to say of someone that "he was moral, but not really good." But it would not sound funny to say of someone "she is a good woman, but not very intelligent," or "he is a good man, but he hasn't accomplished much in his life."
14. Still, perhaps Thoreau's extreme demandingness is not a necessary part of virtue ethics. We may recognize virtue, yet (1) deny that people have a duty to strive to achieve it, (2) deny that people differ much in achieving it, or (3) deny that striving is the proper means to achieve it. The Greek Cynics seem to fit position (2) and the ancient Taoists position (3), which represent perennial alternatives within virtue ethics.
15. Williams, *Limits of Philosophy*, 9.
16. An excellent recent treatment of intellectual virtue is Zagzebski, *Virtues of the Mind*. Not surprisingly, in arguing that intellectual virtues are genuine virtues, she focuses on the connection between virtue and human flourishing.
17. Thoreau, *Correspondence*, 393 (October 16, 1855). The biblical reference is to Psalm 147:10–11: "He delighteth not in the strength of the horse: he taketh not pleasure in the legs of a man. The LORD taketh pleasure in them that fear him, in those that hope in his mercy."
18. Thoreau, *Journal 4*, 59–60 (September 7, 1851). On the related trade-off between an active and a contemplative life, see Thoreau, *Journal 2*, 240 (after April 18, 1846).
19. Thoreau, *Journal 4*, 175 (November 11, 1851). For more on this particular trade-off, see Thoreau, *Week*, 54–56. In his skepticism about the unity of the virtues, Thoreau disagrees with much ancient philosophy, but not necessarily with

the average man in the agora. T. H. Irwin asserts that ancient ethical "common sense" included the belief that "there are different virtues for different people, corresponding to their different circumstances and social roles" (Irwin, "Theory and Common Sense in Greek Philosophy," in Crisp, *How Should One Live?* 39).

20. Thoreau, *Journal 4,* 283–84 (January 24, 1852).

21. My approach here closely follows Nussbaum, "Non-Relative Virtues."

22. Richard Taylor, "Ancient Wisdom," 55–56.

23. Readers interested in the ancient pagan view should review Aristotle's discussion of magnanimity or "great-souledness" in *Nicomachean Ethics,* book 4, chapter 3. Aristotle there defines "magnanimity" (Greek *megalopsuchia*) as a virtue specifying the proper attitude toward honor, stating that the magnanimous man "thinks himself worthy of great honors, and is worthy of them." The associated vices are overvaluation of oneself, on the one hand, and pusillanimity, thinking oneself worthy of little, on the other. Interestingly Aristotle thinks that the latter vice is more usual than the former. One of *Walden*'s most frequently cited virtues is magnanimity, which is also praised as "heroic virtue" (80). Thoreau puts the focus more squarely on great achievements, rather than taking pride in them, but he includes a proper pride within its scope. Thoreau also emphasizes choosing learning and soul-cultivation over the pursuit of wealth as key to developing magnanimity (109, 166, 329).

24. Harding, *Thoreau as Seen,* 101.

25. For a good discussion of cardinality see Wensveen, *Dirty Virtues.* In general, the word "cardinal" is a synonym for "important" in philosophers' discussions. A virtue is a cardinal virtue if it is particularly important in achieving whatever the writer takes to be most important: living a flourishing life for most ancient philosophers, living a godly life for most medieval philosophers, living a moral life for most modern philosophers.

26. These phrases caricature Kantianism and utilitarianism, respectively: our two main modern secular moral theories. Just as Thomas Carew's poem at the end of "Economy" helps rebut Kant (80), Ellen Sturgis Hooper's verses at the end of "House-Warming" rebut Bentham: "Well, we are safe and strong, for now we sit / Beside a hearth where no dim shadows flit, Where nothing cheers nor saddens, but a fire / Warms feet and hands—nor does to more aspire; By whose compact utilitarian heap / The present may sit down and go to sleep" (254–55).

27. For more on the theme that studying and enjoying wild nature makes us better people, see Cafaro, "Virtues of the Naturalist."

28. Thoreau, *Journal 5,* 120 (June 21, 1852).

29. See Richard Taylor, *Virtue Ethics;* Anscombe, "Modern Moral Philosophy."

30. Williams, *Limits of Philosophy,* 175–85. Although perhaps not best characterized as a virtue ethicist, Williams raises common concerns.

31. Thoreau, *Reform Papers,* 67–68. The example of the unjustly seized plank suggests Kant's famous example asserting an absolute duty to tell the truth,

even to an "inquiring murderer" (Kant, "On a Supposed Right to Lie from Philanthropy," in Kant, *Practical Philosophy*, 611–15). However, the differences are as telling as the similarities. While both assert an absolute duty and that one "must do justice cost what it may," Kant asserts a duty to do what is moral (tell the truth) even if that facilitates an injustice (leads to the murder of the man being sought). Thoreau would probably not accept this, since it is the attempt to secure justice, comprehensively considered, that motivates his example in the first place ("If I have unjustly wrested a plank . . . [then] I must restore it to him though I drown myself"). As a matter of fact, Thoreau helped escaped slaves pass through Concord on their way to Canada, using subterfuge to do so. While Thoreau placed a high premium on truthfulness, he was willing to lie to save individuals from the injustice of slavery.

32. Thoreau, *Reform Papers*, 67, emphasis added.

33. Ibid., 96–97.

34. Ibid., 102, 93, 138, emphasis added.

35. Luke 9: 23–25. Thoreau also gave his lecture "Life without Principle" under the title "What Shall It Profit?" (Thoreau, *Reform Papers*, 369).

36. Thoreau, *Reform Papers*, 96.

37. For Nietzsche on Mirabeau, see Nietzsche, *The Genealogy of Morals*, first essay, section 10. It is very illuminating to compare Thoreau and Nietzsche, on Mirabeau and on morals generally. Nietzsche was also a great admirer of Emerson. Both Thoreau and Nietzsche develop heroic virtue ethics that look to the ancients for inspiration. Both criticize Christian morality. But Thoreau keeps a commitment to basic human rights. This makes Thoreau's ethics more useful to us today.

38. Martha Nussbaum argues this point in "Human Nature."

39. Quoted in translator Barbara Stoler Miller's afterword "Why Did Henry David Thoreau Take the *Bhagavad-Gita* to Walden Pond?" in *Bhagavad-Gita*, 155. I have found Miller's remarks very helpful.

40. Cavell, *Senses of* Walden, 117–18.

41. *Bhagavad-Gita*, 133.

42. Thoreau, *Week*, 140–41.

43. Ibid., 133–34.

44. See especially "The Service," *Reform Papers*.

45. Emerson, *Oxford Authors*, 477.

46. Thoreau, *Reform Papers*, 65.

47. Thoreau, *Week*, 135, 136. Thoreau goes on to contrast the progressive and pragmatic moralism of Christianity with Hindu moral stasis (136–41). Here he takes a much more positive view of Christian ethics than elsewhere in *Walden* and *Week*.

48. In an influential essay titled "Moral Luck," Bernard Williams uses the example of Gauguin deserting his family to move to Tahiti, in order to question the claims of morality. Williams suggests that Gauguin might not have had to fulfill his familial obligations, if these conflicted with his project to become

a great painter; or at least, that we might be glad that he did not fulfill those obligations. The parable of the artist of Kouroo suggests that Thoreau yearned for the kind of freedom Gauguin took. But again, he could never have justified such an abdication of duty. See Williams, *Moral Luck*, 22–26.

49. Thoreau, *Correspondence*, 251 (November 20, 1849).

Economy

1. The best scholarly treatment of Thoreau's economic views is Neufeldt, *Economist*. See also Stoller, *After* Walden, and Hellenbrand, "True Integrity."
2. See, for example, the account of a powder mill explosion in Thoreau, *Journal 5*, 429–30 (January 7, 1853).
3. See Sen, *Commodities and Capabilities*.
4. Nor can modern virtue ethics fall back on an Aristotelian sense of "natural" where nature itself is moving toward increased perfection, and hence improving our capabilities completes or perfects our human nature. Modern science does not support such a view of a progressively evolving nature. See MacIntyre, *After Virtue*, 162–63.
5. For a thorough discussion of the appeal to nature in ancient Hellenistic philosophy, see Annas, *Morality of Happiness*, 135–220. Debates similar to those recounted by Annas recur throughout the history of Western philosophy, as recently in connection with the emerging field of sociobiology. See, for example, Ruse and Wilson, "Moral Philosophy."
6. The goal of Hercules' labors was immortality; the labors themselves tasked his abilities to the utmost. This reference and many more in *Walden* enjoin a heroic life, admonishing readers to strive for the highest, rarest forms of excellence (80, 326–27). But Thoreau also asserts the goodness of small, incremental improvements in our lives (328). This dichotomy accurately reflects virtue ethics' reasonable denial of human equality, necessary for the praise of excellence. Heroes really are better than the rest of us, but within each of our lives there is ample scope for improvement or decay.
7. Aristotle, *Ethics*, book 1, chapter 1.
8. See Nussbaum, *Fragility of Goodness*, 290–305.
9. These studies are summarized in Lane, *Market Experience*, 524–47. They show that overall income usually bears a statistically insignificant relationship to feelings of overall satisfaction or happiness. Whether a person is *satisfied* with his or her income, contrarily, has a strong correlation (451–52).
10. The claim is that a "philosophical poverty" can benefit both rich and poor. To evaluate it, we must temporarily set aside issues of economic justice. This neither denies such issues nor presupposes particular answers to them. Justice and the pursuit of personal excellence are both necessary for a complete ethics.
11. Thoreau, "Life without Principle," in *Reform Papers*, 160.
12. Similarly, Thoreau gives the exact measurements of Walden Pond (286). He valued such accuracy, both as a professional surveyor and an expert natu-

ralist. If you are going to measure, measure accurately! But again, such measurements leave plenty out. Most important, they leave out life. Revealingly, Thoreau gives Walden's measurements in the chapter titled "The Pond in Winter."

13. See also Thoreau's letter to Emerson, November 14, 1847 (Thoreau, *Correspondence*, 189–90).

14. Cavell, *Senses of* Walden, 88–89.

15. Ibid., 89.

16. See Lakoff and Johnson, *Metaphors We Live By*.

17. Neufeldt, *Economist*, 38–39.

18. Ibid., 30–31.

19. Ibid., 95.

20. Thoreau, *Journal 5*, 183–84 (July 5, 1852). Interestingly, Lewis Mumford also singled out glass as an especially beneficial technology.

21. For Plato see *Republic*, book 2, 369b–374a; book 9, 580d–588a. For Aristotle see *Ethics*, book 1, chapter 5, and *Politics*, book 1, chapters 2, 8–10. For the Epicureans see extracts from Epicurus's "Letter to Menoeceus" and from Lucretius, "On the Nature of Things," in Long and Sedley, *Hellenistic Philosophers*, vol. 1, 113–14, 119–20. For the Stoics see Seneca, *Epistles of Seneca*, 447–55 (epistle 92).

22. Thoreau, *Wild Fruits*, 38.

23. There is something assertive and confrontational in the act of consumption. It always involves using things, and often, as in eating, it culminates in their destruction. Similarly appetite can be unsettling, tying us to things and thus making possible both dependence and injustice. Thoreau denounced injustice and chafed under the loss of any independence, but there was something more that he disliked about appetite. A person can eat a wild fruit without changing the land, without owning it, without harming the bush it grows on, without taking all the fruit, hence allowing a new generation of plants to grow up and leaving the birds and squirrels their fair share. But such feeding still involves appetite, and Thoreau often seems to wish to get completely beyond this, as in this Platonistic passage: "When I see, as now, in climbing one of our hills, huckleberry and blueberry bushes bent to the ground with fruit, I think of them as fruits fit to grow on the most Olympian or heaven-pointing hills. . . . You eat these berries in the dry pastures where they grow not to gratify an appetite, but as simply and naturally as thoughts come into your mind, as if they were the food of thought, dry as itself" (*Wild Fruits*, 52–53). We have seen that Thoreau's philosophy of economy depends on disciplining our gross physical desires in order to further our higher goals. But to discipline our desires is one thing—to attempt to obliterate them is another. Thoreau's practice is typically the former, but his explicit ethical doctrine often verges on the latter. This position risks devaluing the existing world, in a fruitless and unnecessary quest for purity or autarky.

24. Genesis 3:9, 17–19, King James Version.

25. Thoreau, *Wild Fruits*, 52.

26. The dual identification with Antaeus and Hercules perfectly captures the conflicting tugs in Thoreau's transcendentalism. Both figures are divine, as both the earth and the sky were divine for the Greeks. Finding a transcendence that does not deny or devalue the earth is a central quest for Thoreau.

27. Readers who are uncomfortable with the word "stupider" may substitute the words "less intelligent." Readers who are uncomfortable with the actual stupidity to which such dead-end jobs lead are invited to imagine an economic system in which all of us, including university professors, share in such drudgery, so that no one has to do it for a living.

Solitude and Society

1. Emerson, *Journals,* 238 (August 1848). Compare the second quote with Thoreau's remarks in *Walden* about going many miles to visit particular trees (201).

2. Thoreau, *Journal 4,* 357 (February 19, 1852).

3. In *Solitude,* Philip Koch lists five "virtues of solitude": freedom, attunement to self, attunement to nature, reflective perspective, and creativity. My analysis builds on Koch's work. Indeed, I am much indebted to Koch for deepening my own understanding of solitude and for providing a framework for better comprehending Thoreau's views, which he discusses at length.

4. Emerson, *Essays,* 29.

5. Quoted in Smith, *My Friend,* 130.

6. Koch, *Solitude,* 109–17.

7. See Roszak, Gomes, and Kanner, *Ecopsychology.*

8. Emerson, *Oxford Authors,* 479, 483.

9. One could argue that Thoreau's aloofness and relative isolation from other scientists prevented the full flowering of his scientific powers. Yet his solitary studies of seed dispersal and forest succession stand up well even to modern-day scrutiny, and along with Asa Gray he was probably Darwin's best reader when the *Origin of Species* first reached America. See Robert Richardson Jr., "Introduction," in Thoreau, *Faith,* 11–13.

10. Koch, *Solitude,* 128. As Thoreau says: "You may snore in concert—or you may wake up & talk philosophy" (Thoreau, *Journal 3,* 57 [after April 19, 1850]).

11. Koch, *Solitude,* 137.

12. Thoreau, *Journal 2,* 176 (August 23, 1845), emphasis added. These two passages are compared in Moller, *Thoreau in the Human Community,* 177. I have found this book very helpful in grappling with Thoreau's social philosophy.

13. Thoreau, *Journal 4,* 298–99 (January 28, 1852).

14. Thoreau, *Journal 4,* 336–37 (February 9, 1852). Note that despite his low opinion of newspapers, memorably expressed in *Walden* (93–94), Thoreau appreciates that reading one has educational value for a recent immigrant. For Thoreau and the Riordan family, see also *Journal 3,* 155–56 (November 28, 1850), *Journal 4,* 9 (August 23, 1851) and 216 (December 22, 1851).

15. Moller, *Human Community*, 91.

16. See, for example, Thoreau, *Journal 6*, 219 (June 18, 1853).

17. Harding, *Thoreau as Seen*, 139.

18. Ibid., 218.

19. Ibid., 56.

20. Ibid., 60.

21. Ibid., 60, 109, 112, 137.

22. Ibid., 77.

23. Ibid., 141.

24. See Sayre, *Thoreau and the American Indian*; Burbick, *Thoreau's Alternative History*; Robert Taylor, *America's Bachelor Uncle*.

25. Thoreau, *Journal 3*, 326 (July 21, 1851).

26. Thoreau, *Journal 4*, 311 (January 31, 1852).

27. Thoreau, *Week*, 285–86.

28. Ibid., 261, 262.

29. Ibid., 264, 265.

30. Ibid., 264.

31. Ibid., 265–66.

32. Aristotle, *Ethics*, book 8, chapters 3–6.

33. Thoreau, *Week*, 267, 268.

34. Ibid., 267. See also Thoreau, *Journal 5*, 309–11 (August 24, 1852).

35. Thoreau, *Correspondence*, 420 (March 13, 1856).

36. Thoreau, *Week*, 281–82.

37. Ibid., 265, 268.

38. Ibid., 283, 264.

39. Ibid., 284, 285.

40. My account of Emerson's and Thoreau's friendship draws heavily on Richardson, *Henry Thoreau*, 96–100, 296–300, passim; and on Richardson, *Emerson*, 280–85, 459–64, passim. Also helpful have been Smith, *My Friend*, and Emerson's own essay "Friendship," in Emerson, *Essays*, 111–27.

41. Quoted in Smith, *My Friend*, 15.

42. Emerson, *Journals*, 122 (February 17, 1838).

43. Quoted in Smith, *My Friend*, 53.

44. Richardson, *Henry Thoreau*, 98.

45. Quoted in Smith, *My Friend*, 54. If Thoreau gave Emerson "nature," Emerson in turn gave Thoreau "ideas." "Thoreau found in Emerson a person for whom ideas were as real as things," writes Robert Richardson Jr. "Thoreau once told a mutual friend that 'he found in Emerson a world where truth existed with the same perfection as the objects he studied in external nature, his ideas real and exact as antennai or stamina.'" Richardson, *Emerson*, 283.

46. Smith, *My Friend*, 20–22.

47. Thoreau, *Journal 1*, 104 (January 29, 1840); *Journal 4*, 137 (October 10, 1851).

48. Thoreau, *Journal 4*, 304 (January 30, 1852).

49. Thoreau, *Journal 3*, 26 (after September 11, 1849).

50. Thoreau, *Week*, 109, 382.

51. Emerson, *Essays,* 119–21.
52. Thoreau, *Journal 3,* 26–27 (after September 11, 1849).
53. Smith, *My Friend,* 169.
54. Emerson, *Journals,* 274 (February 29, 1856).
55. Ibid., 203–4 (August 25, 1843).
56. Ibid., 260 (July 1852).
57. Harding, *Days of Thoreau,* 205–6.
58. Emerson, *Journals,* 220–21 (June 1847).
59. Thoreau, *Journal 5,* 250–51 (July 26, 1852).
60. Quoted in Richardson, *Emerson,* 462.
61. Thoreau, *Journal 4,* 435 (April 11, 1852).
62. As Emerson himself wrote: "In reading Henry Thoreau's journal [after his death], I am very sensible of the vigour of his constitution. . . . He has muscle, and ventures on and performs feats which I am forced to decline. In reading him, I find the same thought, the same spirit that is in me, but he takes a step beyond, and illustrates by excellent images that which I should have conveyed in a sleepy generality" (*Journals,* 298 [June 24, 1863]).

Nature

1. Rolston, *Environmental Ethics.*
2. For recent philosophical discussions of environmental virtue ethics, see Wensveen, *Dirty Virtues,* and Cafaro, "Thoreau, Leopold, and Carson."
3. Harding, *Days of Thoreau,* 250–51.
4. Thoreau, *Week,* 26–27, 30–33.
5. Ibid., 26, 29, 37.
6. Similarly, when Thoreau speaks of the fishes' "happiness" being "a regular fruit of the summer," or of the bream's "humble happiness," he is using this word in the ancient sense of "flourishing" or "living well" (*Week,* 26, 27).
7. Rolston, *Environmental Ethics;* Paul Taylor, *Respect for Nature.*
8. In her recent study, Jane Bennett suggests that Thoreau's love of biodiversity led directly to a rejection of hierarchical morality (*Thoreau's Nature,* 53–55). Bennett's interpretation runs into the problem that Thoreau's ethics, like any true virtue ethics, is fundamentally inegalitarian in important ways.
9. Thoreau, *Week,* 37.
10. Ibid., 37–38.
11. The quarrel is recounted in Harding, *Days of Thoreau,* 392–95, which also quotes Thoreau's unanswered letter of protest to Lowell.
12. Singer, *Animal Liberation;* Regan, *Animal Rights.*
13. For a thorough discussion of the sensual Thoreau, see Friesen, *Spirit of the Huckleberry.*
14. Vitousek et al., "Human Appropriation."
15. Locke, *Two Treatises,* 296.
16. Not only does Locke make human use all-important, he slights higher, nonconsumptive human uses and the basic ecosystem services such as clean air

and water on which human life depends. Recent scientific calculations put nature's contributions to human economic productivity much higher.

17. Harding, *Days of Thoreau,* 123–24.

18. Thoreau realized that white settlement had brought great changes to the landscape. The towering white pines were gone, as were the catamount, the wolf, and even the deer. Still, parts of the landscape remained, if not pristine, *wild:* not primarily the product of human manipulation and control, but largely the scene of spontaneous natural productions.

19. "Men do not fail for want of knowledge—but for want of prudence to give wisdom the preference. . . . What we need to know is in any case very simple." Thoreau, *Journal 1,* 308 (May 6, 1841).

20. See for example Thoreau, *Journal 3,* 217 (May 6, 1851) and 305–6 (July 12–16, 1851); *Journal 4,* 415–20 (April 2, 1852); *Journal XI,* 296–98 (November 8, 1858).

21. Thoreau, *Journal 1,* 338 (November 30, 1841).

22. "The Ponds" suggests that a correct environmental ethics must be holistic: valuing wholes as well as individuals, ponds as well as woodchucks. Contemporary environmental ethicists have tried to affirm such holism (see Rolston, *Environmental Ethics,* and Callicott, *Land Ethic*). But it has proven easier for philosophers to extend attention and concern to nonhuman individuals than to comprehend and appreciate nonhuman or more-than-human wholes, such as species or ecosystems. Such wholes are "looser" and more difficult to demarcate. It is not clear that a forest or a pond can have "interests" that may be harmed. Perhaps most important, modern ethicists are more used to valuing individuals than collective entities (in this they differ significantly from ancient ethicists, who usually placed the civic or collective good above the good of individuals). Perhaps one way to meet the difficulty here is to temporarily set aside the theoretical effort to ethically value wholes and to ask instead how we might value them concretely and actually. We may then see *Walden* as a veritable how-to manual for appreciating natural wholes, from woodchucks and trees to ponds and forests.

23. Plato, *Symposium,* 194E–201C.

24. Thoreau, *Wild Fruits,* 37–59.

25. Thoreau, "Walking," in *Natural History Essays,* 112.

26. Ibid., 117.

27. The conclusion of "Slavery in Massachusetts" provides one clear example of this, where the water lily, emblem of purity and spring, temporarily drives away the stench of Southern slavery and Northern temporizing. "What confirmation of our hopes is in the fragrance of this flower! . . . If Nature can compound this fragrance still annually, I shall believe her still young and full of vigor, her integrity and genius unimpaired, and that there is virtue even in man, too, who is fitted to perceive and love it" (*Reform Papers,* 108).

28. Thoreau, *Natural History Essays,* 112, 114, 95–96, 119. On Thoreau's need to "re-ally himself to nature" daily, see also *Journal 5,* 392–93 (November 4, 1852) and *Journal IX,* 112–13 (December 29, 1856).

29. Thoreau, *Journal VIII*, 220–21 (March 23, 1856).
30. Thoreau, *Natural History Essays*, 93, 122–23.
31. *Journal XI*, 450–51 (February 16, 1859). In an earlier journal entry, Thoreau writes of finding a pair of young hawks in the woods, describing their behavior and appearance in detail. "I would rather save one of these hawks than have a hundred hens and chickens," he affirms. "It was worth more to see them soar—especially now that they are so rare in the landscape—It is easy to buy eggs—but not to buy henhawks. My neighbors would not hesitate to shoot the last pair of henhawks in the town to save a few of their chickens—! But such economy is narrow & grovelling—It is unnecessary to sacrifice the greater value to the less" (*Journal 6*, 197 [June 13, 1853]). In these two journal passages Thoreau's response to the "two challenges" to an environmental virtue ethics come together. To the taming and over-economizing of life, such an ethics opposes *wildness:* a soaring hawk. Not just the hawk, though, but the human appreciation of the hawk. An environmental virtue ethics only works if this vision of human life is more compelling, more "vital," than its competitors. If not, it will literally be driven from the field.
32. Excellent explorations of the role of wildness in Thoreau's philosophy may be found in Worster, *Nature's Economy*, 57–111, and Oelschlaeger, *Idea of Wilderness*, 133–71.
33. Thoreau, *Natural History Essays*, 126, 124, 117.
34. Daniel Botkin's book *No Man's Garden* shows what happens when an environmental virtue ethics fails to meet the "two challenges" discussed in this section. Botkin writes in his preface that his "purpose is to help adjust our approach to living within nature and to integrating civilization and nature, in the hope that both can prosper and persist" (xxi). A worthwhile goal. Yet he ignores human overconsumption and over-appropriation of the biosphere. He believes people should manage the entire landscape so as to further whatever goals they might have for it: to scientifically consider our "biospheric options," as he puts it, so as to better choose "what is required for life to persist with the qualities we desire" (193–94). These positions lead Botkin to denigrate wilderness preservation efforts in Maine (161–73) and to calmly countenance the extirpation of native species such as the gray wolf. The endpoint is a selfish, anthropocentric conservation philosophy bearing little resemblance to Thoreau's views.
35. Thoreau, *Journal XI*, 55 (July 18, 1858).
36. Thoreau, *Wild Fruits*, 236.
37. Ibid., 236–37.
38. Thoreau, *Journal 4*, 418 (April 2, 1852).
39. *Wild Fruits*, 237. See also Thoreau, *Journal XII*, 387 (October 15, 1859), and *Journal XIV*, 303–7 (January 3, 1861).
40. Thoreau, *Wild Fruits*, 236–38.
41. Ibid., 238.
42. Broderick, "Thoreau's Proposals," 288–89.

43. Thoreau, *Maine Woods,* 151–52. On the difference between wild and tamed landscapes, a recurrent theme, see also Thoreau, *Journal 6,* 273–75 (July 29, 1853), and 279 (July 30, 1853).

44. Opponents of wilderness preservation sometimes jump on this to argue that Thoreau did not value wilderness preservation. Exhibit A is always the famous Katahdin ascent passage in *Maine Woods* (see Botkin, *No Man's Garden,* 155–56). Thoreau's paeans to the wild and his repeated trips to wild landscapes give the lie to this interpretation. As the quotations from *Maine Woods* in this section indicate, Thoreau was an early, ardent supporter of wilderness preservation. This support grew out of his keen appreciation of nature's creativity, so evident throughout his writings.

45. Thoreau, *Maine Woods,* 156.

46. Ibid.

47. Ibid., 80.

48. Thoreau, *Faith in a Seed,* 128–30, 170–73.

49. Ibid., 166.

50. Ibid., 131; Walls, *Seeing New Worlds,* 275, n. 18.

51. Thoreau, "The Succession of Forest Trees," in *Natural History Essays,* 74.

52. Thoreau, *Faith in a Seed,* 173.

Politics

1. For a summary, see Robert Taylor, *Bachelor Uncle,* 1–7.

2. Thoreau wrote three pieces on John Brown, all found in *Reform Papers.* The last two, "Martyrdom of John Brown" and "The Last Days of John Brown," are shorter and mostly repeat themes found in the first piece.

3. Robert Taylor, *Bachelor Uncle,* 101–2.

4. Thoreau, *Reform Papers,* 97.

5. Ibid., 67.

6. On Thoreau's anti-slavery activities, see Harding, *Days of Thoreau,* 195–96, 315–17. For Thoreau's description of helping one slave escape to Canada, see Thoreau, *Journal 4,* 113 (October 1, 1851). The full extent of his participation in the Underground Railroad remains unclear.

7. Thoreau, *Reform Papers,* 65.

8. Ibid., 72. In an early letter to an abolitionist newspaper, Thoreau had written: "The admission of [Wendell Phillips] into the [Concord] Lyceum has been strenuously opposed by a respectable portion of our fellow citizens, who themselves, we trust, whose descendants, at least, we know, will be as faithful conservers of the true order, whenever that shall be the order of the day" (59).

9. Ibid., 66.

10. Ibid., 72, 87, 98, 103–4.

11. Ibid., 91, 103.

12. Ibid., 85.

13. Ibid., 80.

14. Ibid., 81.
15. Ibid., 80.
16. Ibid., 80–81.
17. Quoted in Hendrick, "Thoreau's 'Civil Disobedience,'" 464.
18. Harding, *Days of Thoreau*, 207.
19. Hendrick, "Thoreau's 'Civil Disobedience,'" 462 and passim.
20. Meyer, *Several More Lives*, 153.
21. Thoreau, *Reform Papers*, 68–69.
22. Ibid., 76.
23. Ibid., 109.
24. Ibid., 72.
25. Ibid., 71.
26. Ibid., 69, 70.
27. Ibid., 104.
28. Robert Taylor, *Bachelor Uncle*, 8.
29. Bennett, *Thoreau's Nature*, 82. Bennett also writes that for Thoreau, "[political] dissent is more a means toward self-refashioning than toward societal reform" (8). I think Thoreau's anguished comments on the slavery issue and his fellow countrymen's mammonism suggest a greater social concern. Bennett is right to see self-development as central to Thoreau's practical philosophy, wrong to see this as trumping practical political concerns. Her Thoreau is a Harraway-esque ironist who would laugh at the naiveté of the contributors to Don Henley's *Heaven Is under Our Feet* and scorn to make common cause with the conservationists of the Walden Woods Project (80–85). But ironic detachment and literature cannot take the place of personal and political action for Thoreau. The fact that he inclines to such detachment yet declines the postmodern surrender gives his practical philosophy added importance.
30. Thoreau, *Reform Papers*, 104.
31. Ibid., 101–2.
32. Ibid., 83.
33. Ibid., 71, 107.
34. Ibid., 106, 133.
35. Robert Taylor, *Bachelor Uncle*, 9, 64–65. Taylor should know better than to dismiss Thoreau's concerns for self-development (and natural history). He well sums up Thoreau's political challenge to his fellow citizens: "Instead of using nature as a resource for living a fully human life, we turn our talents and concerns and energy toward the mastery and domination of nature, even at the risk of pillaging it beyond recognition. Rather than use our talents to develop our moral characters, we assume there is little that can be done in this sphere" (89). It is as if Taylor believes that developing our characters and "living fully human lives" are supremely valuable goals, as long as we do so for the benefit of others. This is absurd; among other things, it ignores the fact, emphasized by Thoreau, that human improvement depends primarily on individual effort.

36. Wilson McWilliams, quoted in Robert Taylor, *Bachelor Uncle*, 72.
37. Thoreau, *Reform Papers*, 129.
38. Ibid., 66.
39. The following two paragraphs rely primarily on Harding, *Days of Thoreau*, 415–26.
40. Thoreau, *Reform Papers*, 112–13, 119, 135–37, 115, 125.
41. Ibid., 114–15, 120, 123–24, 132, 138.
42. Ibid., 69.
43. Ibid., 117–19, 135.
44. Hyde, "Prophetic Excursions," xiii.
45. Thoreau, *Reform Papers*, 132–33.
46. Ibid., 77.
47. Ibid., 68.
48. For these reasons, Hyde is mistaken when he assumes that we can reject Thoreau's rigid adherence to principle, his "love of heroes," and his praise for "manliness" and the martial virtues and still fashion a political philosophy that can stand up for the oppressed (Hyde, "Prophetic Excursions," xlvi). Hyde's position assumes an easy path to political progress that is contradicted at every stage of American history, from the Revolution to the present. It also illustrates the self-doubt that has been one cause of the failure of progressive politics in the United States over the past thirty years.
49. Thoreau, *Reform Papers*, 147–48.
50. Ralph Waldo Emerson, *Oxford Authors*, 51.
51. Thoreau, *Reform Papers*, 155.
52. For an opposing view see Michael Gilmore, "*Walden* and the 'Curse of Trade,'" in Myerson, *Critical Essays*, 177–92. Among other points, Gilmore argues that Thoreau's difficulties in publishing and selling his first book led him to work harder at making *Walden* coherent.
53. Thoreau, *Reform Papers*, 162–63.
54. Ibid., 165.
55. Ibid., 162, 166–67.
56. Ibid., 163.
57. Ibid., 175–76.
58. Ibid., 177.
59. Ibid., 163.
60. Richardson, *Henry Thoreau*, 105–6; Richardson, *Emerson*, 343–44.
61. Thoreau, *Reform Papers*, 177–78.
62. Ibid., 179.
63. See ibid., 102–6, 176, and the first ten pages of "Resistance"; *Journal 1*, 164 (July 31, 1840); *Journal 4*, 172 (November 9, 1851). This second journal entry is richly ambiguous. In it Thoreau refers dismissively to a newly dedicated monument in Acton to the heroes of the Revolution: "It is the Acton flue to dissipate the vapors of patriotism in the upper air—which confined would be deleterious to animal and vegetable health." The monument was of the soaring stone phallus variety. Thoreau opines that a truer monument would

be "a doorstep to the townhouse." Yet doesn't this proposal imply a better patriotism: one that builds positively on the legacy of 1776?

64. Bennett, *Thoreau's Nature*, 5.

65. Stanley Cavell makes the important point that for Thoreau, self-exploration can occur only in siting and exploring our surroundings. Knowing ourselves means "placing ourselves in the world." The way to self-knowledge is neither a pure contemplation nor a disinterested scientific study of human nature, but rather the cultivation of connections to places. The very act of removing to Walden Pond in order to begin a course of self-improvement suggests this. See Cavell, *Senses of Walden*, 53–54, 71–72.

66. Robert Taylor, *Bachelor Uncle*, 13.

67. Thoreau, *Natural History Essays*, 105–6. The full passage makes it clear that in our settlement the character of America is at stake: whether we will journey to the wild or tame ourselves. "Perchance there will appear to the traveler something, he knows not what, of *laeta* and *glabra*, of joyous and serene, in our very faces. Else to what end does the world go on, and why was America discovered? . . . As a true patriot, I should be ashamed to think that Adam in paradise was more favorably situated on the whole than the backwoodsman in this country" (111).

68. Thoreau, *Journal 1*, 164 (July 31, 1840).

69. Thoreau, *Journal 2*, 262–63 (after June 20, 1846); *Reform Papers*, 66.

70. Thoreau, *Reform Papers*, 106.

71. Thoreau, "Autumnal Tints," in *Natural History Essays*, 165, 160, 163.

Foundations

1. I see a strong parallel here between Thoreau's ethics and Charles Peirce's epistemology. Peirce holds on to robust conceptions of truth and reality, while criticizing philosophers' focus on certainty, as an impediment to scientific progress. Similarly, Thoreau holds on to the ideal of ethical truth while giving up ethical certainty and universality, in the name of ethical progress. With both Peirce and Thoreau there is the sense that they rehearsed the main debates of twentieth-century philosophy in their personal journals—and that their mature positions show philosophers the way forward in the twenty-first.

2. See, for example, Stanley Clarke and Evan Simpson, "Introduction: The Primacy of Moral Practice," in Clarke and Simpson, *Anti-Theory in Ethics*, 1–26.

3. A valuable discussion of Thoreau's foundationalism is Walter Benn Michaels, "*Walden*'s False Bottoms," in Myerson, *Critical Essays*, 131–47. Michaels shows the ubiquity of the foundational theme throughout the book and draws an important philosophical moral: "This is what the search for a solid bottom is all about, a location for authority, a ground upon which we can make a decision. *Walden* insists upon the necessity for such a search at the same time that it dramatizes the theoretical impossibility of succeeding in it" (145).

4. Other foundational attempts have appealed to religious revelation (Augustine), universal reason (Kant), or an unchanging structure to human experience (twentieth-century phenomenologists), in addition to human nature. In each case, a rationally justified theory of the way things are grounds a universal ethical theory. Crucially, this putative universality has been seen as key to justifying particular ethical judgments. Thus naturalists, supernaturalists, and idealists may all ground their ethics in an appeal to reality: the way things are. Although my main arguments in this section refer to ethical naturalism as conventionally understood, I think they also have implications for idealistic and theological ethical foundationalism.

5. Thoreau, *Natural History Essays*, 4.

6. An interesting collection treating the attempt to ground ethics in human nature, from Aristotle to the sociobiologists, is Paul, Miller, and Paul, *Ethics, Politics, and Human Nature*.

7. Annas, *Morality of Happiness*, 141.

8. However, Martha Nussbaum presents the beginnings of a discussion of this issue in "Non-Relative Virtues," 266–67.

9. Annas, *Morality of Happiness*, 217.

10. Rolston, *Philosophy Gone Wild*, 48.

11. See also Thoreau's letter to H. G. O. Blake, Thoreau, *Correspondence*, 215–16 (March 27, 1848).

12. I am aware that this is not currently the accepted interpretation of Kant's justification of the moral law. However, it is a plausible interpretation, as H. J. Paton argues in his introduction to Kant's *Groundwork*, 45–46.

13. It is interesting to compare Thoreau's treatment of common sense with that of a well-known contemporary virtue ethicist, James Wallace. In his book *Virtues and Vices*, Wallace attempts to ground virtue ethics in common intuitions about the good life, so as to justify it to its academic critics. In doing so, however, he throws the baby out with the bathwater. Wallace speaks easily enough of "excellences" of character as a synonym for "virtues," but he does not discuss human excellence so much as comfortable human existence, since he never rises above "common sense."

14. Thoreau, *Journal 3*, 274 (June 22, 1851).

15. Aristotle is often interpreted as attempting to ground his ethical judgments in this manner. See, for example, T. H. Irwin, "The Metaphysical and Psychological Basis of Aristotle's Ethics," in Rorty, *Essays on Aristotle's Ethics*, 45–49. This interpretation is contested. But whether or not Aristotle himself is a foundationalist or a naturalistic foundationalist, other virtue ethicists do seek ethical foundations in human nature or Nature itself.

16. The phrase is from Emerson's later work *Society and Solitude*.

17. Aristotle, *Ethics*, 167–68 (book 10, chapter 9).

18. Thoreau, *Reform Papers*, 162.

19. The virtue ethics revival has included some challenges to contemporary ethical philosophy's typical separation of theory and practice. Annette Baier, for example, argues that there is no room for a "moral theorizing" that

is "more philosophical and less committed than moral deliberation." She criticizes theorists who take controversial positions yet fail to work for social reform. Yet this is a minority view within academic philosophy. See Baier, "Doing without Moral Theory?" in Clarke and Simpson, *Anti-Theory in Ethics*, 33.

20. Robert Richardson Jr. takes this last point in a somewhat different direction than I do, arguing that a valid *social* ethics must be built upon such personal, lived foundations. Boldly countering critics who assert the worthlessness of Thoreau's experiment for social ethics, he writes: "*Walden* does not talk as much as it might about the social world to be built . . . but that is because it is intent on getting the foundations right. To build a free and a just society on that foundation is our task still. . . . *Walden* is not the castle in the air, it is the foundation" (Richardson, "The Social Ethics of *Walden*," in Myerson, *Critical Essays*, 246–47).

Death

1. This chapter relies heavily on the accounts of Thoreau's death in Harding, *Days of Thoreau*, 441–69, and Richardson, *Henry Thoreau*, 385–89.
2. Thoreau, *Journal 1*, 201–3 (December 14, 1840).
3. For an amusing account of Thoreau's discovery of a phallus-shaped toadstool—"in all respects a most disgusting object, yet very suggestive"—see Thoreau, *Journal IX*, 115–17 (October 16, 1856).
4. Thoreau, *Journal 1*, 368 (March 8, 1842).
5. Thoreau, *Journal XIV*, 268 (November 25, 1860).
6. Harding, *Days of Thoreau*, 452, 455.
7. Ibid., 456, 460; Thoreau, *Correspondence*, 641 (March 21, 1862).
8. Harding, *Days of Thoreau*, 462, 463.
9. Thoreau, *Correspondence*, 649 (April 13, 1862); Harding, *Days of Thoreau*, 460.
10. Harding, *Days of Thoreau*, 464.
11. Ibid.
12. Emerson, "Thoreau," in *Oxford Authors*, 475, 477, 480, 484, 487.
13. Emerson, *Oxford Authors*, 46. For a very different interpretation of the eulogy, emphasizing Emerson's doubts about Thoreau's achievement, see Sattelmeyer, "Thoreau and Emerson," 36–38.
14. Emerson, *Oxford Authors*, 490.
15. Harding, *Days of Thoreau*, 468.

Bibliography

Annas, Julia. *The Morality of Happiness.* Oxford: Oxford University Press, 1983.

Anscombe, G. E. M. "Modern Moral Philosophy." In *Ethics, Religion and Politics,* vol. 3 of *The Collected Papers of G. E. M. Anscombe.* Minneapolis: University of Minnesota Press, 1987.

Aristotle. *Nicomachean Ethics.* 2d ed. Translated by Terence Irwin. Indianapolis: Hackett, 1999.

Aurelius, Marcus. *The Meditations.* Indianapolis: Hackett, 1983.

Baron, Marcia. "Kantian Ethics." In *Three Methods in Ethics,* by Marcia Baron, Philip Pettit, and Michael Slote. London: Blackwell, 1997.

Bennett, Jane. *Thoreau's Nature: Ethics, Politics, and the Wild.* Lanham, Md.: Rowman and Littlefield, 2002.

The Bhagavad-Gita. Translated by Barbara Stoler Miller. New York: Bantam Books, 1986.

Botkin, Daniel. *No Man's Garden: Thoreau and a New Vision for Civilization and Nature.* Washington, D.C.: Island Press, 2000.

Broderick, John. "Thoreau's Proposals for Legislation." *American Quarterly* 7 (1955): 285–90.

Burbick, John. *Thoreau's Alternative History: Changing Perspectives on Nature, Culture, and Language.* Philadelphia: University of Pennsylvania Press, 1987.

Cafaro, Philip. "Thoreau, Leopold, and Carson: Toward an Environmental Virtue Ethics." *Environmental Ethics* 23 (2001): 3–17.

———. "The Virtues of the Naturalist." *Philosophy in the Contemporary World* 8, no. 2 (2001): 85–99.

Callicott, J. Baird. *In Defense of the Land Ethic: Essays in Environmental Philosophy.* Albany: SUNY Press, 1989.

Cavell, Stanley. *Conditions Handsome and Unhandsome: The Constitution of Emersonian Perfectionism.* Chicago: University of Chicago Press, 1990.

———. *The Senses of Walden.* Chicago: University of Chicago Press, 1992.

Clarke, Stanley, and Evan Simpson, eds. *Anti-Theory in Ethics and Moral Conservatism.* Albany: SUNY Press, 1989.

Crisp, Roger, ed. *How Should One Live? Essays on the Virtues.* Oxford: Oxford University Press, 1996.

Emerson, Ralph Waldo. *The Essays of Ralph Waldo Emerson.* Cambridge: Harvard University Press, 1987.

———. *The Heart of Emerson's Journals.* Edited by Bliss Perry. Mineola, N.Y.: Dover, 1995.

———. *Ralph Waldo Emerson: The Oxford Authors.* Oxford: Oxford University Press, 1990.

Friesen, Victor. *The Spirit of the Huckleberry: Sensuousness in Henry Thoreau.* Edmonton: University of Alberta Press, 1984.

Guignon, Charles, ed. *The Good Life.* Indianapolis: Hackett, 1999.

Harding, Walter. *The Days of Henry Thoreau: A Biography.* Princeton: Princeton University Press, 1992.

————, ed. *Thoreau as Seen by His Contemporaries.* Mineola, N.Y.: Dover, 1989.

Hellenbrand, Harold. "'A True Integrity Day by Day': Thoreau's Organic Economy in *Walden.*" *Emerson Society Quarterly* 25 (1979): 71–78.

Hendrick, George. "The Influence of Thoreau's 'Civil Disobedience' on Gandhi's *Satyagraha.*" *New England Quarterly* 29 (1956): 462–71.

Hursthouse, Rosalind. *On Virtue Ethics.* New York: Oxford University Press, 1999.

Hyde, Lewis. "Introduction: Prophetic Excursions." In Henry Thoreau, *The Essays of Henry D. Thoreau.* New York: North Point Press, 2002.

Kant, Immanuel. *Practical Philosophy.* Cambridge: Cambridge University Press, 1996.

Koch, Philip. *Solitude: A Philosophical Encounter.* Peru, Ill.: Open Court, 1994.

Lakoff, George, and Mark Johnson. *Metaphors We Live By.* Chicago: University of Chicago Press, 1980.

Lane, Robert. *The Market Experience.* Cambridge: Cambridge University Press, 1991.

Locke, John. *Two Treatises of Civil Government.* Cambridge: Cambridge University Press, 1988.

Long, A. A., and D. N. Sedley, eds. *The Hellenistic Philosophers.* Cambridge: Cambridge University Press, 1987.

MacIntyre, Alasdair. *After Virtue.* 2d ed. Notre Dame, Ind.: University of Notre Dame Press, 1984.

Meyer, Michael. *Several More Lives to Live: Thoreau's Political Reputation in America.* Westport, Conn.: Greenwood Press, 1977.

Moller, Mary Elkins. *Thoreau in the Human Community.* Amherst: University of Massachusetts Press, 1980.

Myerson, Joel, ed. *Critical Essays on Henry David Thoreau's Walden.* Boston: G. K. Hall, 1988.

Neufeldt, Leonard. *The Economist: Henry Thoreau and Enterprise.* New York: Oxford University Press, 1989.

Nussbaum, Martha. "Aristotle on Human Nature and the Foundations of Ethics." In *Essays in Honor of Bernard Williams,* edited by J. Altham and R. Harrison. Cambridge: Cambridge University Press, 1990.

————. *The Fragility of Goodness: Luck and Ethics in Greek Tragedy and Philosophy.* Cambridge: Cambridge University Press, 1986.

————. "Non-Relative Virtues: An Aristotelian Approach." In *The Quality of Life,* edited by Martha Nussbaum and Amartya Sen. Oxford: Oxford University Press, 1993.

Nussbaum, Martha, and Amartya Sen, eds. *The Quality of Life.* Oxford: Oxford University Press, 1993.

Oelschlaeger, Max. *The Idea of Wilderness: From Prehistory to the Age of Ecology.* New Haven: Yale University Press, 1991.

Paton, H. J. Introduction to *Groundwork of the Metaphysic of Morals,* by Immanuel Kant. New York: Harper and Row, 1964.

Paul, Ellen Frankel, Fred Miller Jr., and Jeffrey Paul, eds. *Ethics, Politics, and Human Nature.* Oxford: Basil Blackwell, 1991.

————. *Self-Interest.* Cambridge: Cambridge University Press, 1997.

Regan, Tom. *The Case for Animal Rights.* Berkeley: University of California Press, 1983.

Richardson, Robert, Jr. *Emerson: The Mind on Fire.* Berkeley: University of California Press, 1995.

————. *Henry Thoreau: A Life of the Mind.* Berkeley: University of California Press, 1986.

Robinson, David. *Emerson and the Conduct of Life: Pragmatism and Ethical Purpose in the Later Work.* Cambridge: Cambridge University Press, 1993.

Rolston, Holmes, III. *Environmental Ethics: Duties to and Values in the Natural World.* Philadelphia: Temple University Press, 1988.

————. *Philosophy Gone Wild.* Buffalo: Prometheus Books, 1989.

Rorty, Amelie, ed. *Essays on Aristotle's Ethics.* Berkeley: University of California Press, 1980.

Roszak, Theodore, Mary Gomes, and Allen Kanner, eds. *Ecopsychology: Restoring the Earth, Healing the Mind.* San Francisco: Sierra Club Books, 1995.

Ruse, Michael, and E. O. Wilson. "Moral Philosophy as Applied Science." *Philosophy* 61 (1986): 173–92.

Sattelmeyer, Robert. "Thoreau and Emerson." In *The Cambridge Companion to Henry David Thoreau,* edited by Joel Myerson. Cambridge: Cambridge University Press, 1995.

Sayre, Robert. *Thoreau and the American Indian.* Princeton: Princeton University Press, 1977.

Sen, Amartya. *Commodities and Capabilities.* Amsterdam: North-Holland, 1985.

————. *The Standard of Living.* Cambridge: Cambridge University Press, 1987.

Seneca. *The Epistles of Seneca.* Cambridge: Harvard University Press, 1970.

Shanley, J. Lyndon. *The Making of* Walden, *with the Text of the First Version.* Chicago: University of Chicago Press, 1957.

Sherman, Nancy. *Making a Necessity of Virtue: Aristotle and Kant on Virtue.* Cambridge: Cambridge University Press, 1997.

Shi, David, ed. *In Search of the Simple Life.* Salt Lake City: Peregrine Smith, 1986.

Singer, Peter. *Animal Liberation.* 2d ed. New York: Random House, 1990.

Smith, Harmon. *My Friend, My Friend: The Story of Thoreau's Relationship with Emerson.* Amherst: University of Massachusetts Press, 1999.

Stoller, Leo. *After* Walden: *Thoreau's Changing Views of Economic Man.* Stanford: Stanford University Press, 1957.

Taylor, Paul. *Respect for Nature.* Princeton: Princeton University Press, 1986.

Taylor, Richard. "Ancient Wisdom and Modern Folly." In *Midwest Studies in Philosophy,* vol. 13, *Ethical Theory: Character and Virtue,* edited by Peter French,

Theodore Uehling Jr., and Howard Wettstein. Notre Dame, Ind.: University
of Notre Dame Press, 1988.

———. *Virtue Ethics.* Amherst, N.Y.: Prometheus Books, 2002.

Taylor, Robert Pepperman. *America's Bachelor Uncle.* Lawrence: University of
Kansas Press, 1996.

Thoreau, Henry. *The Correspondence of Henry David Thoreau.* Edited by Walter
Harding and Carl Bode. New York: New York University Press, 1958.

———. *Early Essays and Miscellanies.* Princeton: Princeton University Press,
1975.

———. *Faith in a Seed: The Dispersion of Seeds and Other Late Natural History
Writings.* Edited by Bradley Dean. Washington, D.C.: Island Press, 1993.

———. *Journal: Volume 1.* Edited by Elizabeth Hall Witherell, William Howarth,
Robert Sattelmeyer, and Thomas Blanding. Princeton: Princeton University
Press, 1981.

———. *Journal: Volume 2.* Edited by Robert Sattelmeyer. Princeton: Princeton
University Press, 1984.

———. *Journal: Volume 3.* Edited by Robert Sattelmeyer, Mark Patterson, and
William Rossi. Princeton: Princeton University Press, 1990.

———. *Journal: Volume 4.* Edited by Leonard Neufeldt and Nancy Craig Sim-
mons. Princeton: Princeton University Press, 1992.

———. *Journal: Volume 5.* Edited by Patrick O'Connell. Princeton: Princeton
University Press, 1997.

———. *Journal: Volume 6.* Edited by William Rossi and Heather Kirk Thomas.
Princeton: Princeton University Press, 2000.

———. *The Journal of Henry D. Thoreau: Volumes I–XIV.* Edited by Bradford
Torrey and Francis Allen. 1906. Reprint, New York: Dover, 1962.

———. *The Maine Woods.* Princeton: Princeton University Press, 1972.

———. *The Natural History Essays.* Salt Lake City: Peregrine Smith, 1980.

———. *Reform Papers.* Princeton: Princeton University Press, 1973.

———. *Walden.* Princeton: Princeton University Press, 1971.

———. Walden *and Resistance to Civil Government.* Edited by William Rossi.
2d ed. New York: W. W. Norton, 1992.

———. *A Week on the Concord and Merrimack Rivers.* Princeton: Princeton University Press, 1980.

———. *Wild Fruits.* Edited by Bradley Dean. New York: W. W. Norton, 2000.

Tuan, Yi-Fu. *The Good Life.* Madison: University of Wisconsin Press, 1986.

Van Cromphout, Gustaaf. *Emerson's Ethics.* Columbia: University of Missouri
Press, 1999.

Vitousek, P. M., et al. "Human Appropriation of the Products of Biosynthesis."
Bioscience 36 (1986): 368–73.

Wallace, James. *Virtues and Vices.* Ithaca: Cornell University Press, 1978.

Walls, Laura Dassow. *Seeing New Worlds: Henry David Thoreau and Nineteenth-
Century Natural Science.* Madison: University of Wisconsin Press, 1995.

Wensveen, Louke van. *Dirty Virtues: The Emergence of Ecological Virtue Ethics.*
Amherst, N.Y.: Prometheus, 2000.

Williams, Bernard. *Ethics and the Limits of Philosophy.* Cambridge: Harvard University Press, 1985.

———. *Moral Luck: Philosophical Papers 1973–1980.* Cambridge: Cambridge University Press, 1981.

Wolfson, Susan, and Peter Manning, eds. *The Longman Anthology of British Literature.* Vol. 2A: *The Romantics and Their Contemporaries.* New York: Longman, 1999.

Worster, Donald. *Nature's Economy: A History of Ecological Ideas.* Cambridge: Cambridge University Press, 1985.

Zagzebski, Linda. *Virtues of the Mind: An Inquiry into the Nature of Virtue and the Ethical Foundations of Knowledge.* Cambridge: Cambridge University Press, 1996.

Index

(n. 10), 257 (n. 13); and economics, 88–91, 104; experimental, 64–65, 206, 222–26; idealism in, 83, 87–88, 215–22; naturalism in, 207–15; open-endedness of, 26, 28, 31, 64–65, 94; particularism in, 223–26; principles in, 39, 178–80, 187–89, 216–18; striving in, 35–38; trade-offs in, 31–34, 57, 243 (nn. 18, 19). *See also* certainty, ethical; duties; duty, moral; equality, ethical; ethics, foundations of; experience, role of, in ethics; heroes; heroism; justice; metaphors, ethical; nobility; philanthropy; rights; self-development; self-interest; virtue; virtue ethics; virtues

ethics, environmental: appeals to nature within, 213; defined, 139; of Thoreau, x, 91–104, 139–73, 237–38. *See also* consumption; nature, intrinsic value of; wild nature; wildness

ethics, foundations of, 205–29; doing without, 205; experimental, 222–26; ideal, 215–21; limitations of, 221; mixed, 206–7, 221–22; natural, 207–15; and personal commitment, 228–29; philosophical, 226–29; point of, 205, 256 (nn. 3, 4), 258 (n. 20)

eudaimonia, 21–22. *See also* flourishing
Evelyn, John, 47
excellence. *See* virtue
experience: enrichment of, 23; role of, in ethics, 145–46, 214, 217, 222–23
experimentalism, in ethics, 222–26

faculties. *See* capabilities, human
Fall, the, 101–2
Field family (Thoreau's neighbors), 118–21
fish, 140–44

flourishing: connection of, to virtue, 47, 57, 58; of fish, 250 (n. 6); as key ethical concept, 21–22, 25; of nature, human dependency on, 139, 155–73. *See also* good life

focus, as a virtue, 111

freedom, 30, 62–63, 174, 215; deliberation as part of, 18; intellectualized conception of, 41–42; solitude's role in securing of, 108–9; Thoreau's transcendental definition of, 177–78

friendship: between Emerson and Thoreau, 106, 130–38; Thoreau on, 43, 126–30

Gandhi, Mohandas, 174, 178–79, 181–82
Gauguin, Paul, 245–46 (n. 48)
Gilmore, Michael, 255 (n. 52)
gluttony, 96–97, 146–49
Goethe, Johann Wolfgang von, 8
gold rush, California, 193–94, 196
good life: Thoreau's conception of, 29–34, 40–43, 241 (n. 11); wild nature's value for, 162–67. *See also* flourishing
gratitude, 103, 152

Harding, Walter, 123, 239 (n. 1)
health, 31–32, 208–9, 241 (n. 13)
Henley, Don, 254 (n. 29)
Hercules, 49, 80, 101–3, 124, 246 (n. 6), 248 (n. 26)
heroes: challenge of, to democracy, 191–92; as dangerous in ethics, 4; as necessary in ethics, 53–54, 246 (n. 6), 255 (n. 48)
heroism, 195, 202, 203; of John Brown, 186–92; of fish, 143; of Thoreau, 11–12, 104–5; Thoreau on benefits of, 186–92
higher goals, 34–38
holism: ecological, 158, 160; ethical, 251 (n. 22)

Holmes, Oliver Wendell, 1, 9
Homer, 163
Hooper, Ellen Sturgis, 244 (n. 26)
hope, 20
human nature: appeals to, in ethics, 34–37; Thoreau's evolutionary view of, 211
Hume, David, 147
humility, 59–60
Hyde, Lewis, 189–90, 255 (n. 48)

idealism, ethical, 83, 87–88, 215–22
imperialism, 67–68
independence. See freedom
integrity, 61–62
Irwin, T. H., 244 (n. 19)

James, William, 14
joy, 16–18, 27, 207–8
justice: claims of, upheld, 54, 67–71, 74–75; economic, 246 (n. 10); environmental, 141, 155; for fish, 140–41; modern definition of, rejected, 7, 107, 192; for slaves, 174–78. See also duty, moral; rights

Kant, Immanuel, 3, 51, 69, 71, 189, 257 (nn. 4, 12); idealism of, 218; on lying, 244–45 (n. 31); on reason, 147; on self-development, 7, 239 (n. 19); and Thoreau, 176–78; on virtue, 46, 59
Kantianism: caricatured, 244 (n. 26); of Thoreau, 176–78
King, Martin Luther, Jr., 174, 178–79, 181–82
knowledge, pursuit of, 40–44
Koch, Philip, 112, 115, 117, 248 (n. 3)
Kouroo, artist of, 72–75, 245–46 (n. 48)

labor, division of, 2–4, 23, 97–98
landscapes, human appropriation of, 149–55
Lane, Robert, 246 (n. 9)

life: affirmirmation of, by ethics, 16–18; as answer to death, 230–32. See also nature
Locke, John, 151–53, 250–51 (n. 16)
Lowell, James Russell, 1, 140, 144
luxury, 83–85, 210

MacIntyre, Alasdair, 239 (n. 15)
magnanimity, 49, 195, 244 (n. 23)
mammon, worship of, 34, 174, 192, 196
market, the: Thoreau asserts independence from, 99–101; Thoreau challenges wisdom of, 192–93
materialism. See mammon, worship of
means/ends analysis, 80–81, 85, 92, 241–42 (n. 15)
Mencius, 126, 129
metaphors, ethical, 19–25, 28
Michaels, Walter Benn, 256 (n. 3)
militarism, 198–99, 202–3
Miller, Barbara Stoler, 245 (n. 39)
Mirabeau, Honoré, Comte de, 70
Moller, Mary Elkins, 122, 248 (n. 12)
morality. See ethics

national parks, Thoreau's calls for, 171, 237
naturalism: of Aristotle, 207, 218, 246 (n. 4), 257 (n. 15); in ethics, 207–15; in ethics of Thoreau, 132–33, 207–15
naturalist: Thoreau as, 12–13, 133, 158; virtues of, 63, 114, 156, 244 (n. 27)
nature: alienation from, 16–17, 92–95; appeals to, in ethics, 34–37, 79–80, 207–15, 221–22, 246 (nn. 4, 5); beneficence of, 102–3; higher uses of, 151, 164, 167; human connection to, 96, 113–15, 117, 149, 155–67, 251 (n. 28); and human flourishing, 39, 155–73; ignorance of, 161–62; intrinsic value of, 139–44, 149–55, 165; knowledge of, 31; love of, 156–59; management of, 171–72
Nature (Emerson), 8, 9, 12, 116, 156
necessities, 83–85

neighbors: animals as, 124–25; as moral category, 118, 122; of Thoreau, 117–25
Neufeldt, Leonard, 90–91, 246 (n. 1)
New Forestry, 172
Nietzsche, Friedrich, 70, 245 (n. 37)
nobility, 1–9, 22, 24, 55, 120–21, 170, 186, 187–88, 191–92, 195–96, 199
Nussbaum, Martha, 240 (n. 5), 244 (n. 21)

obesity, American, 196
obligation, moral. See duty, moral
Oelschlaeger, Max, 252 (n. 32)
O'Neill, Onora, 239 (n. 19)
overconsumption. See consumption; luxury
overpopulation, democracy undermined by, 185–86, 197

Paley, William, 68
parks, national, Thoreau's calls for, 171, 237
particularism, moral, 223–26
passivity: Emerson on, 1–5; Thoreau on, 16–18, 39
patriotism, 154–55, 198–204, 255–56 (n. 63)
Peirce, Charles Sanders, 14, 256 (n. 1)
philanthropy: as criticized by Emerson, 243 (n. 12); as criticized by Thoreau, 51–55; as synonym for anthropocentrism 141, 145; Thoreau's conception of, 59, 121–22
philosophy: American, x, 14–15; ancient and modern conceptions of, 29, 226–27; and citizenship, 195; defined, 116–17, 161, 257–58 (n. 19); demand of, for action, 5, 37–38, 75, 85; need of, for connection to wild nature, 164, 167; as training for death, 230; as vocation, 226–29. See also Thoreau, as philosopher
Pillsbury, Parker, 234

Plato, 22, 36, 163; on ethical foundations, 209; on friendship, 43, 128–29, 134–35; on love, 40, 159; on virtue, 45; on wealth, 95
pleasure, 35–40
politics: appeals of, to principles, 178–79; of contemporary America, 196; proper goals of, 175, 185, 192, 194–96; Thoreau's frustrations with, 174, 180–85, 197–98; Thoreau's philosophy of, 167–73, 174–204. See also citizenship; patriotism
pride, 59–60
progress, 193–96
property, private, 153–54, 169, 172–73
purity, 179–80

reality, appeals to, in ethics, 215–16
reason: role of, in a good life, 111, 147–49, 156, 162; value of, in ethics, 85–87
reflectiveness, as a virtue, 115–17
Regan, Tom, 145
resolution, 71–75
RESTORE: The North Woods, 171, 237
reverence, 27
Richardson, Robert, Jr., 131, 239 (n. 1), 249 (n. 40), 258 (n. 20)
rights: of animals, 149–50, 165; of minorities, 175; of nature, 155; of people, 67–69, 174–77. See duty, moral; justice
Riordan, Johnny (Thoreau's neighbor), 121–22
Rolston, Holmes, III, 142, 213
romanticism, ethical, 13, 16–17, 23, 63–65
Roszak, Theodore, 112

sacraments, 19, 23, 27, 103
self, Thoreau's conception of, 112–13
self-development, 21–25, 198, 254 (nn. 29, 35); human duty for, 51–52, 120; as proper goal of politics, 195

self-interest, 29, 241 (n. 10); justified, 51–52, 70; role of, in virtue ethics, 243 (n. 12)
self-knowledge, 41–42, 111–13, 200, 256 (n. 65)
self-reliance, 109–11, 200
Sen, Amartya, 79
Seneca, 95
sensuality, 148–49, 250 (n. 13)
settlement, 200–202, 256 (n. 67)
Shi, David, 15
Sierra Club, 238
simplicity, 61, 85, 242 (n. 18), 251 (n. 19)
Singer, Peter, 145
slavery: arguments against, 188–89; as metaphor, 41–42; Thoreau's opposition to, 67–68, 174–81, 186–91, 253 (nn. 6, 8)
Smith, Harmon, 132
society: reinterpretion of, in *Walden*, 30–31; Thoreau enjoys, 117, 122–24, 233; Thoreau eschews, 106, 124, 137–38. *See also* friendship; neighbors; politics
solitude, 108–18; and freedom, 108–9; and nature, 113–15, 117; and society, 117–18
specialization. *See* labor, division of
species, endangered, 140–44, 155, 164–65
Staples, Sam (Thoreau's jailer), 123, 233
Stoics, 32, 40
stupidity, 248 (n. 27)

Taoism, 242 (n. 18), 243 (n. 14)
Taylor, Paul, 142
Taylor, Robert Pepperman, 182, 185, 200, 254 (n. 35)
technology, appropriate, 91–95
Therien, Alek (Thoreau's neighbor), 36–37, 210–11, 242 (n. 18)
Thomas Aquinas, Saint, 76
Thoreau, Henry: abolitionism of, 175–76, 253 (nn. 6, 8); as American,

199–204; on American history, 120–21, 125, 182, 256 (n. 67); as asocial, 106, 124, 137–38; on Bible passages, 69, 101, 148, 243 (n. 17), 245 (n. 35); business lingo used by, 88–91; and children, 123, 233–34, 235; as compassionate, 121–22; and Concord, 107, 225, 234–35; as condescending, 119; connection of, to nature, 96, 137–38, 157–61, 164, 251 (n. 28); conservation ideal of, 167–73; on consumption, 81–83, 96–97, 161–62, 247 (n. 23); death of, 230–36; on economy, later views of, 162; farming of, 98–103; on friendship, 126–38; on heroism, 11–12, 53–54, 104–5, 143, 186–92, 195, 202, 203, 246 (n. 6), 255 (n. 48); on human nature, 206, 211; as Kantian, 176–78; as naturalist, 12–13, 133, 158, 246–47 (n. 12), 248 (n. 9); and neighbors, 117–25; on patriotism, 198–204, 255–56 (n. 63); on philanthropy, 51–55, 59, 122, 141, 145; as philosopher, ix–x, 15, 116–17, 125, 207, 230; on philosophy, 161, 226–29; political philosophy of, 174–204; on private property, 153–54, 169, 171–72; relationship of, to Walden Pond, 156–61; on religion, 25–28, 75, 234; on the self, 112–13; as selfish, 184–85; as sensual, 149, 250 (n. 13); on slavery, 41–42, 67–68, 174–81, 186–91, 253 (nn. 6, 8); as sociable, 117, 122–24, 233; as social critic, 106–7; on wildness, 149, 154–72 passim, 251 (n. 18), 252 (nn. 31, 32), 253 (n. 43), 256 (n. 67)
Thoreau, Henry, compared with: Aristotle, 85, 206, 223, 226; Kant, 176–78, 244–45 (n. 31); Nietzsche, 245 (n. 37); Peirce, 256 (n. 1); Plato, 43, 134–35, 209, 227, 247 (n. 23)
Thoreau, Henry, and Emerson: on civil disobedience, 136–37;

Emerson criticizes *A Week*, 133–34; Emerson criticizes Thoreau's character, 108, 135, 137; Emerson criticizes Thoreau's rhetoric, 136; Emerson's eulogy for Thoreau, 114, 234–35, 258 (n. 13); friendship of, 9–10, 14, 106, 109, 130–38, 239 (n. 1), 249 (nn. 40, 45), 250 (n. 62); on self-reliance, 109–11; Thoreau's challenge of Emerson's ethics, 132–33, 136–37; Thoreau's development of Emerson's ethics, 110–11; Thoreau's reaction to Emerson's challenge, 9; on transcendentalism, 115–16

Thoreau, Henry, ethics of: and anthropocentrism, rejection of, 139–55, 240 (n. 2); broad concept of, 20, 28–29, 43–44; cardinal virtues in, 60–63; egalitarianism in, 48, 68–69, 99–100, 120–21, 175–77, 183–84, 246 (n. 6); environmental, x, 139–73; experimentalism in, 64–65, 206, 222–26; and the good life, 29–34, 40–43, 162–67, 241 (n. 11); idealism of, 83, 87–88, 215–22; justice in, 54, 67–71, 74–75, 107, 140–41, 174–78, 192; method of, 145; moral absolutism of, 189–90; moral duties in, 65–75, 175–78, 181, 187–88, 244–45 (n. 31); naturalism in, 132–33, 207–15; self-development in, 21–25, 51–52, 120, 195, 198, 254 (nn. 29, 35); virtue in, 11, 45–50; and *Walden*'s virtues (listed), 55–56, 57–58. *See also* ethics

Thoreau, Henry, works by: "Autumnal Tints," 117, 233; *Cape Cod*, 182; "Chesuncook," 144; "The Commercial Spirit of Modern Times," 9; *Dispersion of Seeds*, 172–73; *Journal*, 92, 106, 113, 121–23, 125, 131–35, 137–38, 157, 164–65, 167, 199, 202–3, 220, 230–32, 240 (n. 3); "The Last Days of John Brown," 191; "Life

without Principle," 91, 174–75, 192–98, 233, 245 (n. 35); *The Maine Woods*, 117, 170–71, 182; "The Martyrdom of John Brown," 187; "Natural History of Massachusetts," 12–14; "A Plea for Captain John Brown," 69, 175, 187–91; "Resistance to Civil Government," 67–69, 91, 175–82, 183, 184, 188, 189–90, 203; "The Service," 10, 13–14, 188; "Sir Walter Raleigh," 10–12; "Slavery in Massachusetts," 68–69, 175, 176, 181, 184, 203; "Succession of Forest Trees," 172; "Walking," 117, 164–65, 202, 233; *A Week on the Concord and Merrimack Rivers*, 73–75, 86, 126–30, 133–34, 140–44, 182; "Wild Apples," 117, 166, 233; *Wild Fruits*, 96, 162, 168. *See also Walden*

Thoreau, John, 231

Thoreau, Sophia, 233

transcendentalism, 115–16, 235, 240 (n. 2)

transportation, 92–95

utilitarianism, 24, 244 (n. 26)

value, economic, 85–87

vegetarianism, 144–49, 216–19, 233

violence, 189–90

virtue: ancient and modern, compared, 45–47, 50, 242 (n. 2); broad conception of, 11; in business, 89; Christian conception of, 59–60; heroic, 48–50; inegalitarian conception of, 50; intellectual, 243 (nn. 13, 16), 248 (n. 27); justification for pursuit of, 51–55; in nature, 251 (n. 27); physical, 32, 43–44, 243 (n. 17); political, 188; romantic conception of, 63–65; Thoreau's conception of, 45–50; wild, 165. *See also* nobility